Aboriginal Power in Australian Society

Aboriginal Power in Australian Society

edited by
Michael C. Howard

University of Hawaii Press
Honolulu

© University of Queensland Press, St Lucia, Queensland 1982
University of Hawaii Press edition 1982
Printed and bound in Australia by Hedges & Bell

Library of Congress Cataloging in Publication Data
Main entry under title:
Aboriginal power in Australian society.

    1. Australin aborigines — Politics and govern-
ment — Addresses, essays, lectures. 2. Australia —
Native races — Addresses, essays, lectures.
3. Power (Social sciences) — Addresses, essays,
lectures. I. Howard, Michael C.
GN666.A2214 1982 305.8'9915'094 81-16419
ISBN 0-8248-0815-0   AACR2

Contents

Introduction

MICHAEL C. HOWARD

Aborigines lack both the ideological and economic bases of power in contemporary Australian society; for the most part, they control neither things nor ideas. White Australians (and foreign-based corporations) control most resources: they control the means of production and distribution. They are influential in defining needs, and they are able, by and large, to determine how and whether or not these needs are fulfilled. This, of course, was not always so. For thousands of years Australia's Aboriginal inhabitants were, or at least so they thought, absolute masters of the universe — it was their continent. They controlled the physical world that surrounded them, and they defined how power over things and over people was to be obtained and reproduced. This situation changed drastically when European colonists arrived. In a very real sense, Aborigines lost control over things and they lost the ability to define the situation, although recognition of this fact was sometimes slow to materialize. Aborigines were deprived of power, and since their initial incorporation into Australian society they have been searching for a satisfactory place in the new socio-economic order.

The authors of the chapters that follow address themselves to an examination of the evolution of power in relation to Australia's aboriginal population from the pre-contact period to the present. The chapters approach the study of power historically and in a wide range of settings. The book as a whole is especially concerned with Aboriginal power as it has been influenced by Aboriginal incorporation into Australian society, and with the transformations that have occurred as a result of this incorporation.

The initial chapters (those by Kolig, Turner, Maddock, Myers, and Tonkinson) pay particular attention to power relations and ideologies in traditional and tradition-oriented Aboriginal societies, and to the impact of contact with non-Aboriginal peoples. The discussion focuses primarily upon northern and central Australia, although the points raised are of more general relevance.

Examination of the traditional situation is intended to allow for a better knowledge of the precise political effects of integration into

Australian society. An understanding of traditional patterns and concepts is of additional importance because of the central role that *perceived* Aboriginal traditions continue to play in the political dialogue between whites and Aborigines.

The normative basis of power in the pre-conquest setting, and among tradition-oriented Aborigines today, was religious in nature, as expressed in Dreamtime mythology and the Law (see Stanner 1958, Berndt 1965). To traditional Aborigines, power rested on religious dogma and the performance of rituals. Religion and ritual were central to control of the environment, for access to and maintenance of resources; and those possessing the relevant knowledge and the right to perform the necessary rituals were afforded power as guardians of the world order. For individuals, power was acquired through the medium of kinship and by mastery of religious lore.

While virtually all students of Aboriginal society would agree about the basis of power among traditional Aborigines, there has been considerable controversy regarding its social and political manifestaticns in terms of inequality, leadership, government, and the like (see Wheeler 1910; Berndt 1965; Hiatt 1965; Howard 1975; Sackett 1978). On the one hand are Sharp (1958), Meggitt (1962, 1964), Hiatt (1965) and others who view Aboriginal society as being extremely egalitarian, lacking leaders and any recognizable form of government. Then there are those like Elkin (1954), Berndt (1965), and Strehlow (1970) who have a much more hierarchical view of Aboriginal society and who claim that it possessed leaders and governmental institutions. Aboriginal ideology favoured the egalitarian view of a society without "bosses" or need of government.

In practice, Aboriginal society was not entirely egalitarian and there were bosses. Thus, women (in spite of their major role as providers of food) and children generally possessed very little power (see Berndt 1965, pp. 174-75; Sackett 1978, pp. 41-42). This was particularly true in the harsh interior regions, where access to ritual knowledge was most restricted. There were also differences among males as individuals and between social groups and categories of males. Furthermore, there is evidence from at least some regions to support the notion that many traditional Aboriginal societies possessed councils. The councils described include both open ones, in which members of the community as a whole could participate, and councils of a more restricted nature for dealing with Law matters (Howard 1975, pp. 69-71), the latter sometimes being referred to as "councils of elders".

It is apparent, then, that power was not evenly distributed throughout traditional Aboriginal society. There were, however, limitations on the attainment of power by those who were legitimately eligible to seek it. The prevailing ideology and patterns of social organization did not allow for absolute monopolization of religious knowledge or of other resources. Everything was conditional. Kenneth Maddock, for example, in his discussion of traditional land law among Aborigines, points to the division of powers among members of different kin-based groups, as expressed in part by complementary roles performed in the Gunabibi and Jabuduruwa rituals. Furthermore, as Erich Kolig notes in his chapter, the aims of those seeking or holding power were not so much a matter of desire for personal aggrandizement as they reflected a perceived duty to ensure maintenance of the world order. In Fred Myers's discussion of the Pintupi, he emphasizes the reciprocal way in which power is conceived. This is exemplified in the term *kanyininpa*, meaning not only "having" or "holding", but also "looking after". In a way such a concept can be seen as promoting Aboriginal acceptance of white paternalism.

It is also important to recognize that Aboriginal society was not static before the arrival of Europeans. True, the dominant ideology emphasized the unchanging nature of the physical and social universe, but ideology and praxis were not always in congruence (see Kolig 1978). Not only did the nature of power relations vary throughout Aboriginal Australia, but there were also significant changes over the course of time. For example, the pattern of marked status differences between males and females which was evident in the interior of the continent appears to have been expanding outward at the time of European settlement, as evidenced by the spread of male initiation "cults" into coastal areas.

David Turner's chapter, which deals primarily with Aborigines in northern Arnhem Land, discusses potential transformations that might have occurred if the effects of contact had been less severe or if Aboriginal society had continued to evolve slowly on its own. He argues that Aboriginal ideology and social structure contained the potential for the development of a caste-like system similar to that found in early India. He contends that such a transformation had already begun among the Kaiadilt of Bentinck Island before they were relocated by Australian government authorities.

The traditional Aboriginal ways of obtaining power failed them when confronted with the new and very different socio-economic order imposed on them by the Europeans. Europeans, however, were not the first "outsiders" to come into contact with Aborigines. Indonesian seafarers, known as Macassans, had been visiting the coast of northern Australia for centuries before the first European colonists arrived. Initial contact with the Macassans does not appear to have been excessively traumatic. The Macassans did not threaten Aboriginal views of world order. In an analysis of several myths from the Northern Territory, Turner discusses how Aborigines conceptualized relations with non-Aborigines as a result of their early contact with Macassans.

The Macassans came in relatively small numbers and remained only for brief periods, with little thought of conquest or permanent colonization. Aboriginal contact with Europeans was a very different matter, for they came intent upon seizing the land for themselves and settling. The impact of heavy European settlement along Australia's coast was devastating to Aborigines (see Rowley 1970*a*; Evans 1975; Turnbull 1948). The Aboriginal population was decimated, and the economic bases of their lives almost completely destroyed. Aborigines were incorporated into colonial Australian society at the very bottom. In many areas they were denied a significant or effective place in the white-dominated economy and political system. Subsistence came to depend upon receipt of hand-outs and sporadic low-status employment. Among the remmant population, aspects of their traditional culture survived — stories, beliefs, practices, and so forth — but relatively little of what had been before remained. In particular, as Kolig points out, the traditional practice of following sacred precedent as a means of gaining power was no longer of much relevance.

In those areas of central and northern Australia where European settlement was limited, traditional Aboriginal culture was much more durable. In many of the areas occupied by European pastoralists, Aborigines were able to weave "station activity and certain European goods into their social and economic activity and into their psychology without upsetting the fundamentals of their social behaviour and belief" (Elkin 1954, p. 324). In fact, European pastoralism and the maintenance of certain traditional practices by Aborigines often went hand-in-hand, the latter serving to ensure a supply of cheap labour for the pastoral industry (Beckett 1978, p. 6). Jeremy Beckett discusses such a situation in regard to the Torres Strait Islands pearling industry in his chapter under the label of "internal colonialism".

Maintenance of traditional Aboriginal culture has sometimes been achieved by a process of "dissociation" (Beckett 1978, p. 28), involving the maintenance of boundaries between blackfella and whitefella business. For example, Robert Tonkinson reports in his chapter that the people at Jigalong, in the Western Desert, made no attempt at a conceptual integration of the contrasting systems represented by "the camp" and "the mission". While such conservatism may be of value as a means of defence or by serving as a basis for ethnic identity, as can be seen from the discussions in the chapters by Myers and Tonkinson, it alse may serve to hinder the ability of Aboriginal people to deal with the social and political realities of the world they have come to be very much a part of by fostering paternalistic relations with whites.

The ability of Aborigines to maintain a relatively viable structure of socio-cultural duality has depended upon their mode of integration into the wider Australian society. It can be linked to paternalistic control or administration in essentially undeveloped regions or in marginal areas where "internal colonialism" predominates. Changes in the mode of integration tend to result in the destruction of this duality. The expansion of more intensive forms of production has generally destroyed the Aborigines' ability to maintain their separate sphere, duality being replaced by marginality and life as a fringe-dweller (See Dagmar 1978a, 1978b).

Although the power differential between whites and Aborigines is considerable, Aborigines have never been entirely passive in accepting their poor treatment and low status. Many Aborigines violently resisted the European colonization of Australia (see Reece 1974; Reynolds 1972; Robinson and York 1977; Roberts 1978). Aboriginal reaction to their status still occasionally takes a violent form, but less violent means of political agitation are now more the norm.

Many of those who have been most active in trying to gain power within the wider Australian society have functioned as cultural brokers, as intermediaries or middlemen operating within existing gaps between white and Aboriginal society. An analysis of the role of these brokers in relation to white domination of Aborigines is the focal point of my chapter. I argue that these individuals have functioned in many instances, though often indirectly, to maintain existing inequality. For the sake of their own advancement or survival they have tended to become supporters of the *status quo*, although the political ideology imposed by whites assures them that their actions are helping to improve the condition of Aborigines.

Not all Aborigines involved in inter-ethnic politics have been so dependent on or supportive of the system imposed by whites. There have been political activists who have sought to bring about radical changes, although before the Second World War their number was quite small. The extent and level of control exercised by whites simply left little room for those who threatened the pattern of domination. But there were always a few willing to risk the displeasure of those in power. During the early part of this century, these included William Cooper in south-eastern Australia (see the chapter by Delmos J. Jones and Jacquette Hill-Burnett) and William Harris in the south-west (Howard 1978a, p. 20). Cooper and Harris formed Aboriginal organizations and petitioned politicians and administrators during the 1920s and 1930s, in an effort to secure rights and gain power for Aborigines. They were among the first to try to forge a pan-Aboriginal identity. At the time, however, their efforts were unsuccessful. Few whites were interested in what they had to say, and Aboriginal society was in no condition to respond in a meaningful way. More widespread Aboriginal activism did not appear until the Second World War, as white attitudes toward Aborigines became more liberalized and as Aborigines who had served in the military or found work in the civilian labour force sought to prevent a return to pre-war conditions.

The Second World War, as most commentators on Aboriginal affairs have noted, issued in a new era in administrative policy for Aborigines. The immediate post-war period witnessed a flurry of activity as government officials, white non-professionals concerned with helping Aborigines, and even a few Aborigines, sought solutions to "the Aboriginal problem". It was an optimistic time. As assimilation became the policy in Aboriginal affairs, Australia's aboriginal inhabitants were liberated from the most obvious forms of oppression. The high hopes of the 1940s were not immediately realized, however, and Aborigines found that, despite the rhetoric, whites were not anxious to bring about significant changes. There was to be no real transfer of power.

The policies implemented during this period and the goal of Aboriginal assimilation or acculturation reflected a white rather than an Aboriginal perception of the problem. Despite the new, liberalized terminology, the aim remained to control Aborigines in order to force them to comply with the whites' rather narrow world vision. Aboriginal activists who did not share in this vision were either co-opted into becoming part of the system of control or forced to retreat into silence and occasional drunken outbursts against those in authority. As I discuss in my chapter on the south-west, white administrators during the 1950s were able to re-establish their control of Aboriginal politics, which they had been threatened with losing immediately after the war, by concentrating inter-ethnic political activities in a few voluntary organizations which they were able to dominate. Similar patterns were observable in other parts of Australia as well.

Perhaps one of the most important post-war developments to influence Aboriginal power was increased migration of Aborigines to the cities. Before the war, most Aborigines had lived in isolated rural reserves or on the fringes of country towns. In some instances this was by choice, out of loyalty to one's home territory, but there was also an element of coercion in the form of restrictions on Aboriginal movement and place of residence. Thus, Aborigines had been banned from living in the metropolitan area of Perth since the 1920s (Rowley 1970b, p. 375), and even before then there had been forces at work to keep them out of town. After the war, the right of Aborigines to live and work in Perth was supported by the Department of Native Affairs; in 1954, restrictions were completely lifted. During the 1950s and 1960s the number of Aborigines living in cities gradually increased. This movement, by the 1960s, was in part a result of displacement of Aboriginal labourers in rural areas by mechanization in farming (Wilson 1965, p. 158). By the latter part of the 1960s the pace of migration had grown substantially, and today urban dwellers make up a sizeable proportion of the Aboriginal population.

As James C. Pierson points out in his chapter, urban migration meant that Aborigines were closer to the bases of power and influence in Australian society. Also, Aborigines became more difficult to control when no longer concentrated on rural reserves. Although direct control was no longer as easy in the cities, continued impoverishment and discrimination by whites forced many Aborigines to continue to rely on government assistance. For these people, the direct domination encountered on the reserve was gone (this domination, of course, was only apparent when Aborigines did something that posed a threat to the goals of more powerful whites), to be replaced by new, more subtle forms of domination associated with entrapment in a welfare milieu. There were, however, more opportunities for personal advancement in the cities, and a small Aboriginal elite began to emerge.

By the early 1960s, although it was still possible to be optimistic about the chances of improving the Aborigines' lot, it was fairly evident that assimilationist policies had not worked very well and that the situation of most Aborigines remained far from satisfactory. Studies of Aboriginal employment (Broome and Jones 1973; Stevens 1974), health (Moodie 1973; Kalokerinos 1974), treatment by legal authorities (Eggleston 1976; Parker 1977), and so forth, demonstrated how bad things remained. Furthermore, rapid population growth (Broome and Jones 1973; p. 69), less than inspiring advances in education, and the effects of widespread malnutrition and illness (there were indications that health conditions were deteriorating; see Taylor 1977) could only lead to the conclusion that, as bad as the situation was, it would get worse in a very short time unless something was done. Clearly, the programmes initiated since the Second World War had not worked very well, and there was a pressing need to find a new solution.

During the 1960s and early 1970s the foundation was laid for the reformist effort which was to break forth in 1972 following the federal Labor Party victory. The new goal of white policy-makers was *integration*: which meant creating "real and equal opportunities" for Aborigines while allowing them to maintain their cultural distinctiveness (Schapper 1970, p. 56, see also Smith and Biddle 1975, pp. 3-6). On the surface at least, this was a recognition of the need to grant Aborigines more power. Subsequent events were to prove, however, that for Aborigines integration was to mean little more than assimilation, and that most whites in Aboriginal affairs were still not prepared to transfer significant power to Aborigines.

The means of achieving Aboriginal integration proposed by most whites were rather uniform. A situation had to be created whereby Aborigines would be afforded "free and equal access to institutions" purportedly designed to provide assistance (Smith and Biddle 1975, p. 5). Most agreed that "more resources from governments are an essential requirement for Aboriginal integration" (Schnapper 1970, p. 142). Many felt that there was a need to *promote* Aboriginal community leaders (see Rowley 1970c; Schnapper 1970), and to encourage Aboriginal voluntary organizations to assist in providing services for Aborigines (see Gale 1972, pp. 259-62; Rowley 1970c, pp. 425-28). An overall theme common to many of the recommendations was that Aborigines should be given a larger role in the planning process.

In hindsight, there is a certain naivety about these ideas. First, there is the assumption that Aborigines need to be integrated into Australian society, which presupposes that they are not already a part of it. It is essentially a segregationist or plural society (of the anthropological variety) model which emphasizes the discontinuities rather than the interconnectedness of social groups. If, rather than following the intergrationist reasoning, we shift to viewing Aborigines as already being integrated into Australian society, but as being integrated in a very disadvantageous manner, then the problem becomes less one of trying to create opportunities to further integration than a matter of altering the Aboriginal mode of incorporation into Australian society. This leads to the second point, which is that the government (and especially welfare agencies) should not be naively viewed as the good guys. For Aborigines, the government and its agents remain part of the problem, since they are an integral part of the society that has treated Aborigines so poorly. To give those agents more money and to bring Aborigines into those agencies which have traditionally served to discourage Aboriginal freedom is more likely to do harm to Aborigines than to promote their achievement of self-determination, unless very substantial reforms are brought about within the government itself.

Clearly, the success of any proposed reform will depend to a large degree upon the goals and actions of those involved in the administration of Aboriginal affairs. How much difference this can make is highlighted in the contrasting situations in Western Australia, as described in my chapter, and in South Australia, as discussed in Pierson's. In Western Australia there was very little devolution of power during the 1960s. In fact, the department was very adept at maintaining its power despite external factors at work which threatened to undermine it. The situation in South Australia has been somewhat different, and by the latter part of the 1960s Aborigines in that state were clearly better off than Aborigines in many other parts of Australia. The difference was largely due to the willingness of South Australian government employees and politicians to create an environment allowing for greater Aboriginal freedom.

After the Labor Party victory in December of 1972, things began to happen on an unprecedented scale. For one thing, the amount of money spent by the federal government on Aboriginal affairs increased substantially. There was a great deal of activity in the arts, in education, in health care, legal assistance, and in the area of community "development". As always, much of the planning and participation was by non-Aborigines, but there were a number of Aborigines involved as well.

Interrelated with changing white policies toward Aborigines were the activities of Aborigines themselves. Jones and Hill-Burnett, in their chapter, discuss the political activities of Aboriginal militants during the late 1960s and early 1970s and the role they played in intensifying government concern about Aborigines. It is important to note that it was urban-dwelling Aborigines who were at the forefront of this militant movement. It was in the cities, particularly those in the east, that a pan-Aboriginal consciousness first began to emerge, something that represented a considerable threat to white hegemony. Jones and Hill-Burnett discuss the process of ethnogenesis among Aborigines and how it has been related to other developments in Aboriginal affairs. In particular, they note how whites have favoured maintenance of heterogeneity among Aborigines, in part by promoting a localization of loyalties, and point out how this has hindered Aboriginal attempts to gain power.

Perhaps one of the most important political events of the early 1970s was the creation of the National Aboriginal Consultative Committee, a body of elected Aboriginal representatives from throughout Australia which was to serve in an advisory capacity to the Department of Aboriginal Affairs. For Aboriginal political activists, one of the most telling events that demonstrated the government's unwillingness to make substantial concessions to Aboriginal demands for power was the government's reaction to attempts by the NACC delegates to gain power over the administration of Aboriginal affairs. In February 1974 the delegates voted to change the NACC into the National Aboriginal Congress, from a consultative body with no power into one with the ability to make and carry out policy. Their demands included control of the Department of Aboriginal Affairs and of the federal budget for Aborigines. The government's reaction was immediate. The minister for Aboriginal affairs threatened to withhold the delegate's salaries and to disband the NACC. The confrontation ended in a victory for the administration, and the NACC remained powerless. Interestingly, a significant part of the government's campaign to undermine the support for what were perceived to be more radical Aborigines was to emphasize differences between urban-dwelling Aborigines and more tradition-oriented ones.

In addition to the NACC, there were also numerous state and local-level councils established by the government. These included community councils in many rural Aboriginal settlements. Myers discusses the council at Yayayi, with particular reference to the emergence of a new type of "boss" among the Pintupi, the status of the new bosses depending more on personalistic, patron-client relationships than on traditional bases of authority (see the essays on councils in Western Australia by Tonkinson, Sackett, and Douglas, in Howard 1978*b*). Voluntary organizations, which were provided financial support by the government, assumed many of the functions of councils in urban areas. Pierson discusses the role of voluntary organizations in Adelaide, where they have performed valuable political functions, and I write about voluntary organizations in Perth, where they have become part of a structure of indirect rule, serving the aims of the Aboriginal department.

Both formally (e.g., through workshops) and informally, white administrators endeavoured to promote Aboriginal community "leaders". As argued in my chapter, and as Jones and Hill-Burnett discuss in theirs, what this meant all too often was an attempt by whites to promote Aboriginal clients as leaders who were willing to support the whites' view of the situation. There were independent Aboriginal leaders, who often had emerged in spite of or in reaction to white attempts to promote leaders; many of these individuals were eventually lured into the white-dominated administrative structure, out of a desire to try to reform it or for the financial rewards that went with their compliance with continued white domination. What has become even more apparent in recent years is that government actions have served to create a dependent Aboriginal elite which is more responsive to the desires and needs of their white patrons than to the concerns of other Aborigines. It is a development that bodes ill for any chance of Aborigines gaining any real power in Australian society.

Central to the Aboriginal quest for power is the question of land rights. For tradition-oriented Aborigines, maintenance of many of the most fundamental aspects of their lives depends upon their ability to control what happens to the land they live on. Land rights, however, are important not only to more traditional rural-dwelling Aborigines; as the process of ethnogenesis proceeds, the issue of land rights is becoming of interest to all Aborigines.

Although the land rights question has been around for a long time, in essence since the arrival of the first European settlers, it is really only in recent years that it has achieved prominence. This has occurred as a result of a clash between the rapidly expanding mining industry in Australia and the growing concern with securing political and economic rights for Aborigines.[1] The issue subsequently has proved to be something of a can of worms. Maddock, in his chapter, discusses some of the difficulties that have arisen from attempts to come to terms with the problem in the Northern Territory. While it can be argued that a good deal of progress has been made in settling the land rights issue, such optimism may be a little premature. Existing land rights legislation not only fails to safeguard Aboriginal interests, it also favours greater socio-economic inequality among Aborigines. The implementation of policies based upon current land rights thinking among whites, as Maddock points out, benefits only a small number of Aborigines and ignores or works to the disadvantage of a good many Aborigines in the Northern Territory.

As with the immediate post-war period, the 1970s witnessed a major Aboriginal clamouring for power. While it is apparent that some gains were made, by and large whites again remained unwilling to accede to Aboriginal demands and unwilling to create a situation in which self-determination is truly possible. The politics of the 1970s was characterized by Aboriginal demands for greater power and by attempts by whites to channel or control these demands so as not to alter the *status quo* significantly. The *new dependency*, based upon the creation of a dependent elite of Aboriginal administrator/leaders, which began to emerge under the Labor Party government has become more of a reality under the Liberal-National Country Party government, as exemplified in the new, emasculated National Aboriginal Conference which replaced the NACC in 1977.

It would be easy to end on a pessimistic note, for there are many indications that the situation is not improving, but there is some room for optimism. Pierson's chapter implies that Aboriginal self-determination may not be an impossible dream, and the growth of a pan-Aboriginal consciousness, as discussed in the chapter by Jones and Hill-Burnett, has important implications regarding the Aboriginal people's ability to resist white domination. It can only be hoped that white Australians, and foreign economic interests, will not make the future Aboriginal struggle for power too difficult, and that the almost cyclic nature of the Aboriginal quest for power will finally be broken.

Note

1. A special issue of the *Anthropology Resource Centre Newsletter* – vol. 4 no. 4 (December 1980) – provides a useful and succinct overview of the land rights question.

References

Beckett, J. 1978. George Dutton's Country: Portrait of an Aboriginal Drover. *Aboriginal History* 2, nos. 1–2: 2–31.

Berndt, R. M. 1965. Law and Order in Aboriginal Australia. In *Aboriginal Man in Australia,* ed. R. M. and C. H. Berndt. Sydney: Angus and Robertson.

Broome, L., and F. L. Jones. 1973. *A Blanket a Year.* Canberra: Australian National University Press.

Dagmar, H. 1978a. Marginal Australians: A Prelude to Political Involvement. In *"Whitefella Business",* ed. M. C. Howard. Philadelphia: Institute for the Study of Human Issues.

————. 1978b. *Aborigines and Poverty.* Nijmegan.

Eggleston, E. 1976. *Fear, Favour or Affection.* Canberra: Australian National University Press.

Elkin, A. P. 1954. *The Australian Aborigines.* Sydney: Angus and Robertson.

Evans, R. 1975. "The Nigger Shall Disappear . . . " Aborigines and Europeans in Colonial Queensland. In *Exclusion, Exploitation and Extermination,* ed. Raymond Evans, Kay Saunders, and Kathryn Cronin. Sydney: Australia and New Zealand Book Company.

Gale, F. 1972. *Urban Aborigines.* Canberra: Australian National University Press.

Hiatt, L. R. 1965. *Kinship and Conflict.* Canberra: Australian National University Press.

Howard, M. C. 1975. Nyoongah Politics: Aboriginal Politics in the Southwest of Western Australia. Ph.D. dissertation, University of Western Australia.

————. 1978a. Aboriginal "Leadership" in the Southwest of Western Australia. In *"Whitefella Business",* ed. M. C. Howard. Philadelphia: Institute for the Study of Human Issues.

————. 1978b, ed. *"Whitefella Business": Aborigines in Australian Politics.* Philadelphia: Institute for the Study of Human Issues.

Kalokerinos, A. 1974. *Every Second Child.* Melbourne: Nelson.

Kolig, E. 1978. Dialectics of Aboriginal Life-Space. In *"Whitefella Business",* ed. M. C. Howard. Philadelphia: Institute for the Study of Human Issues.

Meggitt, M. J. 1962. *Desert People.* Sydney: Angus and Robertson.

————. 1964. Indigenous Forms of Government among the Australian Aborigines. *Bijdragen tot de Taal-, Land-, en Volkkunde* 120: 163–78.

Moodie, P. M. 1973. *Aboriginal Health.* Canberra: Australian National University Press.

Parker, D. 1977. Social Agents as Generators of Crime. In *Aborigines and Change,* ed. R. M. Berndt. Canberra: Australian Institute of Aboriginal Studies.

Reece, R. H. W. 1974. *Aborigines and Colonists.* Sydney: Sydney University Press.

Reynolds, H. 1972. *Aborigines and Settlers.* Melbourne: Cassell Australia.

Roberts, J. 1978. *From Massacres to Mining.* London: CIMRA and War on Want.

Robinson, F., and B. York. 1977. *The Black Resistance.* Melbourne: Widescope.

Rowley, C. D. 1970a. *The Destruction of Aboriginal Society.* Canberra: Australian National University Press.

————. 1970b. *Outcasts in White Australia.* Canberra: Australian National University Press.

————. 1970c. *The Remote Aborigines.* Canberra: Australian National University Press.

Sackett, L. 1978. Clinging to the Law: Leadership at Wiluna. In *"Whitefella Business",* ed. M. C. Howard. Philadelphia: Institute for the Study of Human Issues.

Schapper, H. P. 1970. *Aboriginal Advancement to Integration.* Canberra: Australian National University Press.

Sharp, L. R. 1958. People Without Politics: the Australian Yir Yoront. In *Systems of Political Control and Bureaucracy in Human Societies,* ed. V. F. Ray. Seattle: University of Washington Press.

Smith, H. M., and E. H. Biddle. 1975. *Look Forward Not Back.* Canberra: Australian National University Press.

Stanner, W. E. H. 1958. The Dreaming. In *Reader in Comparative Religion,* ed. W. A. Lessa and E. Z. Vogt. New York: Harper and Row.

Stevens, F. 1974. *Aborigines in the Northern Territory Cattle Industry.* Canberra: Australian National University Press.

Strehlow, T. G. H. 1970. Geography and the Totemic Landscape in Central Australia: A Functional Study. In *Australian Aboriginal Anthropology,* ed. R. M. Berndt. Nedlands: University of Western Australia Press.

Taylor, J. C. 1977. Diet, Health and Economy: Some Consequences of Planned Social Change in an Aboriginal Community. In *Aborigines and Change,* ed. R. M. Berndt. Canberra: Australian National University Press.

Turnbull, C. 1948. *Black War.* Melbourne: Sun Books.

Wheeler, G. C. 1910. *The Tribe and Intertribal Relations in Australia.* London: John Murray.

Wilson, J. 1965. Assimilation to What? Comments on the White Society. In *Aborigines Now,* ed. M. Reay. Sydney: Angus and Robertson.

An Obituary for Ritual Power

ERICH KOLIG

O'Brien: "The real power, the power we have to fight for night and
           day, is not the power over things, but over men."

Orwell, *1984*

When using the concept of power in the sociological discourse, we
have to realize that it is but a heuristic construct. That is to say,
drawing on a parallel in the "hard sciences", power exists in the same
right as gravity does. Gravity does not share ontological reality with
an atom; it has been made up, as in previous decades phlogiston had
been made up, to be used as a causal concept facilitating explanations
in the physical universe. Similarly, power is an invention serving in
the social universe. Such factors are useful — or have been for some
time so long as they lasted — as they are untrue. (While phlogiston
has been discredited for some time, gravity still remains with us despite
Einstein and quantum mechanics.) Nonetheless, power has a certain
heuristic value as a convenient device that "explains" outcomes in
history and processes of human interaction, that gives reasons why
events have occurred as they did, and facilitates predictions — and
all this despite the lingering suspicion that in reality it yields only
pseudo-explanations; and that saying, for instance, "he won because
he had the greatest power" is just a tautology explaining absolutely
nothing of real causes.

Power, lacking objective reality, may be no more than the phlogiston
of the scientific sociological discourse; yet it is no delusion in the everyday social universe of people. For man as actor in the social universe,
power becomes real. Though a construct of the mind, as part of a
Popperian third world, it assumes a vital role in the dialectical relationship between man and his objectified, institutionalized thought (see,
e.g., Berger and Luckmann 1967). Power becomes an important part
of man's everyday reality, in the way he conceives of it. It is as real
to him as food or the weather on which his crops depend, and as
important. And thus he strives for it, tries to manipulate it, and sometimes falls victim to it.

Man, always and everywhere, has treated power as if it were an existing quality, an ontological entity. Apart from sophisticated sociological interpretations such as Weber's definition of power as "the *probability* that one actor within a social relationship will be in a position to carry out his own will despite resistance, regardless of the basis on which the probability rests" (Weber 1947, p. 152; emphasis added), man usually seems to conceive of power as a mystical quality, free-floating in the universe, which he could bring within his ambit by various means. More than that: power, it often appears, possesses to man all the properties of quantity – which is capable of increase, diminution, displacement, and discharge. Man thinks he can capture it in larger or smaller quantities, and these quanta would attach themselves to him. Or power is seen as a natural resource which man can tap and harness: a universal commodity, precious and much sought after, which some understand to monopolize and use for their own benefit or for societal good.

One might say, then, it is only through ideology that power exists. Ideologies may not bluntly stress power and its importance – few make it a focal concern – but in an indirect, more or less concealed way all ideology deals with power, be it in the weak sense that ideology justifies social and political action (either supportive or subversive of the existing order) – and, in so far as power is an integral part of all socio-political activity, therefore is about power – in the strong sense that cosmically drawn power is seen as essential for man's being and continued survival. In any case, ideologies, or sections of them, contain recipes of how to obtain power and use power; they advise how to bring that elusive quality into the ambit of society, or of specific social strata or, sometimes, of outstanding fortunate individuals. In short, it is through ideology that power becomes to man a tangible reality. (The conceived nature of this reality and details of how to win it, naturally, differ from society to society. See, e.g., Anderson 1972 about Javanese ideology and concept of power.)

This paper is about the ideology, past and present, of Australian Aborigines, and their concept of power. Traditional ideology assured Aboriginal man of a continuing flow of power for all sorts of purposes. But, as one might say tongue in cheek, either the recipes given for obtaining power were faulty or the power obtained in this way was insufficient in quantity, since it could not prevent the demise of this society. Western civilization and its power proved much more potent, effortlessly destroying Aboriginal society. Barely alive after the first Western onslaught had subsided, Aborigines have since found themselves almost totally powerless *vis-a-vis* the wider, white-dominated Australian society. They have shrunk to an uninfluential and rather inconsequential remote minority without power and prestige. Internally the disruption of the traditional power process has widely resulted in anarchical conditions festering within the Aboriginal sub-society, and often one feels distinctly reminded of Durkheim's *anomia*. The traditional ways of obtaining power having failed them, Aborigines are turning now to a new "power ideology" that will teach them effective strategies to regain power in relation to the white society and at the same time remedy the presently abysmal internal situation.

The change in ideology is a slow and rather painful historical process. The strategies of ideology are continually tested against empirical reality, and if they are found wanting in effectiveness — if expected results are glaringly absent — a change in ideology, or the particular section of it, is likely to occur. The historical setting responsible for the transitory process among Aborigines, and in which the gradual, if increasing, abandonment of the traditional power ideology is taking place, cannot be discussed here in any detail. I shall have to confine myself to an outline of traditional Aboriginal ideology — that is, those aspects of it that manifest the power concept — and of that to which Aborigines aspire in the modern Australian nation. My knowledge of the situation is derived primarily from first-hand experience with a certain limited section of Australia and its Aboriginal population. Nonetheless, I consider my presentation as representative of a much wider sector of the present Aboriginal population, caught up as it is in a sweeping movement away from a traditional type *Weltanschauung* toward one that is at least partly Western inspired.

I cannot, and will not, totally avoid a certain comparative perspective on the topic of power. I intend, however, to eschew the temptation of putting my argument into a grossly absolutist, evolutionary framework of interpretation. With greater or lesser persuasiveness, this has often been done in cross-cultural analyses of power and politics (see, e.g., Balandier 1970, Carmack 1974). A comparison of political processes in traditional Aboriginal and Western society lends itself too readily to an evolutionary evaluation: one side seemingly espouses the pristine hunting society with its rather limited power process, symptomatic for this stage of universal development, and the other represents the most advanced, hence most powerful form. (Indeed, a highly sophisticated attempt has been made by Adams [1975], who, following Leslie White, made a case for the evolution of power in terms of the increase in the harnessing and consumption of energy as constitutive for successively progressive and more powerful forms of society.) Yet rather than succumb to this alluring viewpoint, I intend, if I can, to contribute towards discrediting the popular myth of the prevalence of egalitarianism and a totally apolitical life style in simple hunting societies.

This widespread and erroneous notion has it that life conditions would allow for no political flamboyance in such societies in which everybody, being far too busy scraping a meagre living from nature to have any higher ambitions, allegedly shoulders the same measure of instituted pedestrian responsibility. Petty as the traditional Aboriginal scenario of power and politics may appear when measured against world politics of the last few decades, it certainly does not lack in colourful intricacy in its own rights. Yet despite all due admiration, one cannot deny that Aboriginal society easily fell prey, totally succumbing within a few years, to the powerfully advancing Western civilization. It seems glaringly obvious that the reason lies in the inferior power of traditional Aboriginal society. This society, as all simple, hunting-gathering societies, commanded considerably less power than an advanced technological civilization such as the Western one; hence their speedy demise in a culture clash.

Convincing as it may sound, this reasoning becomes invalid as an explanation as soon as one unmasks power as a pseudo-causal factor, as I have indicated earlier. Power is a strictly ideological factor — and all one can deduce from Australian social history is that Western power ideology has apparently been rather more successful than the Aboriginal one. Somewhat mischievously one might assume that Aborigines had a faulty ideology that tricked them into believing that they would have power where they actually had none. Even though one may reject gross, derogatory overtones of that kind, one is nonetheless led to assume that some ideologies are "better" than others in so far as they lead to more effective and better results than others. Ideologies contain knowledge available in a society at a particular time. If one accepts a Popperian scheme of progression of knowledge towards a for-ever-unattainable truth, then it would logically follow that ideologies, inasmuch as they incorporate knowledge, are committed to a similar progression. Matters are, however, not as unambiguous as all that. Ideologies — or, more specifically, political ideologies, which are the major concern in this paper — are multifaceted; they not only contain pure, "scientific" knowledge (i.e., of nature, the universe, causalities, etc.), but also, and equally importantly, incorporate ethical elements. Moreover, ideologies perform certain functions in relation to society and human social existence. (Only a shared ideology makes human beings social.)

Taking these aspects, integral to all political ideology, equally into account makes it abundantly clear that no total ideological advance can possibly be ascertained. A comparative evaluation is only possible in respect of one arbitrarily isolated criterion that is subjected to a value assumption in the process. Aboriginal ideology, for instance, may have been badly founded in respect of power, but it may have been much more successful in integrating society than any of the current

Western ideologies is capable of doing. This statement contains already an implied evaluative judgement that assumes as its basis that ideology should have an integrating function and should muster power. And finally, there is the ethical question I have hinted at through my brief reference, initially, to the Orwellian utopian society and its political ideology. This ideology may draw on advanced insight into human psychological processes — used for brainwashing and mentally controlling subjects — but is it ethically defensible? As this paper is not a theoretical treatise, I shall not pursue this chain of thought any further; I merely hint at this extremely complex problem.

In describing Aboriginal ideology, I adopt Weber's method of *Verstehen,* taking into account that ideology, as part of the larger entity *Weltanschauung,* is expressed not only in the explicit form of theoretical and philosophical thought or in the officially recognized body of doctrines; to an equal if not larger extent, ideology manifests itself implicitly, as Dilthey has argued long ago, in action, aesthetics, art, religious convictions, and so forth (see Mannheim 1964, p. 97ff.) It is through a *Zusammenschau* of all these components that ideology can be constructed as a composite and multifaceted whole. For it is rarely homogeneous: ideology is not equally shared by all supposedly subscribing to it, and it is rarely internally consistent and integrated (Dahl 1963, p. 43). One and the same ideology may produce quite different images and a different sense of purpose in different people presumably sharing it. There is the official version of ideology, accepted by and representative of a society, and then there are more or less divergent personal views, in tacit or overt defiance of official doctrine. In fact, my interpretation of the Aboriginal power process stresses the Janus-faced nature of their ideology. And of course, the social analyst transcends individually and socially held viewpoints by placing them in a context larger than either. As a result, my treatise oscillates between what Mannheim has called objective meaning (sociological description and interpretation), intentional-expressive meaning (meaning intentionally ascribed to action, commensurate with official doctrine), and documentary meaning (unintentionally revealed by actors; viewpoints divergent from and often contradictory to official versions of the meaning of social action or doctrine) (see Mannheim 1964, p. 103f.; Remmling 1975:25).

Gerontocrats on the Power-Board

The traditional cosmology of Australian Aborigines is extremely well documented in the anthropological literature, which makes it superfluous for me to try to add to it with yet another detailed description. Instead I shall confine myself to sketching its features as far as they are of immediate relevance to my discussion of the traditional thaumaturgical power process and its underpinning in the ideology. (In my discussion I present the condition of belief and cognition as it was *before* westernization made its influence felt.) This ideology is characterized by the confluence of religious and political ideas to the extent that they become inseparable: preserving the order of the natural world and maintaining the socio-political *status quo* are virtually identical. Balandier (1970, p. 106) considers it characteristic in simple societies — and for him this has Marxian evolutionary overtones — for religious and political actions to be *related* processes. Religion, he says, contains a certain political element. In Aboriginal society, as it existed traditionally, this interrelation has been carried to the extreme so that religion and politics are inseparably intertwined: religion contains politics and politics *is* religion; and consequently the clergy are politicians and vice versa. (The theme of politics and political power in autochthonous Aboriginal society is a highly controversial subject inasmuch as some anthropologists would see power and political roles as traditionally vested in individual persons, while others attribute political functions to the working-out of abstract societal laws and doctrines. For a summary of this argument, see Strehlow 1970. As becomes consequently obvious, and for reasons I cannot elucidate in this context, I adhere to the former view.)

In traditional Aboriginal belief, the cosmos exists in perfect and eternal shapes and modes. Through the semi-creative processes of the Dreamtime — a cosmogenic phase of unspecified time-depth and duration — the universe as Aboriginal man traditionally knows it became ordered into everlasting, unchanging forms. Ever since, Aboriginal man has found himself living in a perfectly ordered world. If it were not for his traditional inability to conceive of possible existential alternatives, one might say that he saw it, in an almost Leibnizian sense, as the best of all possible worlds. The laws pertaining to its functioning and to organic and social existence are as perfect as they are immutable, and so are the basic shapes and forms in which the operation of the laws expresses itself (see Maddock 1974, p. 109ff.). Changes naturally do occur in the life-world; Aborigines did not deny the empirical evidence of day-to-day transformations, but these were seen as trivial, non-essential in comparison with the basically unchanging ground pattern of the universe. Ephemeral detail unfolds, comes and goes, only in strict accord with the basic and enduring master design that reigns supreme in the universe.

The smugly perfect, eternally immutable universe in which Aboriginal man traditionally lived had an Achilles heel that could prove the undoing of both man and his world. Despite the perfection and immutability of the cosmos and the all-pervasiveness of the existing cosmic order, one element of dialectical contrast is contained in this cosmology: a fleeting vision of total, utter change and radical discontinuation of the existing in all its forms and processes. Aboriginal man's perfect universe was vulnerable and at least potentially ephemeral. For its continuing existence it depended on man and on his purposefully and dutifully maintaining it. Poised like the Sword of Damocles was the grave hazard that if man grossly neglected his duty, if he ignored his obligations, the universe would come tumbling down; it would break apart and bring to an end life as Aboriginal man traditionally knew it. While the religious cosmology did not spell out just what exactly this catastrophe might be like − nor did it say, for that matter, that it would eventually be inevitable, as Ragnarok, Gotterdammerung, or the Day of Judgement are − this danger was distinctly there and was vaguely perceived as devastating and horrific beyond human imagination. To keep this spectre at bay, it needed man's conscious, untiring vigilance.

This cosmological reasoning injected one minute, yet in its consequences awe-inspiring, element of human freedom in an otherwise rigidly deterministic universe that left little choice to man, that credited him with next to no creativity and inventiveness. All he was required to do was to follow sacred precedent. And yet man had it in his power to wilfully terminate, in one maniacal, suicidal frenzy, the existing order and set an end to everything that was familiar to him. At the expense of bringing down the whole universe, man was free.

To prevent the ultimate and irreversible catastrophe, it needed man to follow sacred precedents exactly and minutely. Not only the patterns of everyday life down to the smallest detail had to be repeated over and over again completely unaltered, also the smallest innovation or alteration had to be shunned, and violently suppressed if necessary; for what might have seemed only a most trivial change might trigger the ultimate and absolute "change". For man to discriminate with the necessary precision between established pattern and deviation, it needed precise knowledge. The most mundane activity embodied man's duty to perpetuate it unchanged, if he wished to live. And so that man's path might not be blurred and he stumble into terrible error, exact knowledge was as vital to the survival in the long run as the daily search for food was in the short run.

Man's obligation to maintain and safeguard what existed was discharged in the most concentrated and spectacular way through ritual. Regular performances of commemorative ritual, designed to symbolically re-enact Dreamtime events and creative deeds of the mythic beings, kept the creative essences of the life-giving Dreamtime fluid and oozing forth as, one might say slightly blasphemously, the lubricant of the cosmic cog-work. Fertility ritual was emphatically concerned with natural species and phenomena (such as rain and water), as the continued existence of these things in addition to their value in man's physical survival was essential in the total cosmic order. Thus ritual more than anything else enshrined man's power over nature, the universe, and his own fate — within the limited confines of the contrasting options man had: of either unreservedly embracing the *status quo*, without prospect or hope for a change in all eternity, or of bringing on the final holocaust. And this power rested squarely on *knowledge*; ritual knowledge and knowledge of sacred precedent. Thus truly to Aborigines *knowledge meant power.*

Like everything else that exists in Aboriginal cosmology, power is *a priori* contained in the universe. It is not manufactured by man, and as such it is sacred, eternal, and quite independent of man. This power not only is available to man but can attach itself to objects. Such objects, sacred paraphernalia mostly, assume a thaumaturgical power that enables them to enter a cause-effect relationship with other things or beings — that is, no longer of an obvious, empirical nature. Man so endowed holds causal effects of a nature different from that manifested in killing a kangaroo by throwing a spear. He can hold the universe together; a feat empirically impossible and unprovable. The presence of this power simply opens up a dimension of causality inaccessible to empirical witnessing.

Now the knowledge necessary to maintain and preserve the world was not indiscriminately accessible to everybody in Aboriginal society. The awesome power and responsibility that went along with knowledge lay in the hands of only a few at a time. Shrouded in strict secrecy, only a few were privileged to lift the veil that concealed the most treasured portions of this knowledge. Numerous taboos and death threats surrounded the lofty heights of esoteric wisdom. Monopoly of this knowledge was held, and jealously guarded, by a religious elite. Only through their approval and through gradual ascension could a man — women were excluded in any case — aspire to the highest echelon. Ascent was made difficult through rites of passage which accompanied learning. Many involved excruciating pain, and all contained at least a modicum of discomfort, privation, and humiliation. Only through such indignities and pain, which were the inexorable appendage to learning, could the aspirant work his way up the religious hierarchy. As it took a man the best part of his life to reach the ranks of the elite, elitists were old men by the standard of Aborigines, though not necessarily in Western terms. (Social maturity was more important than actual age, though of course a young man stood little chance of being admitted prematurely to higher esoteric secrets. The term *geron-*

tocracy is therefore slightly misleading in so far as it was not old age that was the absolute determinant but rather a combination of advanced age and social maturity, which excluded the too-young and the old fools.) Effective control of the process of ascension was in the hands of the established elite. And although it was part of the normal expectation that a man should rise throughout his lifetime unless guilty of a crime or mentally deficient, final discretion in this matter was entirely with the elite. No appeal was possible against exclusion. There was no plebiscite or individual will regulating admission. Dissenters bent on changing the system, of course, had no chance ever of reaching the highest stages and thus gaining influence enough to bring to bear whatever innovative ideas they may have had.

At any particular moment in time, then, a relatively small and exclusive elite held knowledge considered vital for the existence and continued survival of society as a whole. This elite stood opposed to a majority of others ignorant to varying degrees: women, children, younger males, and older men considered unfit to gain higher knowledge or simply lacking in ambition. This condition indicates an imbalance of socio-political power in so far as such power directly accrues from religious knowledge. The few truly knowledgeable ones in whose hands lay the "tribal administration" were the wielders of instituted power (or *authority* in Weber's terminology). Although it is doubtful whether Aboriginal society, with its rigid regimentation which stifled all individualism, could ever have fostered flamboyant entrepreneurship lusting for power, an elitist position did offer considerable personal power. Elitists held cosmic power, flowing from their knowledge, in trust for the whole society, and this was the source of their personal power over their fellow men. They could convert their power over nature and the universe into a personal domain, a province others were incapable of usurping. As far as one might surmise, individual arbitrary power was not recognized in Aboriginal society; elitists were considered simply vehicles of power for the good of society and repositories of the necessary knowledge, no more. Aboriginal *Weltanschauung*, consciously, had no room for mundane, whimsical powers of individuals. But although theoretically not recognized, such power did exist: elitists had *de facto* power if not *de jure*. Because of their importance, their fellow men always bowed to their decisions; in any case, the elitists could invoke "sacred power" to press their point *vis-a-vis* lesser persons. They could underpin their decisions by reference to more or less oblique points of the cosmology; they could give exegetical twists to the cosmic laws and bend the situation in their favour. More bluntly, on the basis of their greater knowledge, they could conjure up magical forces to harm their adversaries, both in an everyday and ritual context.

They had every opportunity on their side to get at their opponents of lesser knowledge and hence lesser armour.

What then does socio-political power in traditional Aboriginal society mean? Certainly not the unlimited licence for individuals to dictate to others arbitrarily, or to force their will whimsically on others. There were privileges and high prestige for the elite, but no absolute powers which allowed them to do anything they liked. Elites theoretically had only an exegetical task in mediating eternal laws to their fellow men. Exercising power could only be done within the framework — more bluntly one might say under the pretext — of religious prescriptions. Thus power, and action inspired through it, always referred to a super-individual, religious source, and not to personal will, decision, or insight. Aboriginal man was constrained by his world view to adhere as closely as humanly possible to sacrosanct, eternal laws of conduct. But sometimes his vision might be blurred, causing him to stray from established patterns. Then it was the task of the elite, with their knowledge, to see that the aberration was checked and rectified. Thus the power of the elite was vitally important, and the others freely bowed to it for their own good, since, as we remember, aberration and violation of laws might jeopardize the cosmic *status quo*. Elites managed the necessary power for society, to constrain individuals to obey these laws, which individuals unwittingly or sometimes knowingly might tend to violate. The sacred nature of the elite's power meant that opposition to that power, encapsulated in certain decisions, was sacrilegious and had to be dealt with accordingly. Not only the cosmic order as such was sacronsanct, but also the power policing adherence to it.

Now it is quite clear that this ideology indirectly conceded quite remarkable personal powers to the elite, since exegesis of cosmic order and determining what constituted deviance was its undisputed domain. These powers could be wielded quite whimsically so long as they could be rationalized by the elite as being contained within sacred prescription. There was ample margin for the elite to bend the sacred laws and precedents, either deliberately or unknowingly, according to their personal tastes and views. In fact, this is implicitly part of any social system whose laws and code of conduct are not written up but exist only in the minds of individual people. Such laws are, more than if they existed in written form, subject to exegetical interpretation, wittingly or unwittingly, by those empowered to enforce them; the "public" has no recourse to a body of laws accessible to all and open to collective scrutiny.

Political questions were religious questions to Aborigines, and political problems were matters of religious exegesis. It was only proper, therefore, that religious savants should take charge of political affairs. All situations and conditions of political life were supposed to be contained in the religious cosmology, and if the answer to a problem was not patently obvious to everybody from their more or less limited knowledge, then the religious experts were expected to have the answer. Life was not expected to produce unsolvable problems, but if a situation arose that was not solvable, automatically, by the common stock of experience, it was up to the elite to take charge. The elite in such situations was expected to discharge the power vested in them, to implement the cosmic order and rectify the situation. Even attempts to bring about a redistribution of space and impinge on others' tribal territories, either by strong-arm techniques or by subtler methods, were seen in basically the same light. The rationale was that for some reason the Dreamtime truth, as seen by the usurper, had been deficiently espoused so far in actual reality and an adjustment in real life had to be made, territorially, so as to bring about the necessary conformity with the eternal cosmic order. In intra-group affairs, power was used to enforce individuals to conform to sacred laws. Even though sometimes seemingly for personal ends — such as revenge killings or punishment of adultery — power was applied in the name of cosmic order and not for individual emotional motives. Also, in matters in which recourse to sacred, inviolable cosmic laws could not be taken, the word of the elite weighed heavily.

Synoptically, then, the ideology prescribed that power was to be wielded and held in trust by the elites for the benefit of society — this at least was the official version. A monopoly of power by the elite for societal good was officially condoned. But seeing the situation from the outsider's vantage point, one recognizes that Aboriginal society was caught in an enormous vicious circle. The power-wielders in this society were identical with the intelligentsia — that is, the social stratum that holds monopolistic control over moulding the society's world view, acting as a repository and executor of the societally held ideology (Mannheim 1940, p. 9ff.). In other words, the elite determined, by managing the society's ideology, what is good for this society, and this further enabled them ideologically to justify forming an exclusive elite, wielding power, and, not least of all, preventing redefinition of the cosmoloty and ideology that favoured them. In a curious way the Mannheimian "functional power" — that is, the power to fulfil legitimate functions and activities (see Remmling 1975, p. 129) — is blurred into "arbitrary power" in so far as the elite could more or less arbitrarily define their functional powers.

The continuity of this oligarchial rule was neither physical nor hereditary, but adoptive. The essence of elitism was not one of father-to-son automatic inheritance, but unchallenged persistence of a certain world-view and a certain way of life, imposed by the dead upon the living and policed by the elite. A ruling group remains in power as long as it can nominate its successors and thus control admission to the elite. The Aboriginal ruling clique was not concerned with perpetuating its blood (and therefore was not physically or matrimonially exclusive) but with perpetuating its spirit and in particular the ideology on which the existing social structure rested and by which it was rationalized. Who wielded power was not important, provided that the hierarchical structure remained always the same.

That greater importance was attributed to ideology *per se* than to particular persons indicates that this condition of rule was not the product of a diabolical plot of power-hungry people. It would be quite wrong to charge the elite with "making it all up", with perpetrating an enormous lie to remain comfortably in power, peddling religious opium so as to be ably to carry on merrily suppressing a lower class. The Aboriginal system of rule and ideology were larger than any one man, larger than any group of people at any time. The elite itself was but the pawn in an enormous game, the responsibility (and blame) for which rests with hypothetical inventors at the proverbial dawn of time. (Of course, a political system is hardly ever the product of *ad hoc* creation by individuals; it grows out of often inconspicuous beginnings over a length of time.) Long after this ideology's hypothetical inception, the elite came to believe as genuinely as others in their function of being truly indispensable to society. They as much as everybody else believed in the necessity to perpetuate the system unchanged — including their elitist status — not for their personal sake, but for that of societal welfare. The benevolent despotism of the elite surely was not fraud: power had to be drawn through the ritual process and applied for the good of all.

The Power Cut

Under the onslaught of Western civilization, the Aboriginal thaumaturgical power process failed abysmally. The proud power that Aborigines believe flowed freely forth to them and was demonstrated to them day by day in the continued existence of the universe, eventually proved insufficient to ward off alien intrusion and prevent subsequent subjugation. The power Aborigines were capable of mustering by traditional means turned out to be too weak to repulse an encroaching system that had different means and recipes for obtaining power.

Very little has changed since the days of violent encounter between the two races. Aborigines nowadays still have next to no power. They are trapped in a situation in which their traditional means of procuring power are no longer seen as effective, and power is obtained now in the society at large in ways with which they are still partly unfamiliar or from which they are barred. Aborigines are poignantly aware of their lack of power in relation to man and the universe. They are only now tentatively being placed in a position where they can share, partly at least and modestly, in the power of the society at large. The consciousness of their inability, only partly remedied in most recent years, to obtain and use power in order to shape their destiny as people and as a society, is one of the contributive factors for a state of "alienation" among Aborigines. (Some sociologists see alienation as the direct outcome of powerlessness; but this means presupposing the existence of a psychological reflex reacting to an objective sociological condition. See, e.g., Seeman 1972, p. 88f.) Aborigines conceive very clearly of a vast discrepancy between their realistic expectation for control of events in the social universe — which is almost zero — and their desire for control. As most others would, Aborigines value highly the power that lies in asserting one's independent will *vis-a-vis* a group of people regarded as alien. But this desire contrasts too unfavourably with perceived actuality not to create an acute sense of frustration.

Aborigines have over the past years increased their knowledge of the processes operating in Western society to obtain power. Progressively they approximate current Western paradigms of winning power, in the process detaching themselves more and more from the traditional power concept. This ideological switch has not taken place instantly, in fact it is still very much in a state of flux. The wide spectrum of currently existing, individual views can only be presented in the form of a generalized, highly abstracted picture. (It is hardly surprising that apart from differences in individual views, there are many individuals who seem to hold quite contradictory, irreconcilable notions of power.) Despite history's brusque, unambiguous lesson of the ineffectiveness of the traditional power process, the painful, humiliating conversion to a different power ideology did not occur overnight. External reality and consciousness are two separate, only loosely connected principles, and changes in the former only indirectly influence the latter; it is often with considerable delay that effects become noticeable. For some time after the change in the reality principle has occurred, traditional modes of interpretation, cognitive tools, concepts, and the like will be employed by the people affected. Only gradually does consciousness become adjusted by groping for new modes of comprehending reality. The speed with which changes in consciousness take place in order to adjust to the changed reality principle seems directly proportional to the degree of intensity to which deficiency in the current reality interpretation is experienced. This in turn hinges on the intensity of change and on the strength of existing concepts and the like. (It is an interesting speculation just how drastic change has to be in order to effect an immediate and total adjustment of consciousness without producing lasting disorientation.)

The first real challenge ever to occur to traditional Aboriginal assumptions about the working of the universe was issued by Western civilization. Before, no experience had been sufficiently strong to contradict seriously the Aborigines traditional assumptions. Ritual was carried out, the universe continued to exist, and man went about his daily business in unchanging routine. If pointed at with a magic bone, the victim dutifully died. Rituals brought on the rain in the monsoon season; and if the rain failed to come, there was always the excuse of faults in the ritual or some other interference. There was no need to rethink existing assumptions. This situation dramatically changed with the massive upheavals that came in the wake of westernization. But this did not lead to a speedy abandonment of traditional modes of thought and the equally hasty assumption of new, more adequate ones, as one might slip out of a shirt and into a new one. Only very gradually, and after painful bewilderment, did Aborigines come to realize (and they are still in the process of doing so) that the ritual maintenance of the cosmic *status quo* and the following of sacred precedent hold no real power in the modern world. The universe obviously does not fall apart if traditional ritual is not carried out; the rain comes in due course, with or without rain ritual. Above all, Aborigines realized that the power that accrued from their cosmological assumptions was weak, in fact may never have existed as more than an illusion. It withered away before the bludgeoning power that Western society wielded – and it is to this power, and the ideology behind it, that Aborigines aspire now.

The ideology of power, as prevails in Western society nowadays, stresses the material basis from which power accrues. Power is obtained through control of resources, of goods and raw materials, through economic cunning and material possessions; and the presence of power is demonstrated through economic sanctions and the ability to inflict deprivation. In short, power accrues from economic and material muscle. It is not so much that this power concept is characteristically Marxist and would have crept into even basically non-Marxist ideologies in the Western world, as that it has been latently congenial to Western thought. The Marxist view that power comes from control of real goods and the primary sources of production itself is a product of a societal intellect, a "collective consciousness", that has existed in Western society for some time before Marx. The Protestant ethic does not appear totally unrelated to Marxist thought — and may even have prepared the field for it — and processes of what Weber has termed "eclectic affinity" certainly had a role too in the matter (Weber 1930).

The role of the intelligentsia, the ideology producers, in Western society is quite different from that in the traditional Aboriginal situation. With respect to the power constellation, there is a "division of labour" in Western society which does not apply in traditional Aboriginal society. In Western society the producers and repositories of ideology are not the wielders or managers of power, whereas among Aborigines traditionally, as we have seen, the intelligentsia also holds the power. Of course, this division of specialization in Western society is not total. Power-wielding institutions and individuals do try to manage, even "make" ideology to a certain extent. And the intelligentsia increasingly in recent years has moved into effective power-positions (as Schelsky 1977, somewhat alarmed, has brilliantly pointed up). However, by and large the separation of specialization remains fundamentally intact.

Aborigines are in the process of embracing this power concept and the social constellation that accompanies it. The Aboriginal elite whose power has been constantly eroded to the extent of creating a condition of apparent egalitarianism in Aboriginal society is in a peculiar transitory position. Partly at least, this elite still asserts a measure of power on traditional grounds — that is, it draws power through religious means — but increasingly it seeks to adopt the new strategies of obtaining power. In the process, a new leadership is emerging which is divorced from religious expertise and which manages the collective drive for control of resources, land, and economic development. While leaving religious expertise now to others, the new political elite organizes the impulse toward Aboriginal land rights and economic strength as a means to obtain power mainly *vis-a-vis* the wider society. The power sought is of course ultimately a means — not an end in itself — necessary to achieve, for Aborigines collectively, material betterment and a measure of autonomy from white dominance. (The power that the new Aboriginal leadership attempts to obtain for Aborigines collectively so as to wield it against white society is of course capable of being converted into personal power to be wielded within Aboriginal society.) This bid on the part of the Aboriginal leadership runs parallel with their attempt to gain recognition and standing within Western officialdom and the bureaucratic system. That is to say, they have adopted another Western paradigm of power, namely that involving the power inherent in bureaucracy. The Aboriginal leadership increasingly partakes in instituted political and bureaucratic processes by participating in representative bodies, committees, advisory councils, and the like. Originally following the beckoning of white officialdom without fully appreciating the power potential that lay in active participation, they have gradually come to a full recognition of the advantages involved. For the time being another avenue for power, also suggested by an ideological paradigm existing in Western society, remains largely neglected by Aborigines: namely militant power, the possibility of achieving power through application of forcible means and raw muscle. Aborigines at the present time show little inclination to employ strong-arm tactics. This may be due to a lingering memory of the lesson of the past, but on the other hand the rampant increase of "power movements", guerrilla warfare, and violent struggles of minorities all over the world may sooner or later suggest to Aborigines the usefulness of this paradigm. (Indeed a Black Power movement does exist but is not notable for either its vociferousness or its fierceness.) At the present time, it is still peaceable paradigms that are adopted by Aborigines in their bid to have power restored to them.

The emphasis placed on the control of resources by Western materialist ideology as a means of obtaining power is not totally alien to Aborigines. Aboriginal society traditionally also believed that it was controlling resources, though in a rather non-material manner, and derived power from it. It was through ritual that control was meant to be exerted over primary resources, foods, and raw materials, and ritual was supposed to control the availability of these things. The power, manifested in and derived from this ritual enterprise, was meant to be wielded against enemies if the need should arise. But the power mustered through the ritual control of resources and through other symbolic means manifestly failed to stand up against the power of whites. Only as long as the ritual power was not challenged from the outside could it be kept up. It was illusory in so far as it figured in a perception of reality in which perceived cause-effect relations were highly ineffective. One feels reminded of the story of the man who used to throw paper scraps into the street. One day, somebody who had watched this performance going on for several months asked the man why he was doing it, and got the answer: "To keep the elephants off the street." The startled exclamation: "But there are no elephants in the street" was countered by a triumphant: "That's right — effective, isn't it?" (I am indebted for this anecdote to Gamson 1974) Triumph lasts only as long as the results are not put to the test — and elephants all of a sudden do turn up in the street. But in a more serious vein, this example of reliance on a highly illusory reality points to a very profound difference in Western and traditional Aboriginal power ideology.

Let us go back to the dreaded Orwellian vision invoked by the motto of this paper. Orwell's O'Brien, torturing the novel's hero in a so-called re-education session, states bluntly his party's goal. Big Brother, the party machinery and epitome of the absolutist state, seeks power over man, not things. What he really means is that the state seeks to control minds and derive power from manipulating the citizens' conception of reality. The victim of clandestine or brutal brainwashing is suggestible to anything (as Sargant has sought to demonstrate; see Sargant 1957). As soon as the desired image of reality has been instilled in the victims, by whatever means, it becomes quite unnecessary to change and manipulate external, ontological reality itself. The philosophy behind manipulating people's consciousness directly, in order to achieve any result that is desired, is a gigantic solipsism carried to the logical, terrible extreme. Once the goal has been realized of controlling the mind, power flows richly, and without further effort, for the ideology-managers. At least as long as this system is not challenged by an outside consciousness uncontaminated by this kind of mind-engineering, it will continue to work.

A comparison of Aboriginal society with the Orwellian utopian state may seem a rather dubious venture. Ignoring glaring ethical differences that distinguish one from the other, both had one thing in common: a power process founded on mental and ideological control. Aboriginal society, and the religious elite in its service — it matters little whether wittingly or unwittingly — manipulated consciousness (i.e., epistemological reality, and very little else), which produced a mirage of power that disintegrated readily under the impact of a power built on different premises. This power arose from the ideology emphasizing the control of things in themselves, of vital physical functions, the material basis of human existence. This materially based power — not because it was more true — effortlessly crushed a gnostic power that was unfamiliar with the need to prove itself empirically.

References

Adams, R. N. 1975. *Energy and Structure: A Theory of Social Power*. Austin and London: University of Texas Press.

Anderson, B. R. 1972. The Idea of Power in Javanese Culture. In *Culture and Politics in Indonesia*, ed. C. Holt. Ithaca and London: Cornell University Press.

Balandier, G. 1970. *Political Anthropology*. London: Allen Lane the Penguin Press.

Berger, P., and T. Luckmann. 1967. *The Social Construction of Reality*. Harmondsworth, Mddx.: Penguin.

Carmack, R. M. 1974. Power in a Cross-Cultural Perspective: Tribal Politics. In *Perspectives on Social Power*, ed. J. T. Tedeschi. Chicago: Aldine.

Dahl, R. A. 1963. *Modern Political Analysis*. Englewood Cliffs, N.J.: Prentice-Hall.

Gamson, W. A. 1974. Power and Probability. In *Perspectives on Social Power,* ed. J. T. Tedeschi. Chicago: Aldine.

Maddock, K. 1974. *The Australian Aborigines.* Harmondsworth, Mddx.: Penguin.

Mannheim, K. 1940. *Ideology and Utopia.* London: Kegan.

——— . 1964. *Wissenssoziologie,* ed. K. Wolff. Neuwied and Berlin: Luchterhand.

Remmling, G. W. 1975. *The Sociology of Karl Mannheim.* London: Routledge.

Sargant, W. 1957. *Battle for the Mind.* London: Heinemann.

Schelsky, H. 1977. *Die Arbeit tun die Anderen.* Munich: DTV.

Seeman, M. 1972. On the Meaning of Alienation. In *Sociology: Theories in Conflict,* ed. R. S. Denisoff. Belmont: Wadsworth.

Strehlow, T. G. H. 1970. Geography and the Totemic Landscape in Central Australia. In *Australian Aboriginal Anthropology,* ed. R. M. Berndt. Perth: University of Western Australia Press.

Weber, M. 1930. *The Protestant Ethic and the Spirit of Capitalism.* London: Allen and Unwin.

——— . *The Theory of Social and Economic Organization,* ed. T. Parsons. New York: Oxford University Press.

Caste Logic in a Clan Society: An Aboriginal Response to Domination

DAVID H. TURNER

Introduction

Levi-Strauss has suggested (1966, 1967) that the Indian caste system is a structural inversion of Australian Aboriginal clan organization. With some further refinements, the idea is that as we move from clan to caste the following transformations occur:

1. Totemism, a system utilizing differences to express an overall unity (clan A differs from clan B as species 1 differs from species 2), becomes a system utilizing unity to maintain diversity (caste A corresponds to activity 1, caste B to activity 2 and so on).
2. The exchange of women between clans, an attempt to achieve the *material* reproduction of the clan, becomes an exchange of services between castes to enable the *human* reproduction of the caste.

For Levi-Strauss the transformations here can be expressed in the following terms: the Australian Aborigines culturalize a false nature truly, whereas the Indians naturalize a true culture falsely (Levi-Strauss 1966, p. 127). That is, the Australian Aborigines are faced with the contradiction that their clans are exogamous, while the totemic species associated with them are endogamous. The problem is partly resolved by the cultural principle of patrilineal descent which effectively denies the female role in the reproductive process. When Eaglehawks marry Crows, only Eaglehawks result from the union. Logically awkward, perhaps, but the clan alliance system behind this ideology operates coherently and consistently. The Indians, on the other hand, begin with interdependent, self-reproducing caste groupings and consistently associate each of these groups with discrete, hereditary activities. The erroneous implication of this, however, is that each caste performs only its designated activity to the exclusion of the others. This implication is, however, avoided by a division of activities into two spheres, the practical and the ritual. Ritual activities adhere to the letter of the symbol; practical activities do not. The Australian Aborigines begin with an unsatisfactory *ideology* relating the natural series with the social series, and end with a satisfactory dialectical relationship between groups. The Indians begin with an unsatisfactory *practical* dialectic between castes, and end with a satisfactory ideology associating activities with groups.

Such interpretations as these, however, rest heavily on the analyst's own intuition and ingenuity and can be legitimately criticized on the grounds that they are much too general, frustratingly untestable, and lack a sound data base. In the present case, such criticisms apply particularly to the alleged causes of the transition from the clan to the caste system. Levi-Strauss, for instance, introduces two entirely un-Australian features into his clan-society model in order to effect his transformation: *generalized exchange*, in which A gives a wife to B who gives one to C, who gives one back to A, and *hypergamy*, in which women marry up the scale to higher status groups and men marry down to lower ones (Levi-Strauss 1969, pp. 406–21). This introduction of "foreign" features is entirely unnecessary and undermines the intellectual value of the original statement of structural relationship. The transformation from clan to caste can be effected without introducing anything new into the Australian Aboriginal clan system. The problem has been that the Australian system has not been entirely understood — something for which Levi-Strauss cannot be held responsible.

What adds even further weight to the theory of an Australian Aboriginal-like base for the Indian caste system is the fact that the Australian Aborigines themselves have entertained the possibility of caste-like organization in their myths. The conditions under which they imagine it, moreover, are not unlike those that existed in India during the period of the Aryan conquest (ca. 1500 B.C.). Finally, caste organization in a very elementary and restricted form seems to have actually been practised by the Aborigines of Bentinck Island, though it did not become institutionalized.

Clan and Caste

I have suggested elsewhere (Turner 1979*b*) that if we were to take an Australian society organized according to Aranda-type principles and localize each connubium of intermarrying clans, we would create an arrangement of *independent* villages, each internally divided into four interdependent divisions. These would be theoretically equivalent to the four great Varna divisions of the Hindu caste system.

In an Aranda system the universe is divided into four brotherhood groupings or phratries, each containing a number of totemically linked, "brother" clans. The base-four follows from the prescription that one marry into the father's mother's clan: that is, exchange women with the same clan in alternate generations. There must, therefore, be at least four clans in an Aranda system. In practice, however, there are usually many more clans within each Aranda connubium. This provides some flexibility in marriage choices, given recurrent demographic and political fluctuations that may prevent the ideal marriage rules from being followed.

In order to understand why localization of Australian connubia might occur, and why phratry endogamy, hierarchy, and specialization of ritual and economic functions would follow, it is necessary to locate the basic contradictions structuring Australian societies and examine the variations on Australian social organization that represent attempts to resolve these contradictions. With Maddock (1972, pp. 35–42), I have argued that the various Australian socio-economic systems can be analyzed as responses to the problem of autonomy versus societal security. But I have maintained that the stable configurations are, in fact, interchangeable and that this problem takes its definition, in part, from another, perhaps more basic, one. I have suggested (Turner 1978b) that the clan as such was "invented" to mediate the problem of how to maintain a continuous, regular relation to the land while providing for a continuity of knowledge, of people and environment, under nomadic conditions. The clan principle establishes an abstract, proprietary relationship to the land while allowing ties to be retained to a homeland, which may (theoretically) be occupied by members of other clans without risk of conflict or alienation. By establishing clan jurisdictions in such a way that no one of them can be entirely self-sufficient, and by implementing clan exogamy, alliances are "forced" between clans and co-operation is ensured. Foraging groups are thus formed out of intermarriages between clans; the foraging ranges consist of these clans' respective estates.

Marriage ties to effect linkages between connubia as such, however, would be inappropriate because the estates of the clans in the linked connubia could not be readily utilized for foraging purposes on a regular basis. Instead, ties between connubia are of a fraternal as opposed to affinal nature. The seasonal gatherings that are held between people of different connubia for the purpose of trading, rather than foraging, are occasioned by the celebration of common totemic bonds among the clanspeople involved. The brotherhood relation one has with members of one's own clan is duplicated in another more distant clan through the sharing of a common totemic affiliation. Along with this goes a ban on intermarriage and a sharing of the rights to clan estates. Fraternal ties of the same order are also extended to the clans within one's own connubium into which one may never (in theory) marry (i.e., the mother's mother's clan in an Aranda system).

People of different connubia who share an affiliation with the same totemic being(s) congregate in the territory of one of the constituent clans at a sacred site associated with the activities of the totem(s). In so doing, they are brought into contact with the people of other clans of the local area, most of whom perform different ceremonies associated with different totemic species. A system of ritual inter-dependence binds all the participants together despite opposed ideo-logical affiliations and the absence of marriage and foraging ties. In the ceremonies, a person "works" for, or performs, the rituals belonging to his own clan/brotherhood, but is "bossed", or directed, by people in clans (or in clans totemically linked to those) one's own clan has recently married (e.g., the mother's, or father's mother's). Each participant is both "boss" and "worker" by virtue of either ties of marriage or totemic brotherhood. Because these gatherings shift to different locales along the totemic track and in so far as the connubial areas are to a degree "resource specific", these gatherings vary in composition from season to season and provide the people with access to a wide range of goods and resources they cannot obtain locally.

Once formed, these affinal and fraternal alliance systems, ostensibly economic in origin, become dominated by the totemic and normative ideologies that once served merely as a *reflection* of material relation-ships. This ideological apparatus ensures that the underlying alliance relations will be maintained despite short-term economic needs and fluctuations. Similarly, "spouse exchange" as such now becomes the *raison d'etre* for effecting foraging ties, while ritual association in and of itself becomes the prime motivation for participation in the large gatherings outside the connubium at which trade goods are exchanged. People now come together *because* they have the same totem and perform the ceremonies, people intermarry the way they do *because* they have always exchanged with these clans and had close social bonds with them. To undermine such a system would require a crisis of considerable magnitude.

The various types of Australian Aboriginal social organization, then, represent different means of balancing affinal, foraging ties with fraternal, trade ties. The Aranda, for instance, prefer an exchange of spouses between the same two clans in alternate generations and four brotherhood groups (ignoring their moiety division for the sake of pursuing the formal argument), while the Kariera prefer an exchange of spouses in consecutive generations. What an Aranda clan gains through access to other hunting territories (theoretically two), it loses in access to trading areas (theoretically one in four), what a Kariera clan gains in access to trading areas (one in two), it loses in access to other hunting areas (theoretically, one). Other exchange systems balance gains and losses in basically the same way (Turner 1979*b*). There is one system, however, which instead of balancing affinal and fraternal ties in fact *compounds* them in an effort to secure the maximum benefits of both. Among the Aluridja of the Western Desert one marries a person in the same brotherhood as oneself. This practice follows from the fact that here all clans are totemically linked into a single brotherhood grouping. The relation of people of the same clan is established as the model for the entire social order.

The Aranda Transformation

The "universal" problem of local autonomy versus societal security that underlies Australian Aboriginal societies establishes the limits within which both variational and fundamental change occurs. Taking the Aranda system as our model, we could visualize the conditions under which people might grasp that by cultivating plants growing randomly at habitually used campsites they might achieve a greater measure of clan/phratry autonomy. As I mentioned above, each season, large groups of people sharing close bonds of brotherhood, but who rarely interact outside a ceremonial context, gather to fulfil ritual obligations at a sacred site along the track of a totemic being. To maintain this grouping even for a month or two requires abundant resources: for this reason such gatherings are usually held in the estate of a particularly well-situated clan. To maintain the grouping on a regular basis would require more resources than any one estate could possibly provide. The congregation could only maintain itself as an autonomous body if a permanent, local food supply were available; and this could only be provided through the cultivation of plants and/or domestication of animals. If these connections were in fact all made, it is likely that the clan that "owned" the ceremony and land in question would cultivate the seedlings and establish a permanent settlement — joined at first by members of the same phratry who share a common totemic affiliation (and, by implication, "ownership" of the same area). This group would now be able to reproduce itself both economically and socially. Marriages could be contracted within the phratry; there would be little need for ties to other clans in order to gain access to hunting territories. The problem, though, is that the symbolic apparatus that establishes and maintains rights in land has its own independent logic of clan interdependence. The people in one's own connubium are ritually tied to the owners of the land in question through past intermarriage and through ritual interdependence. Furthermore, utilizing the estates of brotherhood clans as hunting territories to supplement agricultural production would be unpractical; the estates of brotherhood clans are outside the connubium and too remote to be used regularly. The outcome of all this is likely to be a village settlement composed of connubium members and brotherhood-mates of the clan/phratry owning the estate in which the village is located. The owner-clan/phratry would most likely agree to share their agricultural product in return for rights in a common hunting range comprising the territories of the other clans in the connubium.

Functional interdependence at the village level could be implemented according to the same logic as before. But rather than assign specialized territories to particular groups and link them together through an exchange of spouses, the groups could be assigned specialized tasks or services associated with the new mode of production. Each of the four endogamous ritual divisions (the phratries) and each of the subdivisions within these in turn (the clans) would be required to perform a certain function; all functions would have to be performed to ensure the operation of any one division. The system would be "artificial" in the sense that the dominant phratry could be economically self-sufficient in theory but would be forced to uphold the system of ritual interdependence in order to maintain its legitimacy as the dominant division. It is the system of ritual interdependence that establishes the category of "owner", and the clan/phratry in question is owner of the site of agricultural activity, as well as the owner of the most significant ceremony linking clans in different connubia. This phratry would thus become a "priestly" division, responsible for ritual performance; it would also become the final authority on the use of resources. The clan/phratry that had previously "bossed" the "priestly" phratry would assume political authority, overseeing and administering the secular activities (including agriculture production) of the society as a whole. The third phratry might be assigned the job of farming; the fourth, the production of specialized secular and ritual artifacts. Finally, there is the whole mass of people who are not party to the Great Transformation — the neighbouring hunting and gathering peoples outside the Aranda sphere of influence. In so far as the new order is defined as universal — like the old one — allowing nothing alien to remain outside it, these other societies would continue to be regarded as human in nature but would now be differentiated as "primitive" in culture. They are an ambiguous category and would be assigned the tasks associated with the old hunting and gathering way of life — foraging, scavenging, unspecialized manual labour.

Both oppositions — clan autonomy and societal security — in the old contradiction have now been realized simultaneously. All we need assume is that most clans will see the advantages of the new arrangement in realizing a greater measure of autonomy at the clan/phratry level, even if it means accepting another clan/phratry as dominant within the new system. What we would now see throughout the Aranda area in question is a network of separate but ritually linked villages, each formerly a connubium of intermarrying clans. Each village would contain representatives of the four newly endogamous phratries, and each village would be internally interdependent, both economically and ritually.

It is apparent then that there is a basis for occupational and ritual specialization and for a hierarchy of functions among the Aranda (or any people with a similar social system) and that these features resolve the old contradictions that structured their existence as a hunter-gatherer society. Methodologically, it is important to note that the conditions that produced this resolution have been generated out of the internal structure of the Aranda system.

Caste Reality

If the above presentation is consonant with the modern view of traditional case organization, there are objective grounds for accepting this theory, and in fact a survey of the literature does seem to indicate considerable "fit". Texts of the late Vedic period (ending 600 B.C.) distinguish four great divisions in Indian society — Brahmin, Kshatriya, Vaishya, and Sudra. These "Varna" categories were endogamous, hereditary groups, ranked according to their respective degrees of ritual purity and having four different yet interrelated services to perform (at least in a ritual, if not always in a practical, context). At the top of the hierarchy were the ritually pure, twice-born Brahmins; next came the Kshatriya, from whose hands the twice-born could take food cooked in ghee but not water; then came the Vaishya from whose hands the twice-born could not accept any food but could take water; and finally came the Sudra, from whom the twice-born could take neither food nor water. Outside the Varna system stood the Untouchables, whose very touch defiled the orthodox Hindu (see Ghurye 1932/57, pp. 6—7).

The Brahmins controlled access to ritual activity and held only those lands donated to them by the Kshatriya. The Kshatriya controlled the state apparatus, including the military, and were the major land-owners. The Vaishya controlled trade and commerce and did not own much land. The fourth group, the Sudra, were the skilled craftsmen, cultivators, and husbandmen. The Untouchables performed manual labour and "unclean" tasks connected with death and cattle. They alone could eat meat. In the north their segregation was such that they were forbidden from entering the villages occupied by the orthodox castes; in the south they were merely confined to separate quarters within the village. The four Varna divisions (but not the Untouchables) had their mythological origins in the body of the Creator, originating from his mouth, arms, stomach, and feet respectively.

In theory the society could only function properly if all of the four divisions (and by association, the fifth) were represented in each village, performed their separate tasks, and exchanged their own respective goods and services. While all divisions were, in fact, found in each locality, their economic roles were not nearly so specialized in practice. Ghurye (1932/57, p. 15) found that the correlation between occupation and caste was only generally true, and that trading, agriculture, field labour and military service were engaged in by representatives of all divisions. Dumont (1970, p. 92) reports that farming was practised by some 43 per cent of non-farming castes, although 90 per cent of those in farming castes were in fact farmers. Caste specializations were, however, strictly adhered to in the performance of ritual. Only Brahmins could minister; only Sudra could act as drummers, barbers, and so on, for the various subdivisions within castes and Varnas. Indeed, Hocart (1950) and Dumont came to view ritual as the basis of the entire caste system. For Hocart, the caste system was a "sacrificial organization" in which "the aristocracy are feudal lords constantly involved in rites for which they require vassals or serfs, because some of these services involve pollution". Each practical occupation was simultaneously a kind of priestly function performed for a patron or *jajman*. The *jajmani* system of caste interdependence which operated at the village level was as much a ritual organization as it was an economic organization. It was universal in scope and quadripartite in underlying structure. This system cut across India's twelve major linguistic areas, subdividing each of them into about two hundred caste divisions and approximately two thousand subdivisions (Ghurye 1932/57, pp. 25–26).

Hocart, Dumont, and Ghurye consider village affiliation to be subordinate to caste membership, inasmuch as the latter demands one's primary allegiances. They see villages as localized slices of the Varna-caste totality. Indian village life is organized within the framework of a more comprehensive set of caste relations that spans the continent.

The Australian brotherhood-clan system, whether of the one-, two-, or four-phratral type, is universal in scope. In its developed form the brotherhood is, first and foremost, a ritual organization. Although it facilitates trade and other economic activities, these functions are dependent upon the ritual associations of the brotherhoods. In the case of the Aranda model, the four endogamous Varna "descent" categories may be equated with the four totemically linked phratries; the state jurisdiction within which the Varna system operates may be equated with the phratry that "bosses" the clan that "owns" the major ceremony; the Untouchable category may be equated with those who remain outside the Aranda framework. Indeed, in the Hindu system, the Untouchables seem to be a permanent, institutionalized reminder of the ascendancy of the new order — a permanent category of hunters and gatherers forever destined to subordinate their activities to nature and to remain separated from contemporary developments. Finally, the specialized functions performed by each of the four Varna divisions — ritual, administrative, agricultural, and craft production — find their counterpart in Aranda co-operative relations under the new, more fixed conditions of existence, in which marriage between clans is no longer necessary to gain access to hunting territory.

In more specific terms, most accounts agree that in India land is held by the dominant caste in the village; this land is available for use by all castes in so far as each performs a specialized activity that contributes to the productivity of the land. Land holding at the local level is the last link in a chain of administrative jurisdiction extending downward from the king (the dominant figure in the Kshatriya caste and head of state [Dumont 1970, p. 170]). In the Aranda analysis I have shown how village lands might fall under the ownership (in an absolute sense) of one phratry and the control of another, but that all clans and phratries would maintain their ritual relation to the land.

The Hindu "descent" system is also anticipated in the Australian transformation. In caste society, marriages are prohibited between the different subcastes of the same caste. In areas where subcastes are ranked within castes or where castes contain ranked, intermarrying clans, hypergamy may be obligatory, with women marrying up and men marrying down. In this case, subcaste membership is inherited from the father. But even where subcastes do not intermarry, the ideology of common descent within the caste is strong, connecting villages with no history of intermarriages (Beteille 1969, pp. 31–32). This sense of "brotherhood" between villages is also a feature of the Aranda phratry system, though here the ideology is based more on a common affiliation in the present than on consanguinity in the past. Patrilineality is also a feature of the Aranda clan system and might contribute to the continuity of the system under agricultural conditions where constancy in the functional relation between people and resources is required.

Further support for the theory comes from the fact that, even today, tribal peoples outside the Hindu system are usually incorporated at the Untouchable level, as were Europeans when they first arrived in India (Dumont 1970, p. 193).

Caste Logic in Australia

Certain northern Australian myths about the visits of the Macassan traders from Indonesia show that some Australian Aborigines, at least, entertained the possibility of establishing or accepting a caste-like relationship in their dealings with these seasonal visitors.

Macassan Contact

Macassan traders from Celebes and the surrounding area frequented Australia from the early eighteenth century until 1907, when the local authorities banned them from Australian waters (Macknight 1972, p. 294). They came for trepang, or sea-slug, a delicacy they traded to the Chinese, as well as pearl shell, pearls, turtle shell, and timber. Their fleets of thirty to sixty praus, each carrying about thirty men, left Macassar in December and sailed to the Australian coast on the north-west monsoonal wind. In groups of two or three praus, they worked along the coast from Melville and Bathurst islands, then east down the Gulf coast, until April, when they returned home on the south-east wind. As they worked, they established base camps along the shores, where they dried and smoked the trepang. Some of these camps were frequented each season, but there were no permanent settlements. The Macassans seemed content merely to have access to camping areas along the beaches. From the Aborigines, the Macassans obtained labour and trade items such as mentioned above; from the Macassans, the Aborigines acquired food (rice, molasses), cloth and clothing, tools (knives and tomahawks), gin, tobacco, and dugout canoes.

Macknight (1972, p. 285) notes that both sides had an interest in maintaining stable peaceful relations and that the incidents of violence reported in the literature were probably isolated. Circumstances leading to acts of violence included the abuse of Aboriginal women, disputes over trade, and personal injuries demanding redress. This view gains support from Warner (1958, p. 45), who reports that in north-east Arnhem Land the Macassans organized a policing system to prevent their men from having contact with Aboriginal women. On Groote Eylandt, the practice of keeping women secluded from strangers and the requirement of women to wear bark dresses when in the presence of strangers reflect attempts to restrict relations between the sexes. There are many confirmed reports of Aborigines travelling to Celebes with the Macassans; one source records some eighteen Port Essington men living together in Macassar in 1876 (in Macknight 1972, p. 296). On balance, there seems to have been considerable trust on the part of Aborigines in their dealings with the visitors. The general picture is of "two cultures existing side by side involved neither in major co-operation nor in competition" (Macknight 1972, p. 290).

According to Worsley (1954, pp. 13–14) the lasting effects of Macassan contact were, first, the introduction of wage labour into the hunting and gathering economy, but without a fixed medium of exchange; second, the influx of new types of goods in great quantity; third, the introduction of new modes of transportation and communication, fourth, the incorporation of new totemic symbols, such as ship and sail; and fifth, a new emphasis on the production of goods for trade, as well as for local consumption.

Myth Analysis

Elsewhere I have shown that the Aborigines of the Groote Eylandt area imagined, in their myths, alternatives to their Aranda-like system which stood wholly outside the bounds of the Australian framework (Turner 1978a). The alternatives proposed, however, eventually proved to be less appealing than the *status quo*. Ideas such as land holding based on residence rather than clan affiliation and incorporation of aliens into the society without the usual totemic qualifications were entertained, then rejected, as their disastrous consequences became apparent. Such rejection is to be expected when other important aspects of the system, such as the marriage rules and hunting patterns, are held constant in the myths and are all fundamentally incompatible with the proposed alterations. This experimentation seems to have been occasioned by thought on the basic problem of how to ensure continued ownership of clan lands in the absence of the rightful "owners", when outsiders who do not share a common mode of communication (and perhaps not even a common culture) may come to occupy these lands. This particular problem arises, in turn, from applying clan organization under nomadic conditions.

It is likely that the Macassans were both part of the problem here as well as a possible solution. They do not share Aboriginal culture, yet they occupy Aboriginal lands: but if allowed *temporary* access to restricted areas, they may be satisfied and even become useful to the local "owners" as overseers of this land in their absence. In other words, they may become "foreign trustees" (see Turner 1978*a* for an elaboration of this possibility).

The myths under investigation in this paper focus directly on the Macassans and the problems posed by their presence; they afford solutions not unlike the one mentioned above. The myths come from north-east Arnhem Land and Groote Eylandt and for our purposes can be treated as a corpus from the same culture. At the point of European contact and toward the end of the Macassan era when the myths probably originated, both peoples seem to have been organized according to Aranda principles (Turner 1979*a*). The first myth dealt with was gathered by Peter Worsley on Groote Eylandt in 1953, and relates the travels of a Macassan and a European ship throughout the area:

Ship

Originally, a Macassan ship and a European ship came from the south to Groote Eylandt, stopping at Golbamadja on the east coast, where the spirit of a Makassan is still said to live in a cave. As they went on towards Bickerton Island, they stopped at various places in Dalimbo, at Umbakumba, and in Djaragba and Badalumba, and asked the people in the Macassan tongue "What people are you?" The natives, not understanding these words, merely repeated them, an incident in the myth that evokes roars of laughter. At Bickerton Island, they repaired the Makassan ship and made it very long so that it would sail quickly; the European ship needed no repairs. The Makassan ship proved to be too long, however, and a portion was therefore cut off: this still remains at Bickerton Island at Bandu-banduwa.

The ship then went on to Melville Island (near Darwin, called Lau or Lauwa by the Wanindiljaugwa). There the people knew the Macassan language well, and the Makassans stopped and made a huge fire that was blown by the N.W. wind all over the mainland and over Groote, so that the people turned black. Before that they were white or like half-castes. The smoke covered everything like a fog, and the Melville Islanders, being right amongst the thickest smoke, became particularly black. Other tribes on the edges of the smoke-cloud were not so strongly blackened. [Worsley 1954, pp. 98–99].

Following structural precepts, the story can be divided into three major bundles of relations — geographical, territorial, and sociological. Geographically, movement in the myth proceeds from south to north-west in the episode dealing with the movement of the ships, and then reverses itself, moving from north to south-east in the episode dealing with the smoke. These movements parallel the comings and goings of the Macassans each season, although the direction of arrival is reversed: the Macassans always came from the north-west. In the myth, the north-west wind brings the (polluting) smoke to Groote Eylandt.

The symmetry of movement found here seems to be characteristic of the geographical or spatial dimension of "primitive" myths in general, perhaps indicating that natural phenomena like the seasons, the weather, and the topography are beyond human control. By themselves they are unproblematic; but they may cause problems for people − the same wind brings the Macassans to the area each season (see Levi-Strauss 1967). While the myth reverses the Macassans' normal direction of travel, appearing to deny the determining role of nature in human events here, it finally admits "defeat" when the north-west wind brings the "polluting" black smoke back to Groote Eylandt to reverse their political situation *vis-a-vis* the Macassans.

On the technological plane, we begin with two ships, one Macassan, the other European. The European ship is superior to the Macassan one (it is not in need of repair), but both together demonstrate that the outsider's technology is superior to that of Aborigines (who have no ships at all). The "weakening" of the "superior alien ship" category by the breaking down of the Macassan vessel allows mediation of the polar opposition between superior and inferior technologies. Paralleling this opposition is a territorial one between mobile Europeans and Macassans and sedentary Aborigines. Mediation of both technological and territorial oppositions occurs when a portion of the Macassan ship has to be left behind following the completion of repairs. The Aborigines now have a ship, but since the part does not substitute for the whole, their "ship" is as immobile as the landlocked Aborigines.

My Bickerton Island informants told me that when put to sea, this "ship" was transformed into a rock at Midjanga (ship place), off the south coast of the island (Turner 1974, p. 4).

Sociologically, three kinds of relations are explored − those among Aborigines in the Groote Eylandt area, those among Aborigines in Arnhem Land in general, and that between Aborigines and Macassans. This latter set of relations is dominant in so far as its effects cut across the other two sets. In the myth, the Macassan and European ships behave as totemic beings, wandering over the landscape, visiting Aboriginal clan territories and performing significant acts of lasting relevance to the Aboriginal situation. Within the Aboriginal logic of social relations, journeys such as these link the peoples belonging to the estates in question into a single brotherhood grouping; in eastern Arnhem Land these groupings numbered four. It is interesting to note that the ships in the myth in question, in fact, travel through the estates of three of the four phratries of the Groote Eylandt Aborigines and link them to the Melville Island people. What seems to be envisioned here is a universal brotherhood on the Aluridja or Western Desert model: it is universal because the Macassans seem to occupy the status of the fourth phratry. The Aboriginal clans represented in the tale are the Warnindilyaugwa (Dalimbo) of one phratry, the Warnungamagadjeragba (Umbakumba) and Wurramarrba of another (but of the same moiety as the first), and the Warnungwudjaragba and Wurrabadalamba of a third (of the opposite moiety). The Macassans' status as a clan is indicated by two factors: first, they pay a visit to an island on which their dead are said to be buried (indicating they own land on the island); and second, the indigenous phratry missing from the discussion is the one containing the Wurrawilya clan of Groote Eylandt (the one with which the Macassans would have been affiliated had they arrived in the direction set down by the myth). It is common practice in this area for newcomers to be associated with one of the four major wind totems (north-west, south-east, south-west, north-east) when they arrive from the north-west they are affiliated with that wind totem and so on. This procedure is most often applied to non-Aborigines who have no prior "species-connection" in their own society at the general level of the moieties, one signified by the north-west wind and the other by the south-east. Clan affiliation may or may not occur depending on the kind of relationship involved.

In the myth, the Macassans arrive from the south and the south wind is a Wurrawilya totem. This clan itself is said to have had its origins to the south, somewhere along the Gulf coast, and Aborigines arriving from there today are still affiliated with this clan. What is "unaboriginal" about the situation in the myth, however, is that the Macassan "clan" stands over and above all the rest in so far as its "creative being", ship, travels through the territories of the people of Melville Island. As the Macassans now possess the totemic track cross-cutting the greatest number of clan divisions (phratries), in this area at least, they would become ritual leaders. Given their economic specialization, they become a caste in the classic sense of the word; in effect, they become Brahmins.

The myth initially posits this division within an overall unity, significantly a racial one: everyone is at the outset white or like "half-castes". In other words they are all like Macassans. This arrangement is, however, apparently rejected by the end of the myth as a solution to the problem of Aboriginal–Macassan relations. Macassans are separated out on both economic and racial lines; they are white or half-caste and have the superior technology, while the Aborigines become black and have the inferior technology. A unity is still retained between the Melville Islanders and Groote Eylandters, however, and even seems to extend to the mainlanders – they are all a different degree of black. And the Macassan ship track still remains to link the indigenous phratries into a single category. The Macassans thus become an "Untouchable" category standing outside the four-phratry system but still somehow related to it; the Aborigines retain their three- or four-phratry structure, but somehow something has altered. In this connection it is interesting to analyze the relationship between degree of blackness and degree of contact with Macassans. On the question of "race" we would expect that the more contact and intermixture with the Macassans, the "whiter" Aborigines would become. However, in the myth, the Aborigines who become the most black are the ones who had the *most* intensive contact with the Macassans, namely the Melville Islanders (they speak Macassarese in the myth); the Groote Eylandters, with somewhat less of a history of contact, are somewhat less black; and the interior Aborigines with very limited contact are less black still. It is almost as if the mythmakers, having decided on the Untouchable solution, were trying to cover up the fact of racial intermixture between the two groups — a kind of rewriting of history to suit present circumstances.

In the next three myths under investigation, hierarchy is also entertained as a solution to relations between the two groups, and the problems attendant on this solution, from the Aboriginal point of view, are explored further. These myths were collected by Warner among the Murngin.

Macassar White Man and Dog

A very, very long time ago everything was different. People who lived in this place had skin just like Macassar men and Macassar men had skin like black men. Macassar men worked for black men then, just like we work for Macassar men by and by.

Dog was talking to his master. "We better break this house down and throw him away and live without houses."

The master of the dog talked to him. He said, "What do you want? Do you want something?"

Dog replied. He said, "What do you want? Do you want something?" he imitated the master's speech.

The man said, "No, I asked you."

Dog said, "No, I asked you."

They repeated this several times. That dog did not understand what that black fellow–white man was saying. The black man who was a white man said, "You don't understand what I am asking you for." He said that to the dog.

The dog continued acting silly, and said he did not want anything. The white man said, "You're the black man now and I the white. I am the master. I'll give you matches and tobacco and a sailing boat and tomahawks."

The dog said, "I don't want them. You can have them."

That master went back and another headman came. The first headman said, "I have come back."

The other said, "Why have you come back?"

He said, "Because Dog talked badly to me. I offered to give him all of those things and he said he didn't want them."

The other Macassar man said, "All right, all we people will keep all these things and we won't give them to black people because Dog talked that way. We'll let them work for us."

The Macassar men came in their boats for trepang. The black people who belonged to Dog went out to work for them. They became more and more black because Dog had acted so silly. A long time ago we people were white, now we are black. The name of this time a long time ago was Wongar time. This happened when the world started. [Warner 1958, p. 537]

At the beginning of the myth, a hierarchical relationship is established between Macassans and Aborigines within an overall unity. In this case the basis of the unity is not totemic, nor is it racial; rather it is co-residential, with the Aborigines predominating over the Macassans. There is racial differentiation — the Aborigines are white, the Macassans, black — but the two "races" live together. The reversal apparent here, relative to the actual situation that existed between the two groups, is not without its ambiguities; and it is these ambiguities which pave the way for an eventual transformation of the Macassan–Aboriginal relation.

One Aborigine — or rather a class of Aborigines — is singled out and signified as Dog, a category which in Aboriginal thought mediates between animals and humans. Thus, while the Aborigines may be in authority in this original society, Macassans at least can be in authority over dogs. This "substitution" of Dog for Aborigine is what eventually allows a mediation to occur. Dog, as a "silly" Aborigine, can provide the Macassan man, as an incipient "boss", with an excuse for reversing the general form of relations between the two groups. Macassan man generalizes from the individual Dog to the species, now "Aboriginal".

Dog's silliness consists not only of his imitation of what he "understands" of the Macassan's conversation but also of his rejection of the Macassan's technological goods. Since the Aborigines have, through Dog, shown themselves to be too "primitive" to see the advantages of these objects, the two Macassan bosses decide that they will henceforth be in authority and white, while the Aborigines will be subordinate and black. The co-residential unity apparent at the beginning of the myth is now fractured, as the Macassans now only visit seasonally in their boats to obtain trepang. The more the Aborigines work for the Macassans, the blacker (i.e., the more subordinate) they become. The implication is that despite contacts of an economic nature between the two groups, there is little intermixture — also a message of the previous myth.

This myth, then, begins with a caste-like relationship between Aboriginal managers and Macassan workers and ends with a class-like relationship of an employer-employee nature, but with the political situation reversed. However, the final solution still has tinges of caste in that the racial distinction remains important. Co-residence as a principle of group membership, or as a principle by which people may be incorporated into descent groups, is rejected. In class societies, place of work and residence define most of a person's rights and duties.

Macassar Man and Dog

That Wongar Dog always stayed close to the Macassar man when they were in this country. That Macassar big man said to him, "What do you keep your head down for?"

The dog mumbled the same words after his master.

The master said, "I am sorry."

The dog said, "I am sorry."

The Macassar man said, "I am going to give you tobacco, tomahawks, and canoes, and all the things my people have."

The dog replied, "No, I don't want them."

The Macassar man offered the dog a match.

The dog said, "Oh, no, I have fire sticks."

The Macassar man said then, "All right, then. You are going to become a black fellow. I will give you nothing. I'll be a Macassar man and I will keep all these things. You get off that mat and sit on the ground."

Howard Island still has posts of the houses that the Macassar built to give to Dog and which Dog refused, so the Macassar man picked up his houses and went away.

After Dog had refused all the things that the Macassar man possessed, the latter said to him, "Why do you act like this?"

The dog replied, "I want you to be a Macassar man. I am a black man. If I get all these things I will become a white man and you will become a black man."

The dog went away to Elcho Island from Howard Island and when he got to Caddell Straits he made a bark canoe to go across. That is why black men understand how to make these canoes today. After making the canoe he put it in the water but it sank. That canoe can be seen today among the rocks of the straits. The dog sat down and looked at it. He could do nothing. He was defeated. He sat down on the beach and he also turned to stone as his canoe had done.

"Now when we see that water break on that stone which is Dog and his canoe we think about all this and know why black men have so little and Macassar men and white men have so much." [Warner 1958, p. 536.]

In "Macassar Man and Dog", the two principal characters are again co-resident, although there is no permanent unity as the Macassans are only regular *visitors*. Again Dog is silly, again he refuses the goods offered by the Macassan man. Here, though, Macassan man is master (there is no mention of an original state of reversal), and he takes from Dog that which he has *already* given him — the housemat, seemingly a symbol of household existence. Perhaps Dog had been "experimenting" with Macassan goods before his final rejection of them. This would be consistent with the fact that he is active in his rejection, seeing them as undermining his own culture. Acceptance, he says, will make him white. Nor does Dog want the Macassans to become black men or Aborigines. Despite this clear-cut statement of separation, Dog is still ambiguous about his decision and what he has given up. His firesticks may serve as well as matches, but when he builds a canoe to cross open water, like the Macassans, it sinks, and both he and his inferior vessel are transformed into that recurring symbol of Aboriginal immobility — a rock in the sea.

Kolpa Robbers and Macassar Men

In the Kolpa clan's country called Kai-in-i a Wongar Macassar man lived. He was called Pa-po-a. He had built himself a large house with windows and doors and everything. A robber Kolpa man came down from the bush and stole the clothes and blankets from the Macassar man. The Macassar man decided to kill him. When the robber came again to steal from the Macassar man's belongings, the owner stood with his gun and shot at him. The robber stole a lot of the Macassar man's food. After several raids had been made by the Kolpa robber several of the Macassar men marched in a line with their guns to the Kolpa country. They were going to fight this Kolpa robber.
After they had gone a little while Jungle Fowl cried out. Jungle Fowl went into the big house where the Macassar men had left their food. He found many bags of rice. He tore the bags with his bill and scratched them like a fowl. He put over half a bag in his craw. The men came back and tried to shoot him but missed. When they tried to get in the robber's house it was all of stone and they couldn't force their way into it. They all decided to go get some poison and poison the Kolpa robber and Jungle Fowl. The robber overheard them so he stole some matches from them and burned the grass around the house, which finally also burned the house down. The Macassar men gathered up their other belongings and left the country. [Warner 1958, pp. 530–31]

The co-residential unit apparent at the outset of this myth is more pronounced than in the previous two, with the Macassan man described as living in a clan territory in an elaborate house. The myth follows with a successful attempt by an Aborigine to establish political control over the Macassar man, and his unwillingness to behave as an Aborigine. The Macassans here, as in the other myths, have the superior technology. The Kolpa robber attempts to steal the Macassans' goods (the implication being that they will not share them freely, as they should within Aboriginal society), and the Macassans attempt to kill him in retaliation. But, by using his traditional culture (his knowledge of the bush and his totemic connections), Kolpa robber is able to evade his attackers, burn their storehouse, and drive them away. Some ambiguity remains as to the status of Aboriginal versus Macassan culture in so far as it is the Macassans' own technology (the matches) which is used against them to enable their defeat. As before, an overall unity based on residential principles of group formation is implemented, fractured, and finally rejected. The *lack* of hierarchical organization in the last myth compared with the previous three is significant in that it is the Macassans' unwillingness to share which seems to be the reason for the breakdown in relations. Perhaps this myth is trying to explain why hierarchy becomes necessary, given that the Macassans always *do* return, despite being driven out on particular occasions.

These last three Murngin myths all seem to offer some form of separation as a solution to the Macassan problem. The first seems to suggest resignation to the fact of separation on the Macassans' terms, the second idealizes separation, finding each culture suited to its own people, and the third attempts to force a separation on the Aborigines' terms — a truly revolutionary suggestion. The Groote Eylandt peoples' solution seems somehow more creative, if somewhat more conservative. Their myth seems to suggest that relations involving subordination, yet interdependence, might be preferable to no relations at all. The Macassans would come, like it or not.

Caste Practice in Australia

Tindale (1962) has recorded a remarkable example of incipient caste practice among the Kaiadilt Aborigines of Bentinck Island which is uninfluenced by external forces. The Kaiadilt were divided into eight named, patrilineal, territorially defined *dolnoro*, grouped into four phratries along conventional Aranda lines. However, in very un-Aboriginal fashion, some 21 per cent of all marriages were actually within the same *dolnoro*. The neighbouring Laiardili of Mornington Island had almost the same system except that they married in the normal fashion (Sharp 1939).

Close examination of Tindale's data shows that intra-*dolnoro* marriages were confined to four of the island's eight groups, and that within each *dolnoro* in question there were actually no marriages between people possessing the same totem. It is evident, then, that the members of the four *dolnoro* were not marrying randomly within the *dolnoro* but had a concept of an exogamous subgroup. The four in question also held up their practice as ideal, whereas it was rejected by the non-participating groups. Totemic ties between *dolnoro* of the same "phratry" continued to exist despite *dolnoro* endogamy.

Tindale gives us a clue as to why this new arrangement was implemented (Tindale 1962, p. 298). Between 1942 and 1948 the Kaiadilt had been reduced from a population of 123 to 58 as a result of "inter-hordal" conflicts, accidental drownings by loss of small rafts during inter-island crossings, a long continued drought of serious effect, and finally an abnormal tide or tidal wave in February 1948. The members of one *dolnoro,* indeed, had departed for an outlying island after fighting with other Bentinck people. Such incidents may very well have led certain *dolnoro,* particularly those in more abundant resource areas, to have opted for the local autonomy over the societal security pole of the Australian contradiction. Security at the more inclusive level and maintenance of marriage ties to other groups may well have been of continuing interest only for those in particularly difficult circumstances. In any case, a measure of security would be still achieved through retention of totemic "phratral" ties.

The logical outcome of the Kaiadilt predicament may well have been four endogamous phratries with one or two *dolnoro* groupings in control of critical resources, but with all *dolnoro* involved in a system of ritual, and perhaps trade, interdependence. Alternatively, four *dolnoro* might merely have separated off from the rest, leaving the others to fend for themselves. Whether they would, in fact, have done so would have depended on the strength of the ritual connections between the four partly endogamous *dolnoro* and the rest. There is no "one brotherhood" level to Kaiadilt society as a whole which might provide the basis for a new jurisdiction within which hierarchy might be acceptable to all groups.

How all this would have worked out will never be known; the Australian authorities removed the Kaiadilt from the island shortly after the last disaster struck.

Conclusions

We have seen how a five-caste system can be deduced from an Australian base and that the outline of such a system is reflected in the
Aborigines' myths of the Macassans. A rudimentary attempt at caste-
like organization has been located among the Bentinck Islanders of
Queensland. The key to our understanding of these phenomena is
"domination". On one level, the myths analyzed here are efforts to
explain the Aborigines' subordinate position *vis-a-vis* the Macassans
(Worsley 1954, p. 99). But the myths also experiment with ways in
which the reality of domination can be made a part of a new order.
While three of the myth-makers seem to have abandoned their attempts
to work out a new, complementary system, opting instead for a separa-
tist solution, the originators of the "Ship" tale seem to have grasped
the awful implications of the encounter between themselves and the
Macassans. Even so, there is considerable ambiguity in all myths about
the ultimate superiority of Macassan culture, and the question is
raised whether Aboriginal culture is worth abandoning merely for the
sake of a few technological gadgets. The Kaiadilt seem to have gone
beyond mythological expression to actually begin working a caste-like
structure into their society. Domination here was by a few well-situated
groups in a time of extreme crisis. For the less well placed, the alternative was between the new order and starvation.

Whether this all says something about the origins of the Varna
system or whether we have merely located what happens when a
more hierarchical system encounters a more equalitarian one is a
question best left to the Indian historian. Once instituted, however,
an Australian clan-caste organization is likely to expand in basically
the same way as a developed caste system would reach beyond its
own borders. Both systems claim universal applicability, and both
would be in an encounter with a force contradicting that belief – for
one, something out of its past (if our theory is right), for the other,
something in its future. In both cases the response would not be to
annihilate and destroy, but rather to encircle and enfold. Failing in
this attempt, there would be a shift in the attempted level of encircle-
ment and an appreciation of the "other" as either primitive, untouchable, or superhuman – but nevertheless "related" to oneself and
worthy of life.

In neither case can we locate a logic that would lead to the organized
elimination of the "other", as we can in the logic of Algonkian and
European social organization (for instance, see Turner and Wertman
1977, chap. 4). The aim in these and other societies seems to be to
establish jurisdiction over resources and control over an economic base

of sufficient "wealth" that social relations could be more or less confined and reproduced within. This is indeed the logic of the nation state as we know it, and only recently have we begun to realize, and devise arrangements to avoid, the horrendous consequences of following through the implications of this logic under today's technological conditions. The economic philosophy which holds individual nations to be "naturally" endowed with certain advantages which should be developed and traded for the "natural" advantages of other nations is merely a more modern way of artificially spacing people over resources in such a way that co-operative relations of a certain kind must follow. It is a strategy as old as the Australian's hunting and gathering way of life; but perhaps this way was not in Western civilization's own hunting and gathering past. We may be the bearers of a more dynamic yet potentially more destructive tradition.

The problem with applying the Australian logic to modern international affairs in a conscious effort to create a more peaceable world order, through the application of the economic theory of comparative advantage, however, is that unless the "natural" advantages in question are all of equal worth from nation to nation, the resulting system will be hierarchical and centralized, not equalitarian and diffuse. We are still a long way from the global interdependence and equalitarianism implemented by the Australians in their known corner of the world; but then, as we have seen, they too had to face the fact that their logic would not work under conditions they had not imagined. As we seek an escape from the hierarchical-totalitarian implications of our own logic (Dumont 1970) we should be aware that there are models in the world to emulate other than those implicit in our own historical tradition.

References

Beteille, A. 1969. *Caste: Old and New.* Bombay: Asia Publishing House.
Dumont, L. 1970. *Homo Hierarchicus.* London: Weidenfeld and Nicolson.
Ghurye, G. 1932/57. *Caste and Class in India.* Bombay: Popular Book Depot.
Hocart, A. M. 1950. *Caste: A Comparative Study.* New York: Atheneum.
Levi-Strauss, C. 1963. The Bear and the Barber. *Journal of the Royal Anthropological Institute* 93, pt. 1:1–11.
——— . 1966. *The Savage Mind.* Chicago: University of Chicago Press.
——— . 1967. The Story of Asdiwal. In *The Structural Study of Myth and Totemism.* London: Tavistock.
——— . 1969. *The Elementary Structures of Kinship.* Translated by J. H. Bell, J. R. von Sturmer, and R. Needham. London: Eyre and Spottiswoode.
Macknight, C. 1972. Macassans and Aborigines. *Oceania* 42, no. 4: 283–321.

Maddock, K. 1972. *The Australian Aborigines.* London: Allen Lane the Penguin Press.

Mauss, M. 1969. *The Gift.* Introduction by E. E. Evans-Pritchard. London: Routledge and Kegan Paul.

Sharp, L. 1939. Tribes and Totemism in North-East Australia. *Oceania* 9: 254-75, 439–61.

Tindale, N. 1962. Some Population Changes among the Kaiadilt of Bentinck Island, Queensland. *Records of the South Australian Museum* 14: 297–336.

Turner, D. 1974. *Tradition and Transformation.* Canberra: Australian Institute of Aboriginal Studies.

————— . 1978*a* Dialectics in Tradition: Myth and Social Structure in Two Hunter-Gatherer Societies. Occasional Papers of the Royal Anthropological Institute 36.

————— . 1978*b* Hunting and Gathering: Cree and Australian. In *Challenging Anthropology,* ed. G. Smith and D. Turner. Toronto: McGraw-Hill Ryerson.

————— . 1979*a Australian Aboriginal Social Organization.* New York: Humanities Press.

————— . 1979*b* Structuralism, Social Organization and Ecology. *L'Homme,* Spring.

Turner, D., and P. Wertman. 1977. *Shamattawa: The Structure of Social Relations in a Northern Algonkian Band.* Ottawa: National Museums of Man.

Warner, W. L. 1958. *A Black Civilization.* Revised edition. New York: Harper Torchbook.

Worsley, P. M. 1954. The Changing Social Structure of the Wanindiljaugwa. Ph.D. thesis, Australian National University, Canberra.

Aboriginal Land Rights Traditionally and in Legislation: A Case Study

KENNETH MADDOCK

Aboriginal Land Rights Traditionally

The peoples about whom I write originate in and around Arnhem Land.[1] Developments around the periphery broke down the economy and local organization of this region during the first half of the century (grandparental and parental generations). The fatal factors included the rise of towns at Katherine, Mataranka, and Pine Creek, the spread of cattle stations along the east-west line of the Roper River and the north-south line of what is now the Stuart Highway, the founding of missions at Oenpelli and Roper, the opening of mines notably at Maranboy and Pine Creek, and the setting up of the ration depots, army camps, and welfare compounds by which the government tried to control, use, or assimilate Aborigines coming in from the hinterland.

Anthropology had little to say before mid-century about the peoples who were to settle on the Beswick Reserve.[2] A fuller picture of their social and religious organization was obtained only after 1947, when the government bought what is now the reserve as a pastoral training project. My work, like that of Elkin (1946–53) and West (1961–62), was carried out after the traditional economy and local organization had broken down, and there is no first-hand account of these topics. This is a bleak admission to make at the start of a study of powers Aborigines had or have in relation to land, but something has survived the ruin of the rest.

The traditional social organization and religious ritual have persisted in spite of sedentary and controlled conditions of life. Ceremonies keep alive what Mountford aptly calls "totemic geography" (Mountford 1968, p. 111). The most frequent are the Dua moiety's Gunabibi and the Jiridja moiety's Jabuduruwa, each of which is performed once a year with help from the other moiety. Their songs, dances, and material art make memorable and striking the union of man with man, man with place, man with species or spirit, and the union of all these with the mythic times in which the natural and social orders arose. The ritual and mystical aspects of relations to land are especially significant to anyone who tries *now* to portray traditional entitlements to land. In the absence of specifically legal institutions (Maddock 1970), Aboriginal land law can be arrived at only by abstraction from a wide and, legally speaking, undifferentiated web of social and symbolic relationships, the clearest and most conscious expression of which is to be found in ritual and mythology.[3]

Furthermore, although we can no longer observe the traditional land use and settlement pattern, we can infer from what Aborigines say that their local organization must have had much in common with what Hiatt (1962, pp. 279–82; 1965, pp. 14–28) reports for the Gidjingali of northern Arnhem Land. This is a system in which descent groups are connected in the male line with a number of totemic sites. The area containing these sites is a clan estate or territory. Residential groups foraged and camped on a number of adjoining clan estates known together as a range. Most members of a residential group belonged to a clan whose estate lay within the range or had a spouse belonging to one of those clans. The residential group or groups habitually using a range are known together as a band, community, or horde. Their size, structure, and round of activity would vary with seasonal and other factors, but a number would come together at times and perform ceremonies in which the web of social and symbolic relationships to which I referred would be made manifest. Several bands might be represented on these occasions. These economic and residential aspects of relations to land provide a second body of data from which to abstract an Aboriginal land law.[4]

It may be wondered why I should try to construct a system of land law from traditional data if Aborigines had no specifically legal institutions. The short answer is that the land rights' agitation, litigation, and inquiries of the 1960s and 1970s, which culminated in the Aboriginal Land Rights (Northern Territory) Act 1976, raise a question of the extent to which justice can be or has been done to the traditional ideas and relations the denial or neglect of which gave rise to the agitation, litigation, and inquiries. I shall now see what can be made of the two bodies of data available for understanding what land rights traditionally were. It will be necessary in doing so to consider the accuracy of some Aboriginal English translations of key words.

Ritual and Mystical Aspects

The study of a pair of correlated terms, *gidjan* and *djunggaiji,* opens a way to the understanding of relations to land. Each word implies the other, so that it would be as absurd to think of them in isolation as it would be to think of parents without children or wives without husbands.

The *gidjan-djunggaiji* relation occurs at class and personal levels of organization. First, it exists between the patrilineal moieties. Dua is *gidjan* and Jiridja *djunggaiji* for the Gunabibi ceremony, but they reverse roles for the Jabuduruwa. Further, each semi-moiety (a named half) of a moiety is in a *gidjan-djunggaiji* relation with a semi-moiety of the other moiety, but I shall not pursue the details of this. Second, the relation exists between men of opposite moiety, though not necessarily only between men of the semi-moieties paired as *gidjan* and *djunggaiji*.

The relation may be described as asymmetrical, since on a given occasion one class or person will be *gidjan* and the other *djunggaiji*. The asymmetry of the moment is soon corrected between moieties because Gunabibi roles are reversed in the Jabuduruwa and the two ceremonies are performed in rotation (Maddock 1979*b*). Asymmetry can last between persons, however, because a man is normally not *djunggaiji* for his *djunggaiji*, but fills this role for other men of the moiety of his *djunggaiji* (I shall qualify this statement presently). Why this difference?

It might be suggested that symmetry between moieties follows from the fact that they number two: an exogamous moiety is wife-giver to its wife-giver in a two-class system of marriage exchange, and so, in a two-class system of ritual exchange, a moiety is *djunggaiji* to its *djunggaiji*. But the analogy is inconclusive because ritual need not imitate marriage. Exogamous moieties are demographically constrained to take as well as give wives, but one could always be *gidjan* and the other *djunggaiji*. This is, indeed, approximated to in north-east Arnhem Land (Warner 1937, p. 32). Where ritual imitates marriage, as among the peoples of the Beswick Reserve, a general equality results between the moieties. This does not mean a grey uniformity of action, because the Gunabibi and Jabuduruwa are strikingly different ceremonies (Maddock 1979*b*). What a moiety does in its capacity as *gidjan* or *djunggaiji* in one ceremony is therefore not the same as what the other moiety does in that capacity in the other ceremony. The equality is in role categories, not in the action content of roles.

At the personal level, a man is *djunggaiji* for men who belong to his mother's patrilineal clan or to a clan sharing its estate and for men who belong to his father's mother's clan or to a clan sharing its estate. He calls the totemic sites contained in these estates mother or father's mother — that is, he is child or grandchild to them. This suggests that to be *djunggaiji* is to be junior and hence inferior. (A man calls his mother's moiety's ceremony mother, which suggests that they are senior and hence superior to his moiety and its ceremony, but this does not give rise to class hierarchy. The role reversals and rotation of ceremonies to which I referred ensure that each moiety is sometimes mother and sometimes child to the other.)

Marriage and ritual are intrinsically connected at this level. Suppose a woman of clan X marries a man of clan Y. His son calls her mother and uses this term also for her moiety and its ceremony and for totemic sites in the X estate. That is to say, he is maternally filiated to them as he is to her, unlike her brother and his son who are paternally filiated to them as they are to her. Her son's son, too, will be Y. He will call her father's mother and he will use this term also for totemic sites in the X estate, but not for her moiety and its ceremony, because he will be connected to them through his own mother. This analysis shows that men of clan X would be *djunggaiji* to Y — that is, they would call totemic sites in the estate of Y mother or father's mother, only if a woman of Y had married a man of X. Direct exchange is not, however, a normal feature of alliance networks on the reserve.

I have located the *gidjan-djunggaiji* relation. It is time to study the conduct called for between classes or persons so related.

There is, first, a sphere of conduct having to do with the performance of ceremonies. The tasks of the *djunggaiji* moiety include making the symbolic waters which are foci for much of the ritual dancing, making the more important paraphernalia worn or otherwise displayed during a performance, arranging the programme, supervising the correctness of performance, and playing the musical instrument diacritical of the ceremony. Much of their work is carried out in secret. It is noteworthy that men of the *djunggaiji* moiety have access to the whole precinct within which the ceremony is performed, but men of the *gidjan* moiety are restricted; for example, they may not see the symbolic waters under construction or go near the places where certain of the paraphernalia are made. Thus men to whom the ceremony is mother are freer than men paternally related to it. This paradox can be explained if we assume that the juniority of *djunggaiji* — they stand as child to mother — is offset by their masculinity — the *gidjan* moiety's ceremony, being mother, stands as female to them. As child I am mother's junior, but as male I may go where she may not.

Most of the ritual dancing is done by the *gidjan* moiety, and most of the totemic imagery seen during the ceremony is classified with it. If the ceremony has mortuary or post-mortuary significance, the man for whom it is celebrated will be a *gidjan*. We can say that performance of the ceremony enables the *gidjan* to display to an audience of *djunggaiji* a variety of dances and designs associated with the mothers and father's mothers of the audience. The salient elements on display include the design on the dancer's body, the species or spirit it represents, the movements of the dance, and the totemic site at which the performance is symbolically staged. The elements are not an arbitrary assemblage but a mythic configuration, for the design and movements signify a species or spirit that was once at a totemic site to which the dancer is paternally filiated. The configuration is chosen for him by a man maternally filiated to the same site. There can be no ceremony, then, without continuing collaboration for a common end between *gidjan* and *djunggaiji*.

A second sphere of conduct has to do with taking natural products from certain totemic sites. For example, wild honey may be taken from one moiety's sites and eaten only by members of the other. I have seen this privilege exercised and enjoyed the benefit of it at a Jiridja site, for I am Dua. I doubt whether this custom was ever important economically, and nowadays it certainly is not, since bush food is seldom eaten. The significance of the custom lies in what it says about the *gidjan-djunggaiji* relation: there are advantages to being related to a place through one's mother or father's mother instead of in the male line.

A third sphere has to do with movement across country. Certain places may be safely visited only by *djunggaiji* or in the company of *djunggaiji*. A *gidjan* would risk his life by going to them alone or only with other *gidjan*. Here, too, custom is significant for what it says about a relationship.[5]

These usages could be expressed in an old-fashioned idiom as showing mother-right (*das Mutterrecht*) alongside father-right (*das Vaterrecht*) or even in the ascendancy. Whether this division of powers can be traced more widely in the social and religious organization of these Aborigines, or is limited to a few spheres only, need not be investigated here, where the aim is merely to characterize relations to land.

It will be useful now to enlarge upon the references already made to patrilineal clans, since this should clarify the connection between the class and personal levels of the *gidjan-djunggaiji* relation.

Each Aborigine belongs to a *dawaro* with a proper name by which its members may be referred to or addressed. A *dawaro* is associated, often in company with another or others, with an area of country containing some totemic sites (*djang*). A site is normally on a path (*balad*) taken by a world-creative power in mythic times. Other sites will be located along the same path, which is but one of many forming an imaginary network across the countries of an indefinite number of clans. The powers who took these paths are the species or spirits the *gidjan* represent in ceremonies.[6]

A man may be said to be *gidjan* (*a*) for sites in his clan's country, (*b*) for sites outside his clan's country but on a path crossing it, and (*c*) for sites classed in his moiety. He is *djunggaiji* (*a*) for sites in his mother's or father's mother's clan's country, (b) for sites outside his mother's or father's mother's clan's country but on a path crossing it, and (c) for sites classed in his mother's moiety. It is unusual for these distinctions to be made in speech, but the context in which the words *gidjan* and *djunggaiji* are used will often show whether (a) or (b) or (c) is meant. The first of these corresponds best to the personal level at which the *gidjan-djunggaiji* relation manifests itself, but the second belongs also to this level because a *gidjan* may wear the design and perform the dance associated with a (b) site. The third corresponds to the class level, for if a man is *gidjan* or *djunggaiji* to a (c) site, so is each other man of his moiety. Aborigines will indeed often express themselves in class terms at this level and, instead of saying that a named man is *djunggaiji* for the Gunabibi, will say simply that Jiridja is *djunggaiji*.

There are three limitations on a man's right to represent a species or spirit associated with a site for which he is *gidjan* in sense (a) or (b). First, the species or spirit must be associated with the particular ceremony, that is, each ceremony has only some of the powers classed in its moiety. Second, the power must be classed in the same semi-moiety as the man, that is, each clan has two sets of powers distinguished by semi-moiety. Third, the representation must be authorized by a *djunggaiji* in sense (a) or (b).

The survey I have made of the ritual and mystical aspects of relations to land shows that some relations are of men paternally filiated to land because of its association with their father's clan or moiety and that other relations are of men maternally filiated to land because of its association with their mother's or father's mother's clan or moiety. The former relationship is that of *gidjan* the latter that of *djunggaiji* and each carries its own rights and obligations upon the proper exercise of which the other depends.

Problems in Translation

Aborigines translate *gidjan* as "owner" and *djunggaiji* as "manager, boss, worker, policeman". How accurate are these renderings?

The translators have done well with *djunggaiji*. The roles the *djunggaiji* fill include some that are managerial or boss-like in nature – for example, arranging programmes and deciding which configurations of elements will be staged. It may be objected, of course, that a manager in our sense organizes workers and plant at a place of work, but an analogy can be apt even if it breaks down when pushed too far. The *djunggaiji* put in many hours of working making symbolic waters and items of paraphernalia, and they see throughout to the proper conduct of the ritual. There can be no serious quarrel, then, with worker or policeman.

The translation of *gidjan* is less successful. An owner in our sense is in a proprietorial relation to a thing – the thing is his property or, expressed differently, he has property in it. That Aboriginal relations to land resemble property relationships in English law was rejected by Mr Justice Blackburn in the *Gove Land Rights Case.* [7] Although he was giving judgement in an action referring to north-east Arnham Land, there seems little reason for doubting that his observations, which were probably *obiter,* would apply equally to the peoples of the Beswick Reserve. We cannot assume from an Aborigine's use of the possessive that he has property in *his* wife, child, parent, or moiety, even though there may sometimes be a proprietorial relationship, as is likely when a man speaks of *his* boomerang. That is to say, the possessive in *my* land arguably invites comparison with *my* father or *my* mother rather than with *my* spear. This suggests that a man who stands as *gidjan* to a piece of land is not its owner in our sense of the word, and that he has no more (but also no less) ownership of it than has its *djunggaiji.* [8]

That Aboriginal ideas about and relations to land cannot be expressed accurately in the property conceptions of English law need not lead us to deny the legal significance of Aboriginal realities. What is called for is an examination of the Aboriginal ideas and relations to see which constructions are the least forced. The salient point to notice in the case under discussion is that a certain pattern of conduct is prescribed between *gidjan* and *djunggaiji* and between each and the piece of land of which he is *gidjan* or *djunggaiji.* The basis of the distinction between these roles is (*a*) that one stems from father-right, the other from mother-right, and (*b*) that the pattern of conduct prescribed for one is in complementary opposition to the pattern prescribed for the other. It is unfortunate that the vernacular English spoken by Aborigines has been unable to capture these realities in its translation of *gidjan* and *djunggaiji* and has instead confused the issues by introducing the red herring of property law.

Economic and Residential Aspects

I have indicated that the information available here is meagre but that, so far as it goes, it shows some broad resemblances to Gidjingali local organization. There are three reasons for thinking that residential groups – that is, the aggregates of people who foraged and camped together – included members of several clans.

First, it is usual for more than one clan to be totemically connected in the male line with any given piece of land. Second, exogamy means that the members of the clans so connected get their spouses from clans of the other moiety. This gives rise to *djunggaiji* relationships by which people are totemically connected to land through mother or father's mother and have special responsibilities and privileges as a result. Third, Aborigines who talk about things they did in pre-settlement days will often mention such relatives as mother's brother or male cross cousin as having been present. That is to say, men were frequently in the company of their *gidjan*.

If the men as well as the women of a residential group belonged to a number of clans, including clans of opposite moiety, it is a fair inference that most members would have foraged and camped most of the time outside the area to which they were totemically connected in the male line — that is, outside their clan estate. People must have spent much of their time in the other moiety's country.[9]

The inquiries I made into the traditional economy and local organization were insufficient to enable me to go further than these generalizations and inferences; for example, I do not know how extensive were the ranges on which residential groups foraged and camped or whether they overlapped or were discrete areas. Memory data could probably still be obtained on these questions, but it is doubtful whether the answers would force a change in the legal "conceptualization" of the data at present available.

Relations to land in economic and residential contexts may be classified in two groups according to their origin (cf. the two groups of relations to land in ritual and mystical contexts). These can be discovered by asking on what basis a person belonged to a residential group. He belonged by birth if his father or mother was a member of one of the clans having its estate within the residential group's range. The clan estate of father would sometimes fall within the same range as the clan estate of mother, but in other cases they would be on different ranges. A birthright to forage and camp on certain land might thus be maternal or paternal or both, and it would be a nice question whether the combination of the two ever gave a stronger right than one alone.

A person belonged by marriage to a residential group if his spouse belonged by birth to it. Clan estates of opposite moiety are sometimes within the same range, which makes it possible for marriages to have occurred within the band, but often a member by birth would have an in-marrying wife or husband. A marriage right to forage and camp might thus be to the same land as the birthright or to different land, and once again there is a question whether the combination of the two would give a stronger right than one alone.

Traditional Land Rights Recapitulated

The ownership of land by Aborigines can only mean the rights Aborigines had or have in land. The language of jurisprudence being foreign to the Aboriginal tradition, the observer from another society can arrive at those rights only by some such method as inference from the usual or habitual patterns of activity so far as these refer to land — for example, foraging on one's spouse's clan estate or moving freely as a *djunggaiji* at a place where *gidjan* suffer restrictions of access. It is clear that a variety or rights must be recognized — as *gidjan*, as *djunggaiji* as band members — and that rights have different roots — in marriage as well as in birth.

Rights to land may be described as divided in two senses. The first is that there is a variety of rights and that rights arise in different ways. The second sense is more interesting. The nature of the rights is such that they can never be united in one person: a man cannot be *gidjan* and *djunggaiji* in relation to the one piece of land. There is accordingly nothing comparable to the concentration of rights that we find in the fee simple of English land law. Some people can have more rights in a piece of land — e.g., rights as a band member and as a *gidjan* or *djunggaiji* in sense (*a*) — and others can have fewer rights, but although a person might have no rights at all to a piece of land he could not have all the rights. The irreducibly divided nature of Aboriginal property in land is unaffected by the chance that a dwindling of population might leave only one person alive who had any rights in a piece of land.

The usual treatment of Aboriginal rights to land is to impute ownership to a group endowed with legal personality and to accord rights to individuals by virtue of their natal membership of this corporation. Rights that fit this scheme badly tend to be ignored as outside the scope of ownership — for example, rights by marriage, rights as *djunggaiji,* and rights arising from membership of a band. The implication is that something analogous to the English estate in fee simple exists among Aborigines. On this view, justice would be done to Aborigines if their clans were issued with Torrens titles. It will be clear that my approach to ownership takes tacit issue with the usual treatment.[10]

Aboriginal Land Rights in Legislation

Australian law knew virtually no Aboriginal rights to land before the Aboriginal Land Rights (Northern Territory) Act 1976. This act, which provides for ownership and administration of "Aboriginal land", gives effect to many of the recommendations and suggestions of Mr Justice Woodward's royal commission (see Aboriginal Land Rights Commission 1974). Aborigines on the Beswick Reserve were largely untouched by the events that led to the Woodward Commission.[11] The reserve is a backwater, and this no doubt explains why the commissioner did not pay it a visit during his inquiries. But the peoples settled there are subject to the new law, and one may accordingly ask how their rights under it compare with their traditional rights and how they are likely to be affected by it.

Title to Land and Powers of Decision

The operation of section 10 of the act makes the 3,460 square kilometres of the Beswick Reserve "Aboriginal land", defined in section 3 as "land held by a Land Trust for an estate in fee simple". A land trust is defined in section 4 as a corporation the minister (for Aboriginal affairs) establishes "to hold title to land . . . for the benefit of Aboriginals entitled by Aboriginal tradition to the use or occupation of the land". A land trust consists under section 7 of a chairman and at least three other members appointed by the minister for not more than three years but with eligibility for reappointment. These provisions show that the title-holding body will have only a few members and that potentially the minister will control it. Whether these are serious points cannot, however, be determined only by reading the sections about land trusts. The act puts trusts on a middle level between land councils and certain classes of Aborigine and defines their terms of interaction.

Section 21 requires the minister to divide the Northern Territory into at least two areas and to establish for each of them a land council, defined in section 22 as a corporation. There are now three land councils, Northern, Central, and Tiwi, the first two of which go back to 1973 when they formed on an interim basis to make submissions to the Woodward Commission. The Beswick Reserve is within the Northern Land Council's area of responsibility. Before the Tiwi Land Council was established (*Land Rights News*, July 1978), this area covered the so-called Top End of the Territory and included about sixteen thousand Aborigines (*Land Rights News* February 1977). The effect of the act, then, is to lock the Beswick Trust into a larger institutional structure.

The members of a land council are required by section 29 to be Aborigines who live in the council's area or whose names appear on its register of "traditional Aboriginal owners". The methods by which members are chosen and the terms and conditions on which they hold office are subject to the minister's approval. When the minister officially established the Northern Land Council in January 1977, he indicated that its members would remain six months in office and would then be replaced by new members appointed for three years (*Land Rights News* July 1977). The new members, numbering forty-three from twenty-eight communities, were nominated by their communities and include two from Bamyili, the main centre on the Beswick Reserve (*Land Rights News*, September 1977). The full council has elected an executive committee of ten members from nine communities, including one from Bamyili, to run for the rest of its term of office (*Land Rights News*, August 1977).

What is the Beswick Trust's relation to the Northern Land Council? The act states in section 5 that a land trust "(a) shall not exercise its functions in relation to land held by it except in accordance with a direction given to it by the Land Council for the area in which the land is situated; and (b) where such a direction is given to it − shall take action in accordance with that direction". The Beswick Trust is thus fully subordinated to the Northern Land Council.

What are the Northern Land Council's powers and obligations? Section 23 includes among a land council's functions:

(a) to ascertain and express the wishes and the opinion of Aboriginals living in the area of the Land Council as to the management of Aboriginal land in that area . . . ;

(b) to protect the interests of traditional Aboriginal owners of, and other Aboriginals interested in, Aboriginal land in the area of the Land Council;

(c) to consult with traditional Aboriginal owners of, and other Aboriginals interested in, Aboriginal land in the area of the Land Council with respect to any proposal relating to the use of that land . . . ;

(e) to negotiate, on behalf of traditional Aboriginal owners of land in its area held by a Land Trust and any other Aboriginals interested in the land, with persons desiring to use, occupy or obtain an interest in that land . . . ;

(h) to supervise, and provide administrative assistance for, Land Trusts holding, or established to hold, Aboriginal land in its area.

These provisions together with those of section 5 show that the act draws a radical distinction between having title to land and having powers of decision over land. The Beswick Trust has the legal estate in the form of a fee simple to the Beswick Reserve. Such a title confers generally speaking the greatest interest English law allows a person to have in land. He who has a fee simple would normally enjoy a wide range of powers over the land; for example, he would decide whether to lease or mortgage or sell it or whether to grant a right of way or other easement on it. In this case, however, the powers have been separated from the title and the two are in different hands. Certainly the Beswick Trust holds its title under section 4 for the benefit of Aborigines traditionally entitled to use or occupy the Beswick Reserve, but clearly the Northern Land Council is empowered to decide what is beneficial.

How serious is the separation from the viewpoint of Aboriginal rights to land? It might be maintained that powers of decision should go with title to land. The Beswick Trust is potentially closer to the Beswick Reserve and its people than the Northern Land Council could ever be. The trust's members are likely in practice, as at present, though not required by law (see section 7), to live on the reserve or be traditionally connected with it. No more than a few council members can be expected to come from the Beswick Reserve or be connected traditionally with it, and this is bound to "distance" the council from the problems and outlook upon life of the people living there. It is no doubt considerations of this sort that led the people of Melville and Bathurst islands to form their Tiwi Land Council in spite of the Northern Land Council's coolness to fragmentation of its area of responsibility. The present form of the act stands in the way of a union of council and trust, but nothing except ministerial disapproval can prevent the two sorts of corporation embracing exactly the same area.

Some Aborigines might prefer councils to be on the same scale as trusts or wish the act amended to allow a union of council and trust, but there are cogent arguments in favour of the present arrangement.

First, a council's functions can be carried out only with administrative and expert help and advice (e.g., negotiating with mining companies and branches of government), and it would not be practical to provide these at the level of the Beswick Trust. This argument leaves open the possibility that the trust should have some say in what is beneficial.

Second, Aborigines need to agree on some policy issues and to be aware of one another's points of view and the reasons for them, but this requires an administrative and political organ above the trust level.

Third, a separation of title and power is consistent with Aboriginal rights to land traditionally, since these are characterized by their irreducible divisibility. This argument leaves open where the separation can best be drawn; furthermore, tradition knows nothing analogous to a powerless title-holder.

Fourth, the Northern Land Council's superordination to the Beswick Trust and other land trusts need not make it alien to the people on the land. Its activities are generally in accord with Aboriginal wishes and interests — for example, in pressing land claims and in negotiating with mining companies and branches of government — and it is required by the act to consult Aboriginal opinion.

The general tendency of these arguments is to suggest that the Beswick Trust and other land trusts should be seen as bodies having a specialized legal function — the holding of title to land — in a larger system, and that one should take care not to be misled about their role by the usual connotations of the fee simple concept (cf. the need for care in construing the Aboriginal translation of *gidjan* as owner).[12]

Discussion of the pros and cons of councils and trusts is bound to include a large element of the hypothetical, because of the novelty of Aboriginal land rights in Australian law, but it is justified because they form much of the legal framework within which land questions will arise and be answered. It need hardly be said that corporations created by statute are alien to the Aboriginal tradition, and the material I have given shows that their membership is small compared with the number of people they serve. What sort of fit is there, then, between statutory provisions on the one hand and the realities of tradition and population on the other? We have looked up from the Beswick Trust to the Northern Land Council. We must now look down to the people of the reserve.

Aborigines as Traditional Owners and as Traditionally Entitled

The Aboriginal Land Rights Act divides the people who live on the Beswick Reserve into three categories according to their traditional relationship to the land within the reserve.

First, there are "traditional Aboriginal owners", defined in section 3 to mean "a local descent group of Aboriginals who — (a) have common spiritual affiliations to a site on the land, being affiliations that place the group under a primary spiritual responsibility for that site and for the land; and (b) are entitled by Aboriginal tradition to forage as of right over that land".

Second, there are Aborigines who, in the words of section 4, are "entitled by Aboriginal tradition to the use or occupation of the land concerned, whether or not the traditional entitlement is qualified as to place, time, circumstance, purpose or permission". This broadly defined category compromises the people for whose benefit the Beswick Trust holds title to the Beswick Reserve. It includes the traditional owners of land on the reserve, but includes also all other Aborigines who have some traditional relationship with that land.

Third, there are Aborigines who have no traditional relationship whatever to land on the reserve. This residual category includes immigrants (and their children and more remote descendants) from areas whose people did not forage and camp on land now within the reserve or visit it by some sort of "right" (e.g., for taking part in ceremonies). One supposes that most of the sixteen thousand or so Aborigines in the Top End would belong in this category, but in the absence of better information about the traditional local organization it would often be difficult to say confidently whether a man belonged to this or to the second category. Much would depend on where the onus of proof of category membership lies.

The provisions of the act distinguish traditional owners to their advantage from all other Aborigines, as I shall show.

Section 19, which lists circumstances in which a land trust may, at the direction of a land council, grant, transfer, or surrender an estate or interest in Aboriginal land, stipulates that the council shall first satisfy itself that "(a) the traditional Aboriginal owners (if any) of that land understand the nature and purpose of the proposed grant, transfer or surrender and, as a group, consent to it; (b) any Aboriginal community or group that may be affected by the proposed grant, transfer or surrender has been consulted and has had adequate opportunity to express its view to the Land Council". Traditional owners of a piece of Aboriginal land thus enjoy a power of veto over proposed dealings in that land; other Aborigines, no matter how directly or adversely affected, do not.

Section 23, which lists the functions of a land council, makes actions it takes in connection with land held by a trust subject to stipulations like those of section 19.

Section 35, which regulates a land council's spending of money paid to it under certain other sections, stipulates that where the payment was received for Aboriginal land the council shall pay an equal amount to or for the benefit of the traditional owners of that land.

Section 48, which refers to grants of mining interests in Aboriginal land and to the application to such land of acts of parliament authorizing mining, makes the consents a land council gives subject to stipulations like those of section 19.

Section 68, which refers to the construction of roads over Aboriginal land, also makes the consents a land council gives subject to stipulations like those of section 19.

Another advantage that traditional owners enjoy is that they can be eligible for membership of a land trust (section 7) or land council (section 29) even if they do not live in the council's area of responsibility. Other Aborigines are eligible only if they live in that area.

Finally, it may be mentioned that the act provides in section 50 for "traditional land claims" to vacant crown land which, if successful, result in the land becoming Aboriginal. There are extensive areas of vacant land near to or adjoining the Beswick Reserve. The chance exists, then, that the Beswick Trust will extend its holdings. Traditional land claims are defined in section 3 to mean claims "by or on behalf of the traditional Aboriginal owners of the land arising out of their traditional ownership". This is the only sort of claim that may be made under the act.

Clearly it will benefit Aborigines living on the reserve or traditionally connected with it though living elsewhere if they can have themselves accepted as traditional owners of it (or of parts of it). Equally clearly it could be detrimental to anyone wishing, say, to mine or build roads on the reserve if there were traditional owners of the part affected. Traditional owners will, in at least one respect (payments under section 35), be better off the fewer they are.

What advantages does the act give to Aborigines of the second and third categories I distinguished? The expression "any Aboriginal community or group" used in sections 19, 23, 48, and 68 does not distinguish second-category from third-category Aborigines; as members of a community or group affected by a proposed dealing in land, mining grant, and the like, they are entitled to be consulted by the Northern Land Council and to an adequate opportunity to express their view of the matter, but their agreement is inessential. Similarly, the various paragraphs of section 23 referring to Aborigines other than traditional owners do not distinguish between the second and third categories.

Second-category Aborigines are included among those for whose benefit the trust holds its title and third-category Aborigines excluded, but it is not clear from the act that this will make any noticeable difference. To which of these categories an Aborigine belongs will, however, make a difference under some sections of the act that I have not so far discussed.

Section 69 provides a penalty of a thousand dollars for entering or remaining on a sacred site, but this does not apply where the entry or stay is "in accordance with Aboriginal tradition". Presumably this defence would be unavailable to third-category Aborigines – and also to some second- and even first-category Aborigines – for example, if they were of the wrong sex or were uninitiated.

Section 70 provides a penalty of a thousand dollars for entering or remaining on Aboriginal land, but section 71 states that "an Aboriginal or a group of Aboriginals is entitled to enter upon Aboriginal land and use or occupy that land to the extent that that entry, occupation or use is in accordance with Aboriginal tradition governing the rights of that Aboriginal or group of Aboriginals with respect to that land, whether or not those rights are qualified as to place, time, circumstances, purpose, permission or any other factor". The language of section 71 recalls the definition of beneficiaries of a land trust under section 4. Second-category Aborigines are here clearly distinguished from third-category, who would appear to commit an offence by entering Aboriginal land unless given permission under some other law.[13]

An implication of sections 69 and 71 is that an Aborigine may enter or stay on a sacred site or a piece of Aboriginal land only if he is traditionally entitled to be in that area. It would be insufficient to have a traditional entitlement to be in some other area. This means that traditional owners even of parts of the reserve could be "out of bounds" in other parts. Another noteworthy point about section 71 is that traditionally entitled Aborigines appear to be allowed to use or occupy a piece of Aboriginal land only in accordance with Aboriginal tradition. This can only mean that activities not in accordance with that tradition (e.g., surface mining?) are forbidden unless permitted under some other section of the act or under some other law.

It is clear, then, that it matters to which category an Aborigine belongs. Some people on the reserve are substantially advantaged by the act and others are arguably disadvantaged or at any rate will receive no benefit from the act's application to the reserve. First-category Aborigines are at the advantage end, third-category Aborigines at the disadvantage or no-benefit end, and second-category people somewhere in between. These considerations of benefit will affect people who are living away from the reserve — for example, Aborigines who are traditional owners of parts of the reserve but belong to the second or third category where they are living at present. It becomes important, therefore, to assess the fidelity to tradition of the statutory classifications. Do they express the pattern of traditional ideas about and relations to land or do they distort it?

This question bears more particularly on the definition of traditional owners, since it is especially this class which benefits under the act. Aborigines must satisfy four criteria if they are to qualify for membership:

1. They must be a *local descent group.*
2. They must have *common spiritual affiliations* to a site on the land.
3. The affiliations must be such that the group has a *primary spiritual responsibility* for the site and for the land.
4. They must be *entitled to forage as of right* over the land.

The italicized terms, which the Ranger Uranium Environmental Inquiry described as "key concepts" (1977, p. 255), are undefined. They were not terms of statute or common law before being taken up by the act, have been used only sparingly if at all in Australian anthropology, and were not discussed as a set by Mr Justice Woodward. The only real sources of information on the meaning of the definition are the reports of the Ranger Inquiry (1977) and of the Aboriginal Land Commissioner (1978*a*, 1978*b*) none of which is about the Beswick Reserve or adjoining country.[14]

The tendency of these reports confirms the suspicion to which the definition gives rise, namely that the number of criteria and the qualification to each (e.g., not merely a spiritual responsibility but a *primary* spiritual responsibility) will reduce the number of traditionally entitled people who can be owners under the act. The statutory term *traditional owners* is being construed to mean a descent group whose members are totemically connected in the male line to a site or sites. This has three consequences: first, individuals are ignored except as members of groups; second, traditional rights without a religious colouring are insufficient; and third, totemic connections traced maternally are excluded. An implication of the last consequence is that people of mixed descent will fail as traditional owners if they are Aboriginal only on their mother's side.[15]

Traditional ideas about and relations to land do not, on my analysis of them, justify drawing a line where the act does between traditional owners and other traditionally entitled people. The act as judicially interpreted appears in the nature of a quest for the proprietor of an estate in fee simple in English land law and is accordingly unable to accept that traditionally there is a plurality of "rights", some at least of which are equal to each other.

One should not, of course, underestimate the difficulties in the path of giving statutory expression to traditional relationships, and one must admit the wide differences of opinion that can exist about the best "conceptualization" in *our* law of *their* ideas. There is, however, a decisive objective to the present definition. Much of the Territory will never become Aboriginal land. Traditional ownership has little relevance except to land that is Aboriginal already (i.e., the reserves and areas successfully claimed) or that might become Aboriginal in the future (i.e., areas of vacant crown land). The more restrictive the definition of traditional ownership the smaller the number of Aborigines who can be traditional owners of Aboriginal land. The force of this objection diminishes as the area of Aboriginal land increases, since more Aborigines will then have a chance of being traditional owners somewhere, even if only of a place remote from where they are living.

The last point brings us to the migrant character of the Beswick Reserve's population. The *Register of Wards*, an official document conferring status as wards on the persons it named, shows that in 1957 there were 282 Aborigines of twenty-four "tribes" at Bamyili, as it now is, and 53 of ten tribes at Beswick Station, the other centre on the reserve. Three of the Beswick Station tribes were unrepresented at Bamyili, giving 335 Aborigines divided between twenty-seven tribes. The most numerous at Bamyili were the Ngalkbun (Dalabon) 76, Maiali 52, Rembarrnga 42, Jauan (Djauan) 33, and Gunwinggu 29. It is clear that many people on the reserve would have to be regarded as immigrants or as children or grandchildren of immigrants. It is unnecessary here to try to estimate the proportions of first-, second-, and third-category Aborigines: uncertainties about the traditional local organization would often make it doubtful whether a man should be put in the second or in the third category, and the determination of traditional ownership and traditional entitlement is a legal rather than an anthropological problem. The likeliest outcome, in view of the judicial interpretation of the traditional owners definition, is that the first would be by far the smallest category. This is because the Djauan are regarded as the local people.

The 1957 distribution of the Djauan is additional proof of the importance of migration. The *Register of Wards* records, on my count, 228 Djauan of whom 134 were in the Katherine district, 57 in the Darwin district, 33 at Bamyili (then Beswick Creek), 3 in the Barkly Tableland district, and 1 in the Kimberley district. These numbers would perhaps be double by now, for in 1973 the population of the reserve had risen from the 335 of 1957 to 517 (Aboriginal Land Rights Commission 1973, app. A). Granting the chance that only some Djauan would be judicially accepted as belonging to descent groups whose members are totemically connected in the male line to a site on the reserve, it is on the cards that more traditional owners of parts of the reserve would be living off than on the reserve and that the population of the reserve would be substantially greater than the number of traditional owners of parts of it.

Legislative Land Rights Recapitulated

The act appears to have two main purposes regarding Aboriginal rights to land. The purposes are only loosely integrated in the sense that the means adopted for fulfilment of the one could be changed with little if any effect on the other.

One purpose is to establish a legal and administrative framework responsive both to the Australian government and to Northern Territory Aborigines within which title to land can be held and powers of decision over land exercised. The means chosen consist in a hierarchy of corporations in which the lower-level corporations hold title and the higher-level corporations, which are also the less numerous, enjoy powers of decision. That such a system is foreign to the Aboriginal tradition is not an objection. The influx of settlers, who are now in a majority even in the Northern Territory, and the expropriation of land that went with it have meant that Aboriginal rights, however exactly they may be formulated, must be in a workable relation to the law of the land.

The other purpose is to give some sort of recognition to traditional ideas about and relations to land. The means chosen consist in a hierarchy of categories in which Aborigines will be placed according as they are traditional owners (as defined by the act), traditionally entitled in some way less than traditional ownership, or not traditionally entitled at all. Given this purpose, it is unavoidable that some Aborigines who have settled on the reserve will risk not being recognized. There can, *given that purpose,* be no serious quarrel with legislation which exposes some Aborigines to the risk of non-recognition.

There can, however, be criticism of where the line has been drawn between the first two categories and of the tendency of the act to accord members of the second category little more than the right to be consulted and to have their presumed interests taken into consideration when decision are made about the land within the reserve. I have suggested that the act as judicially interpreted puts an undue emphasis on group membership patrilineally defined and that this has unfortunate consequences: many Aborigines living on or traditionally connected with the reserve will not qualify as traditional owners there; some will not qualify as traditional owners of Aboriginal land anywhere, because most of the Northern Territory will not, at least in the foreseeable future, become Aboriginal; and people of mixed descent whose Aboriginality is one the mother's side will presumably be disqualified from traditional ownership. These consequences might be mitigated if statutory amendment or judicial reinterpretation changed the meaning of traditional ownership.

Such a change would leave untouched the subordination of immigrants, traditionally unentitled to use or occupy land within the reserve, to traditional owners. It is easy to see the human problem this creates, but it is harder to see how it could have been avoided in legislation aiming at recognition of traditional relationships.

Mr Justice Woodward inclined at first to favour the community — in the modern sense of the people living at a place — as the basic sociopolitical grouping among present-day Aborigines, and he suggested that Aborigines might register themselves as members of the community of their choice (Aboriginal Land Rights Commission 1973, pp. 34–35). He went on to notice that most anthropologists favoured the clan, and he raised the objection that under present-day conditions members of the same clan may be widely scattered in different communities. His later view was more in line with what anthropologists were saying, and he accepted the Northern Land Council's suggestion that, although it would be impracticable to vest small areas in individual clans, substantially the same results could be obtained through a trust system (Aboriginal Land Rights Commission 1974, pp. 12-13). The Central Land Council had supported the original view. This might have been the better approach for the Beswick Reserve: a community basis makes allowance for the facts of migration; a registration requirement makes allowances for the facts of traditional relationship.

Likely Effects and Possible Remedies

Let us assume that the people of the reserve grasp the distinctions the act makes. What courses of action might then seem best to them?

Those who accepted that they would not qualify as traditional owners of land held by the Beswick Trust might prefer to move to a place where they would qualify. If this commended itself to many people, Bamyili and Beswick Station might not become ghost towns but they would certainly assume a rather deserted appearance. The Aborigines who left would have moved to country over which their forebears had foraged and camped, thus reversing the migrations which emptied the hinterland earlier this century. This would not necessarily lead to a restoration in any exact sense of the traditional local organization but possibly to a patrilineal distortion of it.

Many Beswick Aborigines are children or grandchildren of migrants and might prefer to stay on the reserve, especially as Bamyili and Beswick Station have far more amenities than could be expected at new outstations. This might be the best course of action open to those for whom there is no Aboriginal land of which they are likely to be accepted as traditional owners.

Any loss of population might, of course, be partly offset by the movement to the reserve of Aborigines who at present live elsewhere but have a traditional relationship to the land there. Another possibility to be kept in mind is that traditionally connected Aborigines might like to see the migrants leave the reserve and might try to use the super-ordination the act gives them to bring this about.

A more equal distribution of rights within the existing population might result from statutory amendment or from adjustments the Aborigines made among themselves without legislative interference. Here two possibilities may be distinguished. One is where the traditional owners definition is widened to include all the people traditionally entitled to use or occupy land on the reserve. This would, on my analysis, do more justice to traditional ideas and relationships than does the present definition, and it would have the effect of conflating the first and second categories I distinguished. The thorny problem of outsiders would remain to give trouble. The other possibility is where the full benefits of the act are extended to people ordinarily resident on the reserve as well as to people having certain sorts of traditional connection with it.

It is probable that neither the one solution nor the other would win general acceptance. The trouble with the first is that it turns its back on migrants. To say to these people that they should go back where they (or their parents or grandparents) came from if they dislike having an inferior status seems unsatisfying. It is even less satisfying when their country of origin is not Aboriginal land. The trouble with the second solution is that to grant rights to land regardless of traditional relationships would be to pevert the act's overriding aim, which is to give some sort of recognition to the rights Aborigines had before whites expropriated the land.

The conclusion can only be that thanks to history there is no way to satisfy some persuasive claims to the Beswick Reserve without frustrating others. The root of the trouble is that the reserve shows Australia's problem in a microcosm: how to reconcile the interests of people native to a land with the interests of settlers? The irony is that here settler and native alike are Aboriginal.

Addendum

Although this paper was written in 1978, little has happened since to affect its argument about the Beswick Reserve. The main changes to be noted are in the interpretation of the traditional owners definition and the organization of the Northern Land Council.

First, in the area of responsibility of the Central Land Council, it has become usual to put a broader construction on traditional ownership to include the local equivalents of the Beswick *djunggaiji*. This lessens the patrilineal stress which I criticized, increases the number of Aborigines who qualify for the main powers and advantages created by the act, and expresses more faithfully the reality of traditional relations to land. Unfortunately, the more liberal approach is still unusual in the Northern Land Council's area.

Second, the Northern Land Council was reorganized in 1981 (*Land Rights News*, March 1981) to separate more clearly its Aboriginal members (delegates of communities) from its staff. The former are now known as the Land Council and the latter as the Bureau of the Land Council. This new arrangement, which recalls the division between directors and staff of a company, appears to have resulted from government pressure for "efficiency" — that is, for mediating expeditiously between Aborigines and the outside world. It has been accompanied by a threefold expansion of staff. Quite possibly the growth in efficiency will mean a less personal relation between Aborigines on the land and their land council in Darwin. But a land council is mainly operative in dealings between Aborigines and outsiders, so this change will have little effect on the Beswick people unless their land turns out to be more interesting to outsiders than it has in the past.

Notes

1. I gathered the field data reported here between 1964 and 1970 under the auspices of the Australian Institute of Aboriginal Studies. The analysis offered in this paper had been worked out before the first half of 1978 when I revisited the area with support from Macquarie University and the Northern Land Council. For an account of present-day life on the reserve, see Maddock 1977.
2. Spencer (1914) and Warner (1933; 1937) report a few data, but fuller information comes only with Elkin (1961a; 1961b) and West (1964). Xavier Herbert, Douglas Lockwood, Roland Robinson, W. E. Harney, Tom Ronan and Aeneas Gunn are writers who have given autobiographical or fictional accounts of people and places in the general region, and Bauer (1964) gives a history of it.
3. I am unable, however, to share the Ranger Uranium Environmental Inquiry's view that the Aboriginal relationship to land is essentially religious in nature (Ranger Uranium Environmental Inquiry 1977, p. 270) if this means denying as it apparently does, the importance of relationships of economic nature. Unlike Mr Justice Woodward, I am also unable to accept Berndt's opinion that ownership exists on two levels, of which the religious is primary (Aboriginal Land Rights Commission 1974, p. 32), since such distinctions are pointless in the absence of a proper analysis of the applicability to foreign societies of our legal or quasi-legal concepts.
4. Radcliffe-Brown (1930–31), Hiatt (1962; 1965, pp. 14–28; 1966), and Meggitt (1962), Stanner (1965) are the most instructive contributions since Thomas (1906) to our understanding of Australian local organization. See, for discussion of some of these contributions, Maddock 1978b.
5. For fuller discussion of these spheres of conduct, see Maddock 1974.
6. For discussion of the nature of the world-creative power, see Maddock 1972, pp. 109–30, and 1978c.
7. *Milirrpum* v. *Nabalco Pty. Ltd. and The Commonwealth of Australia,* 17 Federal Law Reports (1971), at pp. 268–74.
8. It is fair to say that the usefulness of the notion of ownership is disputed by writers on English law: "The truth is that words such as 'ownership' and its derivatives are not part of the language of land law" (Hargreaves 1956,

p. 18); "It must be said at the outset that the word is not very often used in the professional literature of English law . . . and that where the word *owner* is sporadically used in statutes it has been given many difficult meanings" (Lawson 1958, p. 86).

9. This is strongly suggested for north-east Arnhem Land by Shapiro (1973).

10. The approach suggested here has been outlined in a recent paper of mine (1978*b*).

11. Some of these events are outlined in *Land Rights News*, January 1977, and discussed in Maddock 1972 (pp. 1–20).

12. It has been suggested that land committees be formed as an intermediary between land trusts and the Northern Land Council (*Land Rights News*, May 1977). Bamyili would be grouped with Borroloola, Elliott, Groote Eylandt, Numbulwar, and Roper River in this system.

13. That this is more than a nominal likelihood may be seen from *Land Rights News*, May 1978, which documents the refusal of the traditional owners of Croker Island to allow free access by people of mixed descent who were raised as children there after being taken from their Aboriginal mothers on the mainland.

14. Mr Justice Woodward thought that his description of the traditional relationship between Aborigines and their land had been accepted by Aborigines and others who have studied the subject (Aboriginal Land Rights Commission 1974, p. 4), but his reference is to an account he published in the first report of his commission (1973, pp. 10–21) and reprinted in the final report (1974, pp. 135–40). The traditional owners definition was given only in the final report and does not follow inevitably from Mr Justice Woodward's description of traditional man-land relationships. For discussion of the statutory definition and its judicial interpretation, see Maddock 1978*a*; 1979*a*.

15. The reports of the Aboriginal Land Rights Commission effectively ignore the problems posed by migrants and people of mixed descent. The commission's definition of traditional ownership reads like an attempt to give substance to the conception of Aboriginal local organization for which the plaintiffs argued unsuccessfully in the Gove Land Rights Case (see judgement at pp. 159–83, 262–74).

References

Aboriginal Land Commissioner. 1978*a*. *Report on the Borroloola Land Claim.* Canberra: Office of the Aboriginal Land Commissioner.

——— . 1978*b*. *Report on the Warlpiri and Kartangarurru-Kurintji Land Claim.* Canberra: Office of the Aboriginal Land Commissioner.

Aboriginal Land Rights Commission. 1973. *First Report.* Melbourne: Aboriginal Land Rights Commission.

——— . 1974. *Second Report.* Canberra: Australian Government Publishing Service.

Bauer, F. H. 1964. *Historical Geography of White Settlement in Part of Northern Australia.* Part 2: *The Katherine-Darwin Region.* Canberra: CSIRO.

Elkin, A. P. 1961*a*. The Yabuduruwa. *Oceania* 31: 166–209.

——— . 1961*b*. Maraian at Mainoru. *Oceania* 31: 259–93; 32: 1–15.

Hargreaves, A. D. 1956. Modern Real Property. *Modern Law Review* 19: 14–25.

78   Kenneth Maddock

Hiatt, L. R. 1962. Local Organization among the Australian Aborigines. *Oceania* 32: 267–86.

———. 1965. *Kinship and Conflict: A Study of an Aboriginal Community in Northern Arnhem Land.* Canberra: Australian National University Press.

———. 1966. The Lost Horde. *Oceania* 37: 81–92.

Lawson, F. H. 1958. *Introduction to the Law of Property.* London: Oxford University Press.

Maddock, K. 1970. Aboriginal Law. *Proceedings Medico-Legal Society of New South Wales* 4: 170–79.

———. 1972. *The Australian Aborigines: A Portrait of Their Society.* London: Allen Lane the Penguin Press.

———. 1974. Dangerous Proximities and Their Analogues. *Mankind.* 9: 206–17.

———. 1977. Two Laws in One Community. In *Aborigines and Change: Australia in the '70s,* ed. R. M. Berndt. Canberra: Australian Instituted of Aboriginal Studies.

———. 1978*a*. Comments on the Aboriginal Land Commissioner's Report on the Borroloola Land Claim. Customary Law Group of Australia *Newsletter,* no. 2, pp. 5–13.

———. 1978*b*. Einige ungeloste Fragen der Okonomie und der lokalen Organisation der australischen Ureinwohner. *Ethnographisch-Archaologische Zeitschrift* 19: 601–11.

———. 1978*c*. Metaphysics in a Mythical View of the World. In *The Rainbow Serpent: A Chromatic Piece,* ed. I. R. Buchler and K. Maddock. The Hague: Mouton.

———. 1979*a*. Comments on the Aboriginal Land Commissioner's Report in the Walbiri Land Claim. Customary Law Group of Australia *Newsletter,* no. 3, pp. 16–19.

———. 1979*b*. A Structural Analysis of Paired Ceremonies in a Dual Social Organization. *Bijdragen tot de Taal-, Land- en Volkenkunde* 135: 84–117.

Meggitt, M. J. 1962. *Desert People: A Study of the Walbiri Aborigines of Central Australia.* Sydney: Angus and Robertson.

Mountford, C. P. 1968. *Winbaraku and the Myth of Jarapiri.* Adelaide: Rigby.

Radcliffe-Brown, A. R. 1930–31. The Social Organization of Australian Tribes. *Oceania* 1: 34–63, 206–46, 322–41, 426–56.

Ranger Uranium Environmental Inquiry. 1977. *Second Report.* Canberra: Australian Government Publishing Service.

Shapiro, W. 1973. Residential Grouping in Northeast Arnhem Land. *Man* 8: 365–83.

Spencer, B. 1914. *Native Tribes of the Northern Territory of Australia.* London: Macmillan.

Stanner, W. E. H. 1965. Aboriginal Territorial Organization: Estate, Range, Domain and Regime. *Oceania* 36: 1–26.

Thomas, N. W. 1906. *Kinship Organisations and Group Marriage in Australia.* Cambridge: Cambridge University Press.

Warner, W. L. 1933. Kinship Morphology of Forty-one North Australian Tribes. *American Anthropologist* 35: 63–80.

———. 1937. *A Black Civilization: A Social Study of an Australian Tribe.* New York: Harper.

West, L. 1964. Sketch Dictionary of Dalabon and Related Languages of Central Arnhem Land. Sydney: manuscript.

Ideology and Experience: The Cultural Basis of Politics in Pintupi Life

FRED R. MYERS

> The politician acts on men in a way that is reminiscent of "natural causes"; they submit to him as they submit to "the caprices of the sky, the sea and the earth's crust". [Valery in Balandier 1970, p. 106]

> Since they have a starting point and foothold in reality (in praxis), or rather to the extent that they do, ideologies are not altogether false. [Lefebvre 1978, p. 71]

General Considerations

This paper is an attempt to explore the cultural basis for politics in the social life of Pintupi Aborigines from the Gibson Desert. Social theorists interested in meaning have emphasized that political processes occur and are realized through what Weber called "shared understandings" (Bendix 1966, p. 286): people set and implement public goals for themselves or allocate power on the basis of some representation of who they are, what is, and what can be. Their actions are guided by symbols, what Geertz calls "extrapersonal mechanisms for the perception, understanding, judgement and manipulation of the world" (Geertz 1973, p. 216). Through such vehicles of conception it is possible to define both order and disorder and to provide instructions for action.

The study of Aboriginal politics requires careful attention to the cultural terms in which political action takes place. Further to take account of the relationship between cultural concepts and their social situation leads to two sorts of distortions in our understanding of Aboriginal social life. I will call these the "saintly elder" view and the "self-seeking elder" view.[1]

The "saintly elder" view. The fact that for many years anthropologists viewed Aborigines as "people without politics" (Sharp 1958), or as people without change, more or less accepted the Aborigines' own view that social life is not based on the human definition of values and pursuit of power.[2] Aborigines understood their lives as part of a cosmic order, an unchanging continuation of the order established once and for all in the Dreaming. Observers assumed themselves to understand what this ideology was about — namely, relations between man and cosmos — and so they tended to ignore the analytical problem this ideology presented to them. What relationship did it have to experience? It will be argued that such a conceived "order of things" — this denial of politics and emphasis on the society as part of nature" — is the result of a particular way of interpreting experience which both expresses and veils important aspects of Aboriginal life.

The "self seeking elder" view. On the other hand, operating with various versions of a simple "base and superstructure" model, many of those most interested in politics would "debunk" culture or ideology as *no more than* the illusory expression of or justification for underlying (and more real) material interests and relations of power. In its most sceptical form, this scheme would view male ritual knowledge not as a continuation of a cosmic order but as the instrument by which male elders dominate women and young men as a means of monopolizing young women. Such a "flattened view of other people's mentalities" (Geertz 1973, p. 210) fails to explain *how* such an ideology might work, ignoring the whole process of symbolic formulation. Similarly, it denies (in some sense) the Aboriginal experience of their cultural representations as "real" or authentic. This would lead to a suspicion that Aboriginal religion is a sham, that the value of the Dreaming (knowledge that old men give to young) is merely a kind of false coin paid for political power. The radical devaluation of knowledge and understanding as epiphenomena is unwarranted both in the general and in the specific case. There is no evidence that elders, young men, or women regard the Dreaming as anything less than the valued ground of all being. Indeed, it regularly acquires such value as people orient their activities around it. The point, surely, is not that it is valueless, but rather that it is controlled.

Both of these distortions are a product of European attempts to grapple with a phenomenon that straddles our distinction between politics and religion along with our distinction between material and ideal. (Cohen [1974] tries to show that symbols and politics should not be dichotomized.) My claim, although not original to me (see Bourdieu 1977; Geertz 1973; Williams 1977), is that we should begin to examine the complex interactive relationship between historically transmitted sets of meanings and symbols and the objective social realities that constitute the world in which actors live. By examining the relationship between ideology (symbols) and experience, we might come to understand *how* ideologies work. As Geertz suggests, a symbol "might . . . draw its power from its capacity to grasp, formulate, and communicate social realities that elude the tempered language of science, that it may mediate more complex meanings than its literal reading suggests" (Geertz 1973, p. 210). We become interested, then, in the persuasive structures of meanings and symbols, seeing them as situated in social contexts, speaking to experience of particular social orders and making them intelligible for action.

The Problem

Like many other Aboriginal groups, the Pintupi at Yayayi, an out-station forty-two kilometres west of Papunya where I spent twenty-one months in research,[3] did not recognize an explicit domain of activity which could be called "politics". Except for the recently introduced village council, neither specific governmental structure nor true "leaders" existed. Like other Aboriginal peoples, the Pintupi appear to have interpreted their society as the continuation into the present of a preordained cosmic order, the Dreaming (Stanner 1956), which it has been men's duty to "follow up". This suggests parallels with Valery's remark that political power may well be represented as part of nature. What should we make of this? Ideologically, public goals are represented as part of the cosmic order, and the Pintupi seem to be "people without politics". But why should this be so, and how is it accomplished? That power — the possibility of constraining others or ruling as one wishes — should be conceived as merely a consequence of some pre-existing "order" may be shown to be a result of the concepts of authority and order which the Pintupi use to understand and act in their social world.

In order to do so requires revealing the social reality underlying use of the important cultural concept of "looking after" (*kanyininpa*) as the content of authority. This paper will show that the concept is used in a variety of domains ranging from child care and generational succession to a justification of male hierarchy as "nurturance", and that its use as an "operator" (Levi-Strauss 1966) to make sense of various kinds of activity gives it a persuasive force that explains its effectiveness as a political ideology. This concept brings together and synthesizes certain key concerns and experiences in Pintupi life — autonomy, freedom, nurturance — in a *convincing* way which places authority in the hands of elder males but denies this to be the result of individual will, struggle, or conflict. It is important to show why "looking after" seems to the Pintupi a satisfactory concept for articulating their social world; what relations and processes — what experiences — does it uncover and present to them? As Lefebvre suggests, "ideologies are not altogether false", and this fact is of great significance. Then, after asking what this ideology "takes for granted", what processes it ignores or conceals, I try to show the problems that have accompanied extension of the concept to the expanded political arena of contemporary life in the white man's world.

Background

Most of the Pintupi left their traditional country in the Gibson Desert between 1948 and 1966 for settled life; so until recently they lived a traditional hunting-gathering life in small bands. The current settlement of 250 people at Yayayi Bore constituted a novel situation for them in many ways, depending on resources very different from the traditional ones. Although funded by the Australian government, Yayayi differed from previous Pintupi settlement life in being run (in theory) by the Pintupi themselves. This provided a unique opportunity to comprehend Aboriginal politics in their terms, their priorities, albeit in a rather new milieu of tents, trucks, money, flour, and rifles. My recognition of the nature and basis of Pintupi politics derived just as much from personal participation as from theorizing.

One day while setting at my "grandfather's" camp, I was abused and threatened by a late arrival who accused me of "writing down" his name and "looking" at him. Although comrades defended me, I departed the camp. Two of my "defenders" (appropriately, I thought, a "mother's brother" and a "cross-cousin") came to join me.

"That's too bad," one said. "He shouldn't talk to you that way, not in cruel way. You look after Aborigines [*yanangu kanyilpa*]. You help us."

The other continued, "You help us with language [English], you explain for us, get our money [from the government]. You are the one who stays here with us, and the notebook is your work."

I was defended not as a kinsman, but rather as one who did things for people. I was the "generous one". Months later, several friends expressed their regret that I was leaving Yayayi: "Who will look after [*kanyininpa*] us now?" Perhaps, they wondered, I would consider staying to be their *mayutju*, their "boss".

Only in these last moments at Yayayi did my tacit understanding of *how* Pintupi do things — after all, I had been there many months —

become explicit recognition of the cultural content of the political activity: "looking after" (*kanyininpa*).

Kanyininpa: A Pintupi Concept

The concept *kanyininpa,* translated as "having", "holding", or "looking after", articulates and unifies several areas of Pintupi life. It may be used to refer to possession of physical objects ("I have two spears", "I am holding two stones"), to the actualized relationship of "parent" to "child" (my "father held/looked after me and grew me up": *ngayuku mamaluni kanyinu pulkanu*). It refers also to rights over sacred sites, ceremonies, songs, and designs, all of which are owned ("dead people held and lost it": *mirrintjanyirriluya kanyinu wantingu*). The concept denotes an intimate and active relationship between a "holder" and that which is "held", as indicated in the primary sense of physically holding. Specifically, the word *kanyininpa* is contrasted with *wantininpa,* which means "leaving" or "losing" something, leaving it behind, breaking off association with it, as for instance in "I left it, that spear" (I didn't touch it) or "I saw the fight and left it alone".

Thus, the Pintupi speak of "holding" a country (e.g., ceremonial rights and obligations associated with a place) or of "carrying the Law" (responsibilities of sacred knowledge), typically with phrases denoting some sort of physical object and indicating a weight burden, or responsibility for the "holder". The aptness of the term comes from its ability to articulate both control and responsibility into a moral order.

Kanyininpa and Kinship

The metaphor invoked by *kanyininpa* is probably derived from the expression used to describe how a small child is held against the chest (*kanyinu yampungka*), an image of security, protection, and nourishment. In this sense, the concept *kanyininpa* is similar to what Turner (1967, p. 30) has called a dominant symbol, having both a "physiological" referent and an ideological or social referent to the relationship between the generations, which comes to include the Pintupi understanding of authority itself. Turner has argued that symbols combine abstract moral values with sensory substance (ibid, p. 54): "The values are saturated with the gross emotions evoked by the symbol's sensory aspects and at the same time the gross emotions are 'ennobled' by contact with the moral values" (Peacock 1968, p. 241).

The personal and physiological referent became clear while I was collecting genealogies, where I found that the notion of "holding" or "looking after" was central to Pintupi ideas of relatedness. One man told me that X was really his "father", his "old man", because: "He took me over, he looked after me." By subsection status, the latter would have been called "father" anyway, but the man's behaviour indicated something more, that he considered his "old man" to be an especially "close" father, one near whom he chose to be and with whom he regularly interacted. Similarly, when a boy was about to be initiated, a young man told me, "They can't initiate him until his father arrives from Yuendumu. He grew up [*kanyinu pulkanu*] that boy." The young man was referring to the boy's lengthy residence at another settlement, where he was looked after and fed by this old man, who was thus a "father" with special concern for the boy. Among women, the person who looks after the younger girls and women in the "single women's camp" (*yalukuru*) is said to "hold" them; she is the focal point of their residence.

Most fully, the concept seems to define a central social fabric of senior persons around whom juniors aggregate and by whom they are "held", rather in the way that these arid-desert people aggregated around important water and resource points. "Holding" depicts authority as deriving from concern and protection. *Kanyininpa* is a concept used by the Pintupi to articulate the moral basis of relationships of authority and respect, to present simultaneously the dual nature of authority and responsibility and to justify authority as the appropriate social relationship among certain kinds of kin. Implicit in the concept is insufficiency on the part of the junior and an activity of transformation on the part of the senior, as expressed in the idea of "growing up" someone. The Pintupi appear to conceptualize many experiences in social life in this fashion, and conceptualizing them thereby reproduces them as a social world.

Generational Succession

Pintupi usage and thinking about kinship gives great importance to the idea of *kanyininpa*. Pintupi maintain that the children of brothers (or sisters) are "family" (pidgin; also expressed as *walytja*) or "really" siblings themselves. If one inquires of an informant, "Who are really your siblings?" the list will include frequently the offspring of the parent's same-sex siblings. Even requests to limit the list to those "from one father" will sometimes include such siblings. The reason given for this is that a person's siblings "look after" his or her children in the event of his or her death. Consequently, there is a tendency, based on typical social experiences of parental death and remarriage, to consider parental siblings as real parents (they are classified under the same kinship term; FB = F, etc.). As the system works informally, all those descended from a common grandparent are considered to be siblings and called by the appropriate term.

Elsewhere (Myers 1976) I have shown that Pintupi relationship terminology should be analyzed into two alternative schemes of organization. One of these schemes, particularly, is of concern in the present context: the system used to organize the universe of "close" kin. A principal characteristic of this scheme is that it presents the social universe as a succession of generations, as those descended from a set of grandparents and grandparental siblings (FF, MF, MMB, MM, FM, FFZ, etc.). This is apparent in diagram 1. The basic criteria of the system are (1) the sociocentric discrimination of two generational categories, reciprocally named "us" (*ngananitja*) and "them" (*yinyurrpa*); and (2) the distinction between "close" and "distant" kin (or consanguines and affines).[4]

The "us" category includes all individuals of ego's own generation and his/her second ascending and descending generations. The "them" category includes all individuals of the alternate generations (see below). These categories, although reciprocally named, are sociocentric and have great behavioural significance on occasions such as male initiation, death, and in considering marriage; they are explicitly endogamous.

No one who is "close" (*ngamutja*) or whose parents are "close" is marriageable, regardless of kintype. "Close" kin are distinguished from "distant" (*tiwatja*) on the basis of frequent coresidence and/or genealogical proximity. Whether a person considered "distant" is a potential affine (spouse, spouse's parent) depends on kintype. In Pintupi expectation, since "close" kin frequently live together, the criteria of geographical and genealogical proximity are ideally homologous. Close relatives should not become affines, so those regarded as "close" are referred to by what I call "consanguineal" terms, used as is appropriate to their generational level but which may ignore other features of genealogical distance (these may be recognized in the second scheme, not treated here).

For the Pintupi, whether someone "looks after" (*kanyininpa*) another is an important consideration in kin relationships and how they are classified, telling us much about the cultural content of kin categories.[5] It implies feeding, protection, and coresidence. In the cultural code employed by Pintupi to articulate their world, those who "look after" you become "close" kin; they are "family" or "one country-men". The code needs no elaboration since most individuals' experiences of these situations are similar (cf. Bernstein 1974 on "elaborated" and "restricted" codes). As a result they are addressed by consanguineal terms, and they or their offspring are not marriageable. Thus, a distant MMBS is called WMB (*tjukunpa*), but one who looked after ego is called "father". Similarly, a distant MMBD is called WM (*yumari*), but if she "held" (*kanyinu*) ego, she is called FZ (*kuntili*), and her daughter is called "cross-cousin" (*watjirra*) rather than "spouse" (*kurri*), because "she is like a sister".

Returning now to the model of the Pintupi social universe, we can delineate how close kin are presented as a succession of generations, each of which is "looked after" or "held" by the preceding generation. From the diagram it can be seen how, at some levels of terminology, kinsmen are lumped into categories based on generation alone: parents and parents' siblings in one category and all their children in the succeeding one. Often "cross-cousins" who are close kin are called by sibling terms, in which case the only discriminations are generation level, affinal status, and sex. The categories are as follows:

(a) Second ascending generation — "grandfather" (*tjamu*, MF, FF, MMB) and "grandmother" (*kapali*, MM, FM, FFZ)
(b) First ascending generation — "father" (*mama*), "father's sister" (*kuntili*), "mother" (*ngunytju*), "mother's brother" (*kamuru*);
(c) Own generation — "older brother" (*kuta*), "older sister" (*kangkuru*), "younger sibling" (*malanypa*), "cross-cousin" (*watjirra*);
(d) First descending — "own son" (*katja*), "own daughter" (*yuntalpa*), "children of opposite-sex sibling" (*yukari*); or alternatively, all children of a sibling set may be lumped together categorically as "male child" (*katja*) or "female child" (*yuntalpa*);
(e) Second descending — "grandson" (*tjamu*), "granddaughter" (*kapali*).

The model is more informative at higher level (superclass) categorizations. On one terminological level, a man *may* differentiate his children from those of his sister and vice versa, a distinction that is important in *some* contexts for discriminating different kinds of rights and duties, but this is not appropriate in all situations. We stress here the importance of another level which lumps all the children of a set of siblings, indicating some identity of those descended from such a set.

Finally, there is yet a third usage, at the highest level, which stresses terminologically the relationship between succeeding generation levels, giving articulate form to this concept of the social process for the Pintupi. The usage is as follows: Ego calls "father", "mother",

"mother's brother", "father's sister" by the term *ngayupula*. Reciprocally, all those named may call ego *ngayumpanu*, a term unmarked
for sex or relative sex of linking kinsman: it designates only consanguines of the first descending generation. The *ngayupula/ngayumpanu*
polarized set thus explicitly recognizes a particular relationship between
adjacent generations: one of "looking after". Examination of expected
behaviour shows that "father", "mother" and the other lumped categories all have a similar obligation or duty towards ego in this regard.
In Goodenough's terms, "looking after" denotes a status relationship,
a bundle of rights and duties, which all four kinship identities share
towards their "child" (Goodenough 1969). The Pintupi themselves
apparently recognize and express this similarity through the term
ngayupula. Members of the *ngayupula* category, if they are coresident,
should "hold" or "look after" their *ngayumpanu* their "child"; they
feed him, they offer protection and security, they "grow him up".
Should they fail in this responsibility, they may be subject to sanction
by others in the same relationship to the "child".

Generally, authority is spoken of as a consequence of relative age:
older people look after or "hold" those who come "behind". Older
children are held responsible to look after their siblings, and this responsibility entails authority, justified by concern for the junior's well-
being. Older siblings may "hold" or "look after" a person until the
latter becomes independent. Responsibility and authority are interrelated in concern for the junior's well-being.

Although the concept of "holding" is by no means restricted
entirely to intergenerational relations, nonetheless it is used by the
Pintupi as a way of schematically representing important features of
their social world to themselves. The hierarchical relations between
generations can be contrasted with those within a generation. The
latter are roughly equivalent or egalitarian, as expressed by the lack
of restraint or "shame" among brothers, in contrast with that between
a man and his "father" or "mother's brother". Brothers may, and are
expected to, fight, but this activity is prohibited between those of
adjacent generations. If one hits a mother's brother, the latter should
not strike back: the relationship is clearly marked as asymmetrical.
Fights between brothers are, on the other hand, "no trouble". Intergenerational relations are seen as being characteristically hierarchical,
represented as conforming to the relation described as "holding".

This analysis of kinship data, then, shows that the Pintupi structure
and experience their social world as a series of generations, each of
which "holds" the succeeding generation. Reciprocally, the succeeding
generation owes obedience and acquiescence to those who "look after"
them. The concept grasps, as it were, their experience of the social
process which is involved in authority and responsibility.

"Boss"

The expectations and the social experience encoded in the concept "looking after" are well expressed in the myth of two young carpet-snakes. It is said that a third snake took care of them: "the old man 'held' those two" (*yinalupulanya kanyinma*). He provided them with food and protection, and as the narrative reveals, they were obliged to heed his advice when he ordered them to cease attacking a woman.

In the Pintupi view, a "boss" is one who looks after his subordinates. For example, one's "father" and "mother's brother" are often referred to as one's *mayutju*, or in pidgin as one's "boss", as those persons who can tell ego what to do. Persons of these categories as well as "mother" are a girl's "bosses" in regard to bestowal. Although there are specializations of status separating "mother's brother" from "father" and from "mother" and so on, the stated duty is that "one should work" for all those of the "parent" category. They tell one what to do, but it is also expected that they will be generous.

Again, both "father" and "mother's brother" are addressed by the respectful term "old man" (*tjilpi* or *yayu*), a term not limited to kin terminology but designating an elder male. "Mothers" and "father's sisters" are addressed as "old woman" (*ulkamanu*). Such terms are partly equivalent to "boss", since old age should be respected. Ideo-logically, the "old men" (*tjilpi tjuta*) are deemed to be the locus of authority within the community and to possess autonomy *vis-à-vis* younger people.

When two men were asked whether they had "bosses" (*mayutju*) in traditional times, one replied first: "No, we could go anyway [wherever/however] we liked", meaning that there were no overriding sources of authority such as the government now constitutes. The second informant added, "Only father" (*mama*). Both then continued: "or older brother [*kuta*] or own mother's brother, those who gave us meat." In general, the criterion for inclusion in the "boss" category for ego is that a person "looked after" ego. Authority, the right to constrain others to one's wishes, is seen as a complement of the duty to look after, to grow up — to transform — ego. (Two other usages of the category *mayutju* will be discussed later, in reference to the Aboriginal village council and with reference to whites who work for the government or employ Aborigines.)

The moral basis of authority differential, as we saw in the kinship domain, is that the "boss" does more, contributes more of value to the junior. Aboriginal societies have been described often enough as "gerontocracies" (Rose 1968), implying rule by the elderly males. In the Pintupi view, elders "look after" the rest of the group, and their authority is legitimized by the way in which they "hold" those who follow. The authority of the elders is not absolute, but has its locus primarily in the domain of ritual, sacred sites, and marriage, in and through which the elders have considerable "power" over their juniors. Outside of these areas, social relations are generally more egalitarian, access to natural resources is relatively free, and there is no monopoly of force (Maddock 1970, p. 183).

Kanyininpa and the Social Order

In this section, we will see how the content of and basis for authority (like the divine right of kings or the Constitution for other societies) finds its ground in the Pintupi conception of human nature and its place in the cosmic order. As in other egalitarian societies (Read 1959), hierarchy and consensus for public goals present difficulties which the Pintupi solve through presenting such goals as sacred law. People are bent to the pre-existing consensus, the Dreaming or "Law".

It has been frequently remarked how traditional cultures without separate political domains often employ comprehensive, unspecialized models (Levi-Strauss 1966) — very general cultural orientations (Geertz 1973, p. 219) — to integrate diverse domains. As a dominant symbol, "looking after" has a similar place in Pintupi life, drawing together several domains into a single process. This concept assimilates kinship, temporal progression, political power, and the natural order into a single social process, representing their social world as a moral order. In traditional life, the Pintupi experienced these analytically separable dimensions as one process, which they represented as the passage of the Dreaming through the generations, the continuous manifestation of the Law in the phenomenal realm. "Holding" is a collective symbol of authority experienced not in the abstract but as part of this context.

The concept of "holding" examined thus far may be viewed as an ideology which "makes sense" out of Pintupi experience of the social world. The schematic image of social order it offers is that of generations succeeding one after another, each nurturing and mediating authority to the next. This social model is articulated through the kinship system's succession of generations.

The model, in this form, corresponds to a more general notion in Pintupi cosmology that what comes first is an important and definitive model (or *mould*) for that which follows. It is by virtue of their idea of the relationship between generations that the Pintupi are able to represent their society to themselves as conforming to the cosmic order, being but a manifestation of these first principles. As Munn (1970) points out for related groups, the ontological orientation to experience of the physical environment (the "totemic landscape") and to experience of the social order are identical. The concept of "holding" integrates these assumptions into a shared understanding, a theory of authority and obedience.

Kinship does not constitute the whole of Pintupi social life; it does not provide their most general orientations. As Durkheim perceived for the Aranda long ago, the Pintupi understand themselves most fully as a "society" through the idiom of "religion", or Law. This complex of initiation and cult-ritual is also the basis of the most prevailing and enduring power relations in the society. Through control of ritual and ritual knowledge, initiated males (particularly elders) exercise considerable authority over male juniors and the whole body of the uninitiated.

The source of male authority is the very basis of authority itself, as the Pintupi see the world: knowledge of the Dreaming (*tjulurrpa*), or Law. By these items, Pintupi refer to what is for them the origin of all things, all being. In the Dreaming, the world was given its significant shape, and the subsequent plan of life was laid down. What happened then is seen as the definitive plan for how things should happen now — a plan known through myths, songs, and ceremonies related to the actions of Dreamtime ancestors at known geographical places. If life is to be maintained, Pintupi believe each generation must *learn* and *conform* to the Law.

Elder males are deemed more valuable, more competent, more knowledgeable, and thereby more powerful, in regard to the Dreaming. Through "giving" (*yunginpa*) the Law — revealing ceremonies and giving instruction — they validate their authority, their right to implement goals for the society. These goals, however, are not thought of as man-made but as being legitimate through continuity with the preexisting cosmic order which male elders mediate and in whose name they rule.

The power that males exercise through their control of the Dreaming is of two sorts. One kind of power, direct and dramatic, is the power exercised by senior males over novices in periods of seclusion and the power exercised by males over the uninitiated during ritual: shouted commands, belligerency accompanied by threat of violence if disobeyed. Not all authority relations involve giving commands in this fashion. Often, public goals are set or power exercised through limiting participation in decision-making, limiting the opportunities of speaking publicly (Bloch 1975). Such is the case with much of Pintupi gerontocracy, wherein "authority" is simply the right to speak. The moral basis for both kinds of "power" in the Pintupi case is the same, the survival and security of the subordinates. Elders conform to this criterion by the representation of gerontocracy as "looking after", or nurturance. Just as seniors physically "look after" juniors, so is a similar process experienced as taking place at more profound levels, in the transmission of sacred knowledge. Power has its base in control of this major resource in Pintupi life: esoteric knowledge.

The Pintupi see esoteric knowledge as the basis of authority and also as a responsibility, having the same duality as the concept of "holding" or "looking after". Those who hold (*kanyininpa*) the story of a place have the right to decide when, where, and who will perform the associated ceremony; they decide what is correct and they take priority in discussions of it.

A good deal of "impression-management" is involved in maintaining and legitimizing this power. Prominence or priority in public discussions depends upon convincing others that one truly knows more about the story, the ceremony, or the place than anyone else. Such men have "power" which is as jealously guarded as any copyright. Concomitantly, the "holder" is held responsible by his fellow men to see that everything is carried out properly, that the sacred sites in his care are "looked after". Should he fail, everyone may suffer. Because looking after sacred sites is necessary to maintain the world and its resources, to hold the Law is both a privilege and a responsibility. The pidgin description of ritual responsibility as "men's work" is the Pintupi way of explicating its obligatory characteristics.

In this gerontocracy, then, "old men" present themselves as "looking after" the rest, their ability to do so based in large part on the possession of special knowledge: the Law. The passage of Law through the generations is seen as the passage of responsibility and authority from senior to junior, from one generation to the next. It is said that when a man dies, his "son" (*katja*) "takes on" his country and its ceremonial associations; the image of a burden or responsibility is striking. His "son" (or "sister's son") is said to "carry the Law" (*kanyininpa*). Or again, the dead man "loses" (*wantininpa*) the Law and the succeeding younger men "grab" and "hold" it. In this way, the social order is presented as a series of generations "holding" and "passing on" the Law. A similar concept of responsibility is applied to "holding" children. When an older sibling dies, his younger brother "takes on" his children, to look after them. An important feature in both domains is that the authority of one generation over the next is experienced as following "naturally" from their priority in the temporal transmission of the Dreaming: power is not the result of personal struggle, and it cannot be achieved through egotism. In Pintupi theory, the authority of seniors derives from having undergone the process of transmission first, a circumstance that leaves plenty of room for impression-management. No one *knows* what an elder has learned.

In fact, much of the "power" of older men derives from their oratorical abilities, the priority they have in speaking publicly. Young men are "too shy" to speak because they have not mastered the speech forms or the traditional and often secret lore which is frequently the subject of discussion. Were they to speak, they might embarrass themselves through ignorance or clumsiness or both. Disputes over points of esoteric Law leave younger men in the awkward position of being uncertain about what they know. In other words, the concept "looking after" *assumes* these aspects, because (in Pintupi experience) "looking after", age, and ability to speak are part of an inseparable process. By virtue of these circumstances, only the older have the ability to "look after" the rest.

A body of esoteric knowledge called Law provides an ideal medium through which elders can assert precedence and priorities in the name of the whole society. Young men who aspire to power see that the course to authority and autonomy is *through* the Law, through submission.

Such knowledge is a great source of power and responsibility, but it is a resource which is *not* freely available. It is thought of as deriving from the Dreaming and as being transmitted from "older" to "younger" through the generations. It is passed from the "old men" (*tjilpi tjuta*) to "all the boys" (*katjapiti*: "the group of male first-generation descendants"). Care in transmission of esoteric knowledge preserves it and keeps it out of the hands of the uninitiated, retaining power among those who "know". Because knowledge is dangerous, as the Pintupi see it, only the mature and responsible are to be entrusted with it. This is important in validating the "truthfulness" of the symbolic system in relation to social experience. Without gaining knowledge of the Law, males cannot "grow up", cannot marry and take on adult status. To be without Law is to be "powerless". To have it is to be in a position to look after dependants.

The domains co-ordinated by the single image of "holding" – of knowledge and children – are both depicted as a chain of transmission from senior to junior, a transmission of authority pictured as a transformation between polarized statuses in the social order (Munn 1970, p. 154). Each generation must incorporate the Law through subordination to it and become thereby the mediators of the Dreaming for the next generation. Ultimate authority and potency are in the Dreaming, the cosmological datum given once for all and to which all persons are subordinate.

Individual males have authority and autonomy just because they have incorporated the Law. As noted, most of this authority is exerted in ritual and Dreaming-related contexts, those concerned with maintaining and transmitting the Law. This view of the world and the source of authority allows men to enforce "public goals" without seeming to do so on the basis of their personal, egotistical wishes. They are only passing on the Dreaming. As conceptualized by the Pintupi, legitimate authority is without despotic or personal overtones, taken on as a responsibility to ensure the security and benefit of its objects. Having internalized the Law and been thereby transformed, the wishes of the mature men are viewed not as their personal whims but as externalizations of that which they have previously taken in.[6] And to this juniors must conform. As men say, "It is not *our* idea; it is a big Law."

What elders tell one to do is "right"; its legitimacy is assured by its continuity of passage from the Dreaming.[7] Examples are cited, frequently enough, to convince power holders and subjects that ignoring or rejecting this "protective restraint" will have disastrous consequences and that performance of obligation will prove beneficial. As the Pintupi say, does not the black currant grow year after year because we do the ritual?

This does not mean that individuals follow the Law *automatically*, out of moral imperative alone. Normative obligations for behaviour among kinsmen, affines, and in ritual are, to be sure, transmitted as "from the Dreaming", but violations occur. Conflict is as much a part of Pintupi life as it is in any other group. The Law provides, instead, a basis on which individuals can mobilize others to defend their interests, a standard against which the whole community can judge the merits of a case. The medium is impersonal, and does not, theoretically, reflect the interests of any individual or group.

For example, if X's "mother's brother" fails to protect his nephew, another "mother's brother" may abuse the first for failure to uphold his responsibility. Whether or not others will intervene or defend the first depends on how they view the merits of the case against him. In other words, what *is* appropriate is not usually a matter for dispute; problems arise deciding whether an action conforms or not. The Law itself as a set of stock solutions for expected and repeated situations is seen as beyond question or criticism and as binding – representing the "good" of the society.

Typically, then, failure to conform to the Law is sanctioned by the party who is thereby injured in his rightful expectations, be it a kinsman deprived of his share of meat or a ritual elder whose rights to be consulted in a particular religious performance are ignored. Whether the nonconformist is punished depends on establishing the violation of a norm and convincing others to consent to this interpretation. Thus, decision to take action depends on widespread consensus on the legitimacy of the norm, the Law. Similarly, there are two constraints on personal abuse of the Law by the old: (1) other elders know the Dreaming, so *significant* departures arouse protest; and (2) older men have internalized the Law, have become structured by it.

That knowledge of the Dreaming also confers "power" on the elderly through negative sanction is also clear. One old man, it was said, always wanted to get the emu heart. A young man explained to me, "If we didn't give it, he might sing the sun to stop. Those old men have a lot of tricks." He further explained that one could never know for certain the extent of their powers or knowledge. It seemed safer not to test. Part of the power of the old men (and women) seemed to rest on just this uncertainty, that they have a lot of tricks, that there may be something they know which is dangerous. Threat, therefore, may be an important aspect of their power.

Male Life Cycle

For the Pintupi, submission to authority is a stage in the succession to authority and with it to *responsibility* and duty. This transformation from passive receptivity and subordination, from being "held", to autonomy and authority, to "holding" and "looking after" others, is a significant theme in male cult and in the life cycle of males. As the following account shows, experience of this life cycle validates the ideology of authority as a "true" representation of the social world: ideology is shaped by experience of the social order.

As a child, a male is subject to the authority of all his seniors, male and female. They "look after" him. Along with all the uninitiated males and females, he is in a polar position of subordination and passivity over and against the group of initiated men. This is manifest on occasions of secret male ritual when all persons of the uninitiated category are subservient to the dictates of senior initiated men (and to the Law of the Dreaming which they embody). This constraint may take the form of avoidance by junior males of designated geographical areas; at other times they must cover their heads and avoid looking at a ritual occurring almost within their reach. Failure to observe such regulations may, in serious cases, result in punishment of death. Senior males seem to emphasize their autonomy on ritual occasions, shouting orders, and threatening violent sanctions for disobedience, but also viewing their own actions as benevolent in warding off the dire consequences of misbehaviour. Outside of such periods as ceremonial, the lack of discipline and control towards the very young is, for an American observer at least, remarkable.

As a young child, one is thought to be "unknowing, unsensitive" (*patjarru*) and unable to know when to be "ashamed" (*kunta*). Later, restraint becomes customary. Relations with the parents' generation ("them", *yinyurrpa*) are supposed to be characterized by "shame" (*kunta*), and this is especially true towards those whose age mirrors the generational separation. From the age of eight or nine years, boys are resident in separate "single men's camps" (*tawarra*), which are, ideally, of one's own generation category ("us"). Here they are under the authority of older boys and young men who are "older brother" to them. I rarely observed, for example, boys hunting with their fathers. They travel, rather, with age-mates and young men only slightly their elders. Boys, however, continue to be fed by their "parents" and "parents' siblings", who are still concerned for their welfare.

There is a violent change when the time of initiation comes, around sixteen years. During this and subsequent periods of seclusion from the uninitiated and women, young men come under the watchful eye of their elders; this instruction, accompanied by discipline and a series of physical ordeals (things done *to* him: tooth evulsion, nose-piercing, circumcision, subincision, fire ordeals, fingernail pulling), produces — over a period of time — real personality changes. During periods of ritual seclusion, following instruction in and revelation of Law, the young men must go out and hunt meat for the senior men who "give" them such knowledge. Novices may be beaten and threatened for too much talking, inattention, misbehaviour, or insolence, as well as for previous offences against individual older men. Young men in seclusion now refer to this period sometimes as "high school" and sometimes as "prison", emphasizing both tutelage and restriction of personal freedom. The novices are dependent on their seniors to bring them food, although it is prepared often by women in the ordinary camp, and the period is one of relative privation as regards food. The young men are awakened at any hour of night and chased with bullroarers on enforced hunts, often leaving at night. They are lined up, heads bowed, symbolizing their subordination to those of greater autonomy towards them. Decisions for such procedures are made by all of the older men in discussion. The superordinates see their responsibility as "holding" the subordinates and training them.

Within the overall group of initiated "men", the Pintupi distinguish several relative stages which represent a series of polarized positions relative to each other; each is subordinate to those higher in the hierarchy and superordinate with respect to those below. The basis of the graduation is "knowledge" of myth, ceremony, and song. Each man experiences the Law, then, through members of the next higher superordinate category, which is, as regards ego, an objectification of the Dreaming and a restraint on one's freedom. It is usually these men of the next higher status who most actively interact with novices and who "hold" (*kanyininpa*) and "train" them.

Young men who have finished their instruction and other mandatory ceremonial obligations describe their situation as that of a "free man", as the absence of restraints formerly imposed. They can go where they want, because there is no danger of stumbling onto a male ceremonial performance they are not permitted to see. Learning the Law is seen as an obligation and as a constraint on one's movements and free will. By being subjected to it, one eventually reaches a position of "freedom", lack of constraints — that is, what we call autonomy (cf. Fried 1967 for a discussion of "autonomy" as the ultimate goal in egalitarian political orders). The freedom is, of course, ultimately the freedom to follow the Law which they have incorporated and to impress it upon successors. Those who have passed through the Law make decision about when and where the ceremonies will take place, who will be instructed, who take part — participation in this domain is a source of prestige, accomplishment, and personal pride. Finally, having passed through the Law, one may take a wife.

At each stage reached, a man has both a wider domain of autonomy and is seen to have a greater responsibility. This "ideal" and structural picture corresponds with other facts of personal development as described in individuals' accounts of their youth. One man told me of his illegal youthful spearings of cattle, his many fights, trickery, and wild travels, saying, "I was a 'silly man' then, but now I have children" (and responsibility). The periods of seclusion, ritual discipline, and subordination, then, seem to develop in men a sense of responsibility and duty. Such is the Pintupi experience of the male life cycle. This life cycle is seen, then, as a continuous progression towards autonomy and potency, a progression (in Pintupi eyes) towards greater identification with the moral order. The consent of younger males to the authority of the older seems to rest on the expectation that there is something to be gained — something of value — both for them and for the whole "society". It is something they do for themselves but also something they do for the continuation of life itself. The power and authority of older men is seen as necessary to make everyone conform to the cosmic plan; essentially their ability to "look after" the juniors, the legitimacy of their decision, is guaranteed by their proximity to the Law.

Although this authority is not usually viewed as personal gain-seeking or aggrandizement, the Law they pass on as value is still the instrument of their power. Through it, men come to exert power and authority without accusation of being non-egalitarian or egoistical: they only mediate the Law. Thus is hierarchy achieved in an egalitarian society and thus is social consensus maintained for important social regulations. The social order and the prevailing power relations are secured through presenting the political order as the social organization of esoteric knowledge, presenting the power and domination of males as a result and mainstay of the cosmic order.[8] This view of authority depicts as *natural* and *necessary* the protracted immaturity of younger males while they pass through the ritual cycle, allowing the older men to keep the women for themselves while providing them with a domain in which to exercise their authority.

Freedom and Responsibility

The symbolic emphases of the widespread Kangaroo Dreaming Circumcision ceremonies confirm this interpretation (for more details of the analysis, see Myers 1976). This first ceremony of manhood is a dramatization of a man's becoming responsible for himself, a negation of being "looked after" by "fathers" or "mother's brothers". This theme is presented through the initiate's continual separation from the alternate generation and the latter's relative inactivity in the event. "Own" generation men instruct him in the duties and knowledge of manhood at this time, and responsibility towards the wider society is assumed, symbolized by taking on affines: these seem to mark the terms of his new identity as a "man".

Emphasis is on equivalence and equality, symbolized by *intra*-generational relations rather than hierarchical, intergenerational ones. Thus, the initiate becomes one of the equal men of the male ritual corporation over and against the uninitiated. Subsequently, with the physical marks of initiation (circumcision, subincision), he can "pay" for his ceremonial breaches or other wrongdoings by offering his penis to be held. Men told me, "With this one you can go anywhere", and that it is "like a hundred dollars" with which you can pay. Hereafter, as well, he begins to be concerned with his obligations to his potential affines, giving them gifts of meat. These are long-term relations of reciprocity, involving prototypically one's circumciser who "cut" the initiate and who must repay him for the injury with a wife; in return for this, the initiate must give meat and otherwise help his circumciser. The young initiate is now no longer cut off from the activities of men's ritual cult life, which he enters, however, as passive and subordinate in relation to seniors, but as superordinate regarding females and the uninitiated. He is "free", but now responsible, and he begins his career towards full autonomy.

Taking on Responsibility

Taking on responsibility has political ramifications in Pintupi society, as a way of advancing one's personal position. Men who are desirious of enhancing their reputations and esteem do all they can to "help" others. Typically, the arena for such activity is in white-Aboriginal relations. The aspiring "leader" offers his abilities to translate for other Pintupi into English, and to translate English into Pintupi, voicing their concerns and interests to the white representative of the government (usually) and explaining the latter's concern to the Pintupi. He may show initiative in requesting help for individuals, interceding with Europeans for them. In the cases I observed, men of previously low esteem gained much credence for their opinions; people listened when they spoke at meetings. One was considered, as a result, to be a councillor. Another man, long ago, became spokesman for and "king of the Pintupi", by building his status through helping others. He decided where he and his people would camp and guided their relations with whites, but his position declined when people began to suspect that he was not really looking after them.

We should note that these sorts of patron-client relationships are different from the traditional Dreaming-derived authority relations, for important reasons. The former concern special abilities of the patrons for dealing with whites. Traditionally, the only similar "specializations" were those of the older men regarding the Dreaming and those of "parents" to feed their children. What politics there were, then, derived from the maintenance of a monopoly on ritual knowledge.

The Pintupi concept of hierarchy and authority recognizes a status relationship in which the superordinate's obligation is to "look after" (*kanyininpa*) the subordinate, in return for which the subordinate owes his "boss" deference, respect, and a degree of obedience to his wishes. It is felt that he can tell one what to do, although we shall see how problematic this becomes in regard to the range of his authority. Ascendance to authority and autonomy is gained through acceptance of responsibilities, through generosity and concern for the welfare of others.

Pintupi ideology and experience sees these conditions as being "naturally" met through the gerontocratic mediation of the sacramental plan of the Dreaming on which the welfare of future generations depends. The authority of elder males is legitimized as acceptance of a responsibility to "carry" and "pass on" the Law and to "look after" those who follow. Thus can we regard "holding" (*kanyininpa*) as a dominant symbol in Pintupi social life, a schematic image of social order.

We are also now in a position to better appreciate some of this symbol's particular value for the Pintupi. The image depicted by "holding the child at the breast" (*kanyininpa yampungka*) can refer, ambiguously, to nursing as a primary experience of social concern. Our argument that this concept is extended to the hierarchy of elder males seems to lend some credence to Roheim's analysis of male initiation as a symbolic declaration that henceforth it is men who will be nurturant and protective (Roheim 1945). In other words, through control of the Dreaming and male ritual, it is senior men who will "look after" and "hold" younger men. The data Roheim gathered among neighbours of the Pintupi on the symbolic emphases of male "motherhood" (his term, no theirs) could be brought in here as well. The special ability of Pintupi conceptions of hierarchy is that authority and control are presented in the guise of concern and nurturance. Indeed, it seems we must go further and see in the Pintupi conception of these "opposites" as a necessary unity – a mature and transcendant grasp of the complexity of social life – similar in type to the Ndembu notion of matriliny as simultaneously nurturance and authority (Turner 1967, pp. 57–58).

Reciprocity

The talk about one's "owing" obedience and work to those who "look after" one – of authority as the complement of generosity – deserves some elaboration before touching on its implications for contemporary politics. Reciprocity – an expectation of transactions resulting in parity – is a vital and central principle in all Pintupi social interaction, from "revenge parties" to the bestowal of women. Giving, they maintain, should not be "only one side"; rather it should be "level", "square and square", or *ngaparrku*, signifying an equivalent return.

When I refused to give up my shoes, my brother Pinta Pinta reminded me of the cigarettes he had recently given me. Requests are often phrased to remind one of previous actions, just as men remind their juniors, "I was at your initiation." Men to whom I was generous in non-pay weeks insisted on my eating with them when food was abundant, so that it would not be "too much one side". The expectation of fights similarly is for a transaction of equal exchange: X spears Y and then offers his leg to be speared in return (*ngaparrku wakanu*). A young man whose broken leg had been repaired by surgery in a hospital assured me that the doctor would pay him – because the latter had *cut* him, a situation parallel to expectations of a wife from one's circumciser.

Conversely, unfulfilled expectations of reciprocity – what Sahlins (1965, p. 148) calls negative reciprocity – often lead to conflict and social disturbance. The vast literature on disputes about bestowal is testament to this.

In the acquisition of ritual knowledge, novices especially must reciprocate the "gift" of each ritual revelation with a ceremonial gift of meat to the "old men" who showed it to them. All stages in the accession to important ritual status seem to be accompanied with the novice undergoing an ordeal and pain, as a kind of payment. As the Pintupi say, ritual knowledge is "dear". Older men "give" knowledge and instructees "pay" with pain, meat, and obedience, the sort of transaction I describe as transformative (and hierarchical). As a result of the transaction, there is an increase of "value" on the part of the junior. In these kinds of transaction, what is exchanged is *not* similar in kind or value. Since elders "control" the specialized resource, juniors can never overcome the differential.

This kind of exchange constitutes and continually revalidates the *value* of knowledge; it is "dear" because access is difficult and restricted. This is the way, of course, that the Durkleimian circuit (which brings together experience and symbol) works: what Geertz has captured in his definition of symbols as "models of and for behavior" (Geertz 1965, p. 207). Thus does the Pintupi image of their social order as generations "looking after" successors inform their lives and reproduce their social mode of being.

Village Councillors: A Differentiating Society

In the traditional situation, "looking after" in a material sense was seen as homologous with mediating the authority of the Dreaming. The physical and the metaphysical were articulated as aspects of the same social process, presenting an image of the social and natural order as identical, and rationalizing the "power" of initiated males as a natural fact, unquestionable. Those who "came before" did, in fact, possess both attributes, and there was no reason to discriminate between them. The use of the same concept and the same rationale for both domains created a unified world, a sensible and understandable world in which the political order and the kinship order were both seen as parts of the natural, temporal progression of the generations. This corresponds to the social experience of a society without an autonomous polity, one in which consensus was maintained by common adherence to a shared, external code. There were no single leaders, no single "boss", for a whole group. Nor were there sudden, unexpected problems that demanded radically new solutions. Yet it is precisely this model of social relations which the Pintupi have tried to use to organize and interpret new and different kinds of experience. This can be seen clearly in the Pintupi conception of the Aboriginal village councillor as "boss" and their notion of political relations.

The village council is an institution created by the Australian government, establishing a democratically elected group of councillors to represent and govern Aborigines in their community. Whereas traditional authority derived from and existed mainly in the exercise of ritual knowledge and power, corresponding to biological aging and the succession of generations, here now exists an autonomous institution, differentiated from the rest of a unified world. The Pintupi have sought to integrate the new autonomous domain with the old, but "democratic representation" is a cultural construct that is not first nature to all people.

The village councillor is conceptualized in terms of the relationship between succeeding generations. It is felt that these "bosses" should "look after" their charges, and a frequent criticism made of councillors (as it is of Congressmen in the United States) is that "they don't look after the people properly". Councillors are expected to break up or prevent fights, not to contribute to them, especially on occasions of drunkenness. Criticism, in the form of private grumbling, is quick to follow on such failures. "Leaders" explicitly used the concepts discussed here.

One "leader" frequently asserted, "I look after all this mob", and in disputes about his position as number one councillor, he justified his right to it by maintaining that *he* had got money, tents, and vehicles for the community and that they should treat him as befits a "boss", not fight with him, and should allow him to speak first and so on. Such deference, he felt, was his right and the community's duty to him.

At one period, this man was deposed as number one councillor because he had taken the council truck, belonging to the Yayayi community, and gone to another settlement in the south to settle a personal dispute. This left those who remained at Yayayi without transportation to get food or medical help. There was much criticism during his absence that he was "not properly looking after the people" and that he had never asked the other councillors if it was all right to take the vehicle. Subsequently, he was sacked from his position.

The expected duty of the councillor — to look after his people — is highly problematic when there is no agreement about what constitutes appropriate action, the common good, or even the "society" itself. In any case the duty is a two-edged sword which effectively counters the practical effects of their authority over community property. By Pintupi definition of the role, a councillor should help the people. Consequently, he cannot deny anyone the use of the corporately owned truck without accusations that he is not helping *them*. The right of the councillor in his social identity is that he be asked for use of the truck; his duty, it seems, is to grant its use. This patron-client conception of the rights and duties surrounding authority consistently undermined the ability of the councillors to organize the community effectively. Equally detrimental and perhaps vital is the overriding concern of individuals with "egalitarianism",[9] roughly defined as "No one is better than me." In many areas, the relationships between men, if not always equal, were "mutual complementary" (Maddock 1970, p. 184): X was leader in one ceremony and Y was leader in the next, and so on.

Traditionally, authority was, among men, limited to specific ritual situations and specific kinship domains, in which the nature of one's duties to a "senior" was both well known and thought of as Law. These were not rules or regulations created and imposed by other men; they are not questionable in authenticity. To violant one of these is to violate a socially accepted norm which other individuals are obligated to defend with known sanctions. By contrast, village councillor decisions and rules simply do not have social consensus: their authority is more of a personal matter with individual followers rather than the result of their representation of a "society". Their decisions are seen not as a principle transcending time but as a man-made product and therefore as non-authoritative in the accepted sense of legitimacy (Meggitt [1962, p. 254] comments similarly for the Walbiri). Councillors are not mediating authority: the two aspects no longer coincide. Except for that decreed by Law, one's power and authority depend on how much respect (generosity) one has built up, a kind of assurance of concern with the followers' interests. Credibility depends on past comportment – how selfless and concerned one has been. People evaluate their interests and their self-image in deciding whether to accept authority, so that one will do much more for really "close" kin than for distant, because one feels obligated. Those "fathers" who ask for obedience without prior concern are likely to hear, "You never loved me, only that other man was really my father." However, should council decisions not benefit them, there is no reason to accede to them.

As the Pintupi see it, the councillors – as "bosses" – are free to talk to the government, to take priority in meetings of a current political nature (deference), and to make decisions, but as they have no real power of sanction or denial, few feel binding obligation to follow or police these decisions if their own interests should conflict – although the rulings are not entirely ignored. To understand this problem requires comparison of past and present Pintupi life. Traditionally, the Pintupi had occasion to make relatively few binding, collective decisions. Where and when to hunt, gather, or move camp were largely matters of individual decision, although the lead of a respected person might be followed. Few subsistence tasks required extensive co-operation. Should conflict arise, the final solution was to put distance between the parties, to move to a more favourable place. The resources and productive techniques made this the most sensible resolution of repeated difficulties.

Few public goals were established, then, which coerced individuals to follow or take part. An important domain in which this did occur was that of men's ritual,[10] and in this domain, consensus was a matter of following the pattern of the Dreaming: decision consisting of pursuing a "plan" long established and of which the legitimacy was assured. In the relatively constant world in which they acted, the Pintupi had pre-existing, legitimate solutions (in the Dreaming) for the important problems they were likely to encounter, solutions that bore compelling moral imperative for individuals.[11] Innovation did occur; we know that the Dreaming was constantly revised by dreams, strange encounters, mystical experiences (see Stanner 1966; Myers 1976, pp. 212–15), but innovation took place in the idiom of the Dreaming itself.

The situation of the contemporary settlements is different, with resources that are not easily replaced, dependence on wages and store food, lack of mobility, and large populations. New occasions, new resources, and new problems demand innovations, but how are decisions of men to be made morally binding? How can they be considered "legitimate" and representative of the "social good", when this requires that they be derived from some ontological source of authority beyond their reach? Nor can they simply move away to fairer pastures. Important resources are scarce and no longer available to any man.

The "rise to power", then, is no longer a matter of accession to the right to pass on traditional solutions to repetitive problems. The councillor's problem is to convince people to accept his decisions, to gain consensus for them as public goals. Numerous cases show that when these are seen as contrary to the desires of individuals or groups, the leader is considered to be no longer "looking after" them: hierarchy is exposed as non-nurturant and rejected. Never in the past did a single person have to represent the desires of such a group, of conflicting interests; this was managed through the Law, whose authority was incontestable. Thus, in one area of constant concern, repeated council decisions to ban liquor from the camp were to little avail. As a mechanism to organize Pintupi settlement society and allocate value, the system fails. When a councillor seeks to implement a decision, it is seen as his personal wish and encounters resistance. As a "man", he has no legitimate power over equal men. Even Law would be violated were there not sanctions, but the Law provides that even close kin will be punished for violating the social code: it is every person's obligation to do so. Cataclysm follows failure to observe one's duty. Violation of councillor law does not compel sanction; there is no basis to organize punitive action. People feel this is the council's problem, and to whom can they turn?

Pintupi and the Government: A Broken Code

> White and native are foreigners to each other, getting what they can from each other, but sharing little. [Elkin 1967, p. 56]

The Pintupi conception of the white "boss" is an extension of the same concept: authority based on the "boss's" reciprocal obligation to look after or help the "workers" and the latter's obligation to show respect and consideration for and work for the "boss". The kinship-based model of social relations is extended to organizing the political realm of white-Aboriginal interaction. In such action across a boundary, no longer do models *of* behaviour become models *for* behaviour. Instead, as we shall show, much experience simply does not make sense.

What is happening is the emergence of an explicit political ideology as the Pintupi attempt to make sense out of otherwise incomprehensible social situations, to "construe them so as to make it possible to act purposefully" (Geertz 1973, p. 220). As Geertz argues, ideologies come most crucially into play in situations where the particular kind of information they contain is lacking (ibid., p. 218). But this ideology, coming as it does out of very general cultural orientations, seems inadequate to the novel situation. The Pintupi conception of the reciprocal relationship does not match the European economically founded notion of bosses and workers, especially in regard to the boss's obligation to look after the people. That they do not share the same code for interpreting and evaluating the behaviour and intentions of the opposite party has caused dissonance, mutual resentment, frustration, and disillusion on both sides. As the ideology is inadequate to defining the situation, so do they find it difficult to act purposefully. The problem is that they lack what Weber understood as the "shared

understanding" necessary for social relations. Such shared understandings are lacking in two areas, (1) the basis and nature of authority,
and (2) co-ordinate concepts of value.

The Pintupi model of social relations – of hierarchy and reciprocity
– has been used by them to construe their relationship to the government. They see the latter and its representatives as "bosses", largely
autonomous, to whom deference and obedience is owed but who in
turn are obliged to "help" and "look after" the Aborigines. Past government behaviour, to the Pintupi, signals the appropriateness of this role,
on the following bases:

1. The government gave them food.
2. The government gave pensions to the old.
3. The government says and has said repeatedly that it wants to
   "help" Aborigines (in pidgin, *help* is a synonym of *look after*).
4. Others (especially politically radical Aborigines) say the government should help and is not helping enough.

It is not difficult to see that the Pintupi have interpreted governmental actions and their social relations with the government on the
basis of their own political theory. The Pintupi do, in fact, alter much
of their behaviour in the presence of whites so as to show respect for
the latter, as befits a "boss".

In their own eyes, the Pintupi have maintained their side of the
relationship in reciprocal obligations, and their actions are a further
ground of their expectation that the government should "help" them.
The following examples are illustrative:

(a) Two informants described to me the historical basis of Pintupi-
European relations. Sometime in the 1930s, when they were children,
a European missionary met them and their group near Mount Liebig.
He offered their group wheat flour and rice, and they gave him various
kinds of Aboriginal food. They saw this transaction as forming the
foundation of a reciprocal relationship between whites and themselves.

(b) The same two informants and a few others told me that they
should get pensions and that the Pintupi should be allowed to stay in
the area of Haasts Bluff and Papunya. *They* (the Pintupi) built Haasts
Bluff for the government, and they built Papunya settlement (i.e., they
provided labour). They had worked for the government, and therefore
the government should "look after" them.

(c) The most poignant case is that which resulted from a trip to
the sacred site *yawalyurrunya* with a member of the Department of
Aboriginal Affairs and myself. The trip was initiated at the request of
Aborigines to enable them to visit a sacred site. Yet, in their eyes, they
were doing something for the whites and the government, "showing"
their country. They believed that the government would henceforth
"hold" the site for them; admission to secrets usually implies a res-

ponsibility by the initiated. In any case, many of the men expected to be paid for going. Undoubtedly this was based on the precedent of previous similar trips which had, however, been for filming of ritual, for which men were paid. There was no such filming; the custodians of the country had prohibited it. Contrary to their hopes and expectations, there was no pay for their work as "guides". They pointed out to me that they had done such work, but this really was a minor part of their expectations. The idea grew later that in return for its representative having been to the site, the government would put a bore down near by and establish a settlement there — which some people wanted. This did not occur, although it was still being considered when I left Yayayi.

The implication of all these cases is that they claim to have done something for the government and maintain that it should, reciprocally, help them.

Conversely, and fairly, some of the Pintupi men viewed the avoidance of work by their compatriots as a breach of "contract". It was "no good", they remarked, "to rob the government". These others did no work and still got their pay. "Government gives money for work, that's all." Not to work but to get money was "to rob", not to give equivalent value in return. They did not, I think, expect to get something for nothing and therefore always — as all men do — tried to justify their claims, to phrase their claims to make themselves look the injured party.

The Pintupi almost always phrase their expectations of government help in terms of this model: we helped the government, and they should help us. The number one councillor, Shorty Bruno, also felt he was "helping" the government and therefore was entitled to special consideration. Unfortunately, this code is not shared by the whites, who typically take a very different view of the same social relations.

It is the particular conception of reciprocal obligation described above that ultimately informs the Pintupi category of "boss" and the appropriate relationship entailed by this designation and their view of "work". Men would often ask the community adviser to drive them to Papunya. If he refused, for whatever reason he may have had, most men simply accepted the refusal. It was not infrequent, however, to hear men assert that the "boss" should help them because they worked for him: "I helped you build that fence." It must be remembered that all such workers received financial compensation for work; but in their view the relationship was not simply economic. Rather, it constituted a series of obligations that extended beyond the "work" domain. Men will accept verbal abuse from white bosses that they will not accept from equals, just as they will "listen" to a father. The emotional attachment of Aborigines to their "boss", the one with whom they work, is partly explained by this conception. It is, usually, to a "boss" that an Aborigine goes for help – as when he is out of food or his car is broken down. Those who fulfil the expectations of this role are highly thought of. But it must be emphasized that, in the Aborigine's eyes at least, he has "earned" the help. Like all people, the Pintupi feel that their requests are justified, that they are not asking for more than they give; and they always justify their claims, citing occasions on which they "helped".

As I have tried to show, the Pintupi are not just "having the whites on", as some whites are prone to think. When refused by another Aborigine, a man is just as likely to cite precedents on which he gave the other man "a lot of meat".

In the Pintupi view, their expectation of "help" is fully justified by all the work they have done. This, I am arguing, constitutes a political and bargaining transaction in which each side must evaluate its own reciprocal obligations. Such a "measuring", if it is to satisfy both parties, requires a shared concept of value and equivalence. The Pintupi do have ideas of "enough", "more than", and "less than", although they have no "market". The traditional system of equivalence did not involve a wide variety of items, so that everyone knew how much was enough. In the Pintupi manner of social relationships, there is no outside party to decide when equal value is met. Rather for satisfaction to be reached, both parties must be satisfied. When a notion of equal value is shared, this requires an emotional satisfaction with parity, which is ingrained in Pintupi children.

Many cases, however, especially in the white-Aboriginal domain, are not characterized by a shared system of equivalence. In fact, the Aborigines seem usually to be uncertain whether they are being cheated or not. This situation continues especially in so far as the Pintupi are insulated from direct interaction with an "economic market" where value might be established. They do not see value being established in processes of transaction and choice, because they have worked only for the government. As a result, they have a distorted conception of what the whites are getting and conclude that *maybe* they are being "cheated".

There is a basis for this in Pintupi experience. When they worked at Haasts Bluff settlement twenty years ago, men were paid very small wages, called "pocket money", and were given government rations for food and clothing, as well as other services. Sometime before the move to Papunya in 1960, the wages were raised but were still rather low (to keep Aborigines from going to town), and at Papunya everyone was fed in the government kitchen. Along with the changing ideas about Aborigines that characterized the 1960s, the government began to opt for a programme emphasizing Aboriginal self-reliance and greater self-determination. Wages were raised and rations were cut off; people were expected to take care of themselves. Many of the Pintupi continue to think of their wages as pocket money, to be spent on luxuries. They find it hard to understand that they should use this for the necessities of life. In the view of many, the government is expecting them to use their own "private" money. They wonder why rations were cut off. Still continuing to think of their wages (although more substantial than previously) as pocket money, they feel that they are being cheated, that the government is not properly looking after them: they wonder what has become of rations which they still seem to expect. It must be remembered that in the contemporary world they have been visited by persons who tell them they have been cheated. How, then, are they to conceive of the breach between their expectations and what they receive? Are they being cheated? The difficulty lies entirely in their isolation from the processes of the economic world and market.

Many of the most sophisticated Aborigines continue to think that white people's houses in Melbourne are given to them by the government, and most were greatly surprised to learn that they would have to pay rent to live in the new houses being built for them in Papunya. They have nothing with which to compare their situation, to match the value they receive against that which others receive. Without the shared notion of value and of equivalence, the entire code based on reciprocity cannot work. They do not know "how much is enough" and therefore do not know how much to ask for. This uncertainty underlies much of the claims-making that goes on towards whites, in which Aborigines emphasize what they have done for whites but do not know how much is enough in return.

The final problem with the Pintupi political theory as extended to the white-Aboriginal domain is that it does not explicitly recognize negotiation. They do not, as yet, recognize an autonomous political order, and the concepts by which they seek to articulate political activity have many unspoken assumptions and expectations which experience has not yet separated. In the Pintupi view, consensus is maintained by common adherence to a shared, external, and autonomous code, a cosmological datum. The decisions of men can never be accorded a similar status, a status of Law which must be followed. Thus, the Pintupi seem constantly to try to make of each important event an objectification similar to that constituted by the Dreaming, to view relationships as essentially unchanging, to find a "once and for all" to which they may conform. Theirs is a view of "once a precedent, twice a tradition". Although in relationships among themselves the Pintupi do negotiate and transact, this transaction is never *explicit* and the ideological interpretation of every outcome is that it is a manifestation of the unchanging Dreaming — for example, that all the

people of the country look after it. Transaction is not seen as capable
of altering the basic structure of things. With such a view they seem
unable to comprehend that they *can* alter the structure of their
relationships with whites. Instead, to better their situation, they seek
always to find a better "boss" to look after them. It is true that now
they say that the "boss" works for them, that they can sack him if
he does not do the right thing. Yet, they continue to seek a "boss".

Why they do so is an interesting question which I shall try to answer
briefly. A "boss" is someone outside the community. His decisions
are similarly "outside", beyond the system of kinship. Decisions made
by the council, even though they are conceived of as the heads of the
community, are usually taken to the white boss for ratification. If
these decisions then come to have unfortunate consequences, the blame
is often shifted to the white boss. So, when a "worker" is fired from
his job or his wages reduced for lack of work, it is usually the white
boss who will take the blame. The advantage, then, of having such a
"boss" is obvious. He becomes the external object around which
negotiation and transaction can take place. He becomes, as it were,
the Law. If a councillor wants to be sure that a vehicle will not be used
by anyone in the community, he will ask the white boss to hold the
keys. The white boss, the Aborigine feels, can refuse its use whereas he,
bound in the web of kinship, cannot.

The white "boss", outside the community, is used as a way of pro-
jecting and transforming man-made decisions into an externalized
"object" — turning a "subject" into an "object" — making man-made
decisions into Law, which must be followed.

Summary and Conclusions

> Ideologies are thus ignorant of the exact nature of their relations
> with praxis — do not really understand their own conditions and
> presuppositions, nor the actual consequences to which they are
> leading. [Lefebvre 1968, p. 71]

This account of Pintupi politics may be viewed as a gloss on the theoretical underpinnings of both Marxian and Durkheimian analysis, which
relate ideology to experience and the processes underlying experience.
I have tried to show how the visibility of the Pintupi concept of
authority as "holding" or "looking after" depends for its legitimacy
on a set of expectable social processes and experiences in the lives of
individuals. Parental care, the system of kin classification, the nature

of knowledge as a resource, free access to other resources, the control of knowledge by older males, male initiation, and the high value on egalitarianism all converge as formative elements. Because these central experiences intrude into the life of every Pintupi — indeed, constitute that life — they are so common and expectable that little conceptual effort has gone into distinguishing them one from another. The situation is similar to that noted by Stanner (1966) among the Murinbata: the Pintupi appear to have little objectivity or critical distance in their experience.

They have had little contact with varying cultures and little experience of that internal variation which might exist through a more specialized division of labour. Nor, apparently, was Pintupi history marked by the sort of dramatic and sudden changes which provide the evidence that things could in fact be different, that, in fact, things *are* a certain way as opposed to another.

What Durkheim called "mechanical solidarity", it seems, provides the conditions that make it possible for a single concept or symbol to articulate several domains of activity. My argument has obvious affinities to Bernstein's use of the contrast between restricted and elaborated linguistic codes (Bernstein 1974), affinities based on similar attention to the relationship between symbol and experience. Characteristically, restricted codes arise in small-scale social situations "in which the speakers all have access to the same fundamental assumptions" (Douglas 1973, p. 43), they constitute highly "condensed" symbols. Bernstein argues that, because the restricted code is deeply enmeshed in the social structure, every utterance both conveys information *and* affirms the social order. Elaborated codes, on the other hand, are "adapted to enable a speaker to make his own intentions explicit, to elucidate general principles" (Douglas 1973, p. 44) — that is, to bridge *different* initial assumptions. Presumably, elaborated codes arise from social differentiation.

As Bernstein has defined these codes "in terms of the relative ease or difficulty of predicting the syntactic alternatives which speakers take up to organize meanings" (Bernstein 1974, p. 145), so have we noted the frequency with which Pintupi use *kanyininpa* as an "experience-near" concept to order and act in their world. Traditional Pintupi society, with its repetitive and highly shared social experiences (as in the life cycle), is typified by use of a "restricted code", precisely the kind of symbolic structure that does not make explicit (or even recognize) its assumptions, does not elicit general principles. Such a code, by assuming the regularity of experience, hinders recognition of the activities that regularly constitute that experience as a "fact of nature". Stanner, in his extraordinary way, called our attention to the "embeddedness" of Aboriginal thought, its profoundly analogical quality: "some kind of initiative fitting together of the primary conceptions" (Stanner 1966, p. 15), thought that is "innocent of detached intellectualism" (ibid., p. 44).

Regularity in traditional Pintupi life is a consequence of an extremely stable and continuous adaptation to a fairly constant environment which has produced little specialization of labour and which provided free access to most resources. The experiences of differentiation — as in male/female, uninitiated/initiated — are highly repetitive and expectable, and therefore manageable conceptually by stock, pre-existing solutions. This is also true of "economic" and "social" problems: repetitive and expectable, they can be managed through answers already at hand. When these conditions are not met, as in the contemporary examples, the code begins to lose effectiveness in providing a guide to action and some of its contradicitions may come to light.

Within these constraints, I have argued that the image of the Pintupi as "people without politics" is the consequence of a particular concept of authority as "looking after" which presents hierarchy as nurturance. The employment of this same metaphor to "grasp" several domains of Pintupi life depicts the world as proceeding from and being defined by a set of first principles, familiar to students of the area as the Dreaming. Such a view and justification of "political power" by initiated, mature males as part of nature rather than as a product of human activity (or history) is typically validated by experiences in individuals' lives: maturity and responsibility do come to males after ritual instruction, and it is then that they may marry. The very symbol of "holding", linking parental concern and social authority, presents society as a natural order.

It could be argued that parental concern and old men's authority are not the same, that parents give something in return for respect while old men extract obedience and give only meaningless songs and words. Besides imputing a kind of "bath faith" to older men which is belied by all accounts, to call this a "mystification" in the sense of intentional deceit misses the point that actors' experiences conform to the ideological view: elders do nurture (give things of value). This is a mystification only in so far as, like all ideologies, actors are largely unaware of the social and productive processes, "taken for granted", on which the "truth" of their representations relies.

The concept works. Through the long period of submission, it appears that rebellious young males will internalize and come to identify with important aspects of the Law, eventually taking on responsibility for its enactment and transmission. Learning the Law is a route to the achievement of power, but the despotic qualities of that power are greatly constrained by previous submission to an internalization of a set of norms representing the social good. Thus, geron-tocracy exists and is justified in the Pintupi view because fully initiated older males "look after" and protect those without knowledge.

I have explained the contemporary situations as representing a de-parture from traditional politics because the Durkheimian constraints underlying restricted codes no longer exist. The Pintupi are no longer "producing" and "reproducing" the world they experience in isolation. Thus, the contemporary situation seems to demand some elaboration in the code, some explicit rendering of what constitutes legitimate authority in different domains. In displaying contradictions within the traditional concept of authority, the contemporary cases illuminate the analysis of the cultural basis of Pintupi politics.

In the case of the village councillor, the difficulty can be traced both to the need to gain social consensus for solutions to *new* problems and also to the nature of important resources like trucks, tools, and money, which are not easily "managed" for the good of the subordinates. On the other hand, the Pintupi-government misunderstanding illustrates the difficulties of political interaction without "shared understandings". The tragedy in this kind of interaction is the likelihood that it will validate and continually reproduce racial stereotypes.

Finally, I think it is clear that the Pintupi seek to continue their world as it has been, to impose on time and change an image of per-manence and continuity. When they left the desert to take advantage of new resources, they surely did not foresee the implications this decision would have. In the fact of so much new experience and so many alternatives, their conception of authority seems inadequate to the social world they inhabit. The extent to which they can survive as Pintupi will depend on the way in which they elaborate on their most vital views of the world and human society: that is, on how they come to bring ideology and experience back together.

Notes

1. It is interesting that versions of these distortions also once reflected Euro-pean attitudes to Aborigines. In the nineteenth century, many writers de-nounced the oppressive evils of Aboriginal society as superstition and cruel-ty; later, there followed the period of apologetic defence of Aboriginal life, old men often being presented as wise and concerned for the good of all.
2. We might excuse the "without politics" view as consciously referring to the absence of separate political institutions (i.e., the "kinship" and "govern-ment" distinction), but many of these writers simply regarded the Dreaming as "religion" and failed to consider its relationship to political processes. Thus, they fell prey to accepting the Aboriginal ideology without awareness of its pre-conditions (see Summary and Conclusions).

3. Field research with the Pintupi was supported by NSF Dissertation Improvement Grant No. GS 37122, an Australian Institute of Aboriginal Studies Living Stipend, and NIMH Fellowship No. 3FOIMH57275-01. Invaluable help in the Pintupi language was provided by Ken Hansen of the Summer Institute of Linguistics. This article is based on chapters 10-12 of a Ph.D. dissertation written at Bryn Mawr College under the direction of Jane C. Goodale. I gratefully acknowledge the helpful suggestions of Bette Clark, Don Brenneis, Nic Peterson, Michael Goldstein, Bob Rubinstein, and Jane Atkinson, who have read or heard the present version.

4. These criteria constitute the basis for the four-section systems so widespread in Australia.

5. Freddy West tjakamarra considers Yanyatjarri tjampitjinpa to be a "close" relative; they say they are "from one country". Ordinarily men of the *tjakamarra* subsection refer to *tjampitjinpa* men as *tjamu* (a term often glossed as "grandfather", but which also marks degree of genealogical distance. However, Freddy calls Yanyatjarri "elder brother" (*kuta*) and Freddy called to Yanyatjarri's father (*tjangala* subsection) by the term "father" (*mama*) instead of the "wife's mother's brother" (*tjukunpa*) term ordinarily used between men of their respective subsections. Freddy calls Yanyatjarri's daughter by the "daughter" term (*yuntalpa*), although she is of the subsection that usually entails the affinal term "wife's mother" (*yumari*) and strict avoidance. He said, "I looked after her. She's no mother-in-law". Examples like this can be multiplied, but they follow a consistent pattern.

6. The extent to which males are truly transformed by initiation is described by Stanner (1960).

7. Pintupi youths, of course, feel somewhat differently, and the supposedly impersonal authority of elders is often used personally enough to punish a youthful violator of one's sexual rights to certain women.

8. Although the ideology we are examining maintains that the hierarchy derives from the Dreaming and the natural order of things, the orientation to the natural world is itself a projection of experience of the social world, as Munn (1970) has argued a la Durkheim. A similar argument has been made by Barth (1975) regarding the relationship between epistemology and experience of esoteric cults.

9. Myers 1979 provides further elaboration of the emotional basis of this egalitarianism.

10. Marriage and the coercion involved in bestowals can, with extended argument, I believe, be accommodated to our view of authority, but the problem is omitted from consideration here.

11. Robert Rubinstein has suggested to me that the relationship of the Dreaming to men's ritual and to society as a whole needs clarification. The view I am taking here is that the Pintupi attempt to understand their whole society as coming from the Dreaming *on the model of* the relationship of ritual to the Dreaming, especially since men's ritual is the content of most "public life".

References

Balandier, G. 1970. *Political Anthropology*. London: Allen Lane the Penguin Press.

Barth, F. 1975. *Ritual and Knowledge among the Baktaman*. New Haven, Conn.: Yale University Press.

Bendix, R. 1966. *Class, Codes and Control.* Volume 1. New York: Schocken Books.

Bloch, M. 1975. *Political Language and Oratory in Traditional Society.* New York: Academic Press.

Bourdieu, P. 1977. *Outline of a Theory of Practice.* Translated by R. Nice. Cambridge: Cambridge University Press.

Cohen, A. 1974. *Two-Dimensional Man.* Berkeley: University of California Press.

Douglas, M. 1973. *Natural Symbols.* New York: Vintage Books.

Elkin, A. P. 1967. Reaction and Interaction: A Food-Gathering People and European Settlement in Australia. In *Beyond the Frontier: Social Process and Cultural Change,* ed. P. Bohannon and F. Plog. Garden City: Natural History Press.

Fried, M. 1967. *The Evolution of Political Society.* New York: Random House.

Geertz, C. 1965. Religion as a Cultural System. In *Reader in Comparative Religion,* ed. W. Lessa and E. Vogt. 2nd edition. New York: Harper and Row.

———. 1973. *The Interpretation of Cultures.* New York: Basic Books.

Goodenough, W. 1969. Rethinking Status and Role. In *Cognitive Anthropology,* ed. S. Tyler. New York: Holt, Rinehart, and Winston.

Lefebvre, H. 1968. *The Sociology of Marx.* Translated by N. Guterman. New York: Random House.

Levi-Struass, C. 1966. *The Savage Mind.* Chicago: University of Chicago Press.

Maddock, K. 1970. *The Australian Aborigines.* Harmondsworth, Mddx.: Allen Lane the Penguin Press.

Meggitt, M. J. 1962. *Desert People.* Chicago. University of Chicago Press.

Munn, N. 1970. The Transformation of Subjects into Objects in Walbiri and Pitjantjatjara Myth. In *Australian Aboriginal Anthropology,* ed. R. M. Berndt. Nedlands: University of Western Australia Press.

Myers, F. 1976. To Have and To Hold: A Study of Persistence and Change in Pintupi Social Life. Ph.D. dissertation, Bryn Mawr College.

———. 1979. Emotions and the Self: A Theory of Personhood and Political Order among Pintupi Aborigines. *Ethos* 7, no. 4: 343–70.

Peacock, J. 1968. *Rites of Modernization.* Chicago: University of Chicago Press.

Read, K. 1959. Leadership and Consensus in a New Guinea Society. *American Anthropologist* 61: 425–36.

Roheim, G. 1945. *The Eternal Ones of the Dream.* New York: International Universities Press.

Rose, F. 1968. Aboriginal Marriage, Land-Owning Groups, and Initiation. In *Man the Hunter,* ed. R. Lee and I. DeVore. Chicago: Aldine.

Sahlins, M. 1965. On the Sociology of Primitive Exchange. In *The Relevance of Models for Social Anthropology,* ed. M. Banton. A.S.A. monographs. London: Tavistock.

Sharp, L. 1958. People without Politics. In *Systems of Political Control and Bureaucracy in Human Societies,* ed. V. F. Ray. Seattle: American Ethnological Society.

Stanner, W. E. H. 1956. The Dreaming. In *Australian Signpost,* ed. T. A. G. Hungerford. Melbourne: Cheshire.

———. 1960. Durmugam: A Nangiomeri. In *In the Company of Man,* ed. J. B. Casagrande. New York: Harper and Brothers.

———. 1966. *On Aboriginal Religion.* Oceania Monograph No. 11. Sydney: University of Sydney Press.

Turner, V. 1967. *The Forest of Symbols.* Ithaca, N.Y.: Cornell University Press.

Williams, R. 1977. *Marxism and Literature.* Cambridge: Cambridge University Press.

Outside the Power of the Dreaming: Paternalism and Permissiveness in an Aboriginal Settlement

ROBERT TONKINSON

For Western Desert Aborigines, emigration to fringe settlements brought contact with whites, who represented an alien culture and alien power.[1] The desert people apparently made no attempts at a *conceptual* integration of the two contrasting systems; they acquiesced to the presence of the whites, accepting them as a major new given while they concentrated their efforts on adaptation and survival in what was a dramatically different social environment. The Aborigines knew nothing of the nature, distribution, and dynamics of power in the contacting society. Accordingly, in the paternalistic milieu of the mission settlement Aborigines permitted the agents of white society relatively free exercise of their power, judging it to be an intrinsic component of their being as whites.

At Jigalong, an isolated fringe settlement that is the setting for this paper, there evolved in the Aboriginal view two conceptually quite distinct social fields. One, "the mission" (the area of white settlement) was the white's domain and their arena of power and control; the other, "the camp", was Aboriginal space and not a legitimate domain of the whites. Whether or not Aborigines were directly involved, most of what happened in the mission was essentially "whitefella business" (cf. Tonkinson 1978*a*) and the power exercised there was that of the whites. The Aborigines jealously guarded their prerogatives of power and control in the camp arena, while largely ignoring much of what happened a few hundred yards away in the mission — or more correctly, while not comprehending the implications of some of the exercise of paternalistic white power there.

Where Aborigines have developed a clear dichotomy between their own and alien social fields, the exercise of power by whites has had vitally important "masking" functions, blurring Aboriginal perceptions of certain developments that now assume the status of "problems". With fundamental changes in governmental ideologies during the 1960s and 1970s from paternalistic control to Aboriginal self-management and the encouragement of Aboriginal initiative, it has become impossible for Aborigines to sustain a clear conceptual distinction between "mission" and "camp" and between "whitefella business" and "*mardu* [Aboriginal] business". The Aborigines at Jigalong now find themselves having to respond to "problems" they never knew they had, problems located in the "mission" arena and therefore "whitefella business". Because in the post-contact era the Aborigines were preoccupied with adapting to changed and continually changing circumstances, they did not become aware of certain other changes occurring at the same time. A major focus of this paper is one such hidden problem, that of disciplining children in the settlement context. Given the values of self-reliance and independence of children in pre-contact desert culture, this did not emerge as a problem for the Aborigines until after the paternalistic regime of the missionaries had ended. A new generation of white staff has refused to assume a disciplinarian role, since it contravenes contemporary policies directed towards Aboriginal initiative and problem-solving.

Elsewhere I have discussed Aboriginal-missionary relationships at Jigalong in detail, noting that there was a deep-seated and mutual distrust and that the Aborigines regarded the end of the mission era as a triumph for Aboriginal Law over Christianity (Tonkinson 1974). That some Jigalong Aborigines have in recent years expressed nostalgia for certain aspects of the mission period might at first sight seem surprising. In explaining this seeming anomaly, I suggest that what the Jigalong people seek is the return of whites who will exercise their power in those aspects of "the mission" social field where the Aborigines feel unable or unwilling to act.

The appeal to a locus of authority outside themselves is a strategy having continuity with the pre-contact past, but it reflects as well a continuing refusal to attempt an integration of traditional and alien kinds of power. For Aborigines, power lay in the spiritual realm of the Dreaming, where creative ancestral beings saw that the flow of power into the physical world was maintained in response to ritual action and the faithful following by Aborigines of the life-design bequeathed them from the Dreaming (cf. Stanner 1958; Tonkinson 1978*b*). Power, like knowledge, resided in the spiritual realm and was "given" to human Aborigines, through spirit intermediaries, so it was not viewed as a product of human intellect and secular endeavour. In the contact situation, where Aborigines lack understanding of the nature of the power of the whites, it is simpler and more pragmatic to maintain the dichotomy between "whitefella" and Aboriginal business by having whites exercise what is seen as their power. If this tendency is widespread among Aboriginal communities, it has significant implications for the direction and ultimate outcome of contemporary policies concerning Aboriginal self-management.

The Setting

Jigalong, a community of about five hundred desert Aborigines, lies on the western fringe of the Gibson Desert in north-western Australia. Its inhabitants are immigrants from the desert proper who abandoned their former nomadic existence for a settled life that has led to an increasing dependence on the wider Australian society. Even after several decades of contact with whites, these Aborigines remain tradition-oriented in many important values and behaviours, and they continue to follow many of the major dictates of the Law of the Dreaming. Jigalong became the site of a fundamentalist Christian mission in 1946 and remained under missionary control until 1969, when the missionaries withdrew, having won only one convert to their faith. Since 1973 the settlement has been an incorporated Aboriginal community, with an all-Aboriginal governing council which is assisted by white advisers and heavily dependent on government financing for social and economic development. The transition from extreme paternalism to self-management is taking place at a time when the community is attempting to cope with increasing pressures from the outside world. The situation is unstable, and the Jigalong Aborigines are beset by a number of unprecedented and difficult problems.

Child Discipline and Property in Pre-Contact Aboriginal Society

In the desert environment, children were allowed free rein to do as they pleased within very broad limits. Australian Aboriginal culture is noted for the extreme permissiveness of adults toward children, who were generally indulged to a remarkable degree (Berndt and Berndt 1964). Children were accustomed to getting their way and were rarely subjected to physical punishment by adults. If chastised or hit, their typical reaction was a violent and prolonged temper tantrum, which included verbal and physical abuse of their adversaries until their feelings were assuaged by capitulation, bribery, and great shows of affection. One of the only non-negotiable stances was that of men refusing to allow their children to accompany them when their intended business included secret-sacred aspects. For girls, the transition to the adult female roles of provider and wife began well before adolescence, but boys were allowed to continue a free-and-easy, playful existence until their mid to late teens, when suddenly and traumatically they were launched on the decade-long path to full social adulthood and eligibility for marriage.

As a consequence of nomadism, the lack of agriculture and domesticated animals, and the extremely marginal nature of their desert environment, the Aborigines possessed relatively little "property" and had very few rules pertaining to its use or abuse. The only major crime against property was the theft of sacred objects, and this was apparently a rare event. Initiated men took great pains to keep sacred paraphernalia and activities well hidden from women and children. At a very early age, children were taught to avoid trespass into "men's country" and other tabooed locations. Everywhere else, children could work their will on the face of the land and on the few material possessions of their families without fear of anything more than a gentle rebuke. A man might sit by and watch his small child hammer on his elaborately carved shield with a sharp stone and make no firm attempt to intervene, lest he incur the child's loud and prolonged wrath. Children were permitted to play with fire and engage in the same kind of mild pyromania that everyone else did. There were no houses to burn down, and in the desert there was little danger of a blaze getting out of hand.

Although from infancy children were continually reminded by adults of their kin relationships to others and of the correct behaviours expected between such kin, they were free of the need to observe the dictates of kin behavioural patterning. When small children engaged in sexual experimentation, this evoked at worst a light-hearted scolding, especially if the pair concerned stood in an incestuous relationship to each other. Adults were most likely to turn a blind eye and make joking references amongst themselves to what was going on. In a band of perhaps twenty or thirty adults the half-dozen or so small children would have spent much time in the company of their mothers and older females. But once they were considered capable of looking after themselves, children spent much time playing beyond the range of any adult supervision and their activities were of minimal interest to adults. Such a separation was doubtless mutually valued. Desert life involved dispersal in small groups most of the time, and population densities were extremely low, so children had limitless room to express themselves, and their parents were happy to give them this freedom.

The Mission Era and Discipline

In the Jigalong area, the first encounters of many desert immigrants were with frontier white men, whose behaviours and values were in most cases radically different from those of the missionaries who arrived later on the scene. White men on the outlying pastoral leases had specific exploitive interests in the desert people: they exchanged food, axes, and other goods for dingo scalps, labour, and in many cases for sexual access to Aboriginal women. Otherwise, they interfered little in the lives of the Aborigines and were not interested in "civilizing" them beyond what was necessary to accomplish their immediate objectives.

So marked was the contrast between the frontiersmen and the Jigalong missionaries that the Aborigines categorized the latter as "Christians", people quite distinct from other "whitefellas". The missionaries behaved differently and voiced objections to many aspects of Aboriginal culture, which they regarded as the work of the devil and as something to destroy. Viewing the adults as so steeped in evil as to be beyond redemption, the missionaries concentrated their efforts on the children, whose souls they believed could still be saved for Christ. They felt it necessary to remove the children from the adults and the alleged iniquities and depravities of the camp life, so as to enhance their chances of weaning the children from the devil. They therefore put all the school-aged children into single-sex and spatially segregated dormitories, and overcame initial parental objections by invoking "government law" as validation for their actions.

In both school and dormitory situations, the children were confronted with rigid discipline for the first time in their lives. Rebellion or physical attacks on their punishers brought only severe beatings and the threat of God's wrath. The latter peril did not trouble them, since they and their parents had no understanding of Christianity as relevant to their lives. Parents whose children were beaten sometimes became angry enough to venture a confrontation with the missionaries. But they were uncomfortable about intruding into the "mission" domain, where Aboriginal power was neither understood nor heeded, and they feared the power of the missionaries and "the government". So they rarely resorted to violence, and even co-operated by returning runaway children to the dormitories, lest the missionaries call in the police.

The schoolchildren learned about "property" and its high valuation in European culture. They were taught its proper care and maintenance, and soon became acquainted with the rod and its use to teach them respect for property and to discourage them from un-Christian behaviours, particularly sexual activity of any kind. For the children, the mission domain was a rule-ridden one, but daily escape to the camp for brief periods occurred. The missionaries found it impossible to prevent children from spending some of their spare time in camp. There they were indulged by their elders and had ample opportunity to internalize the kinds of values that would prevent them from identifying with the relatively oppressive world of their Christian guardians. They adapted quickly to the routines of school and dormitory and for the most part obeyed the rules of the mission order. But they were no closer to becoming Christians than were their parents. The Aborigines sensed no threat of having their children alienated from them, and there was little essential difference between desert and settlement in respect of the daily separation and autonomy of parents and school-aged children.

The only potential converts to Christianity, and the group that did cause Aborigines worry, were some of the older teenage girls who exploited a strong missionary opposition to their arranged marriages to much older men. These girls were housed in a special, closely guarded dormitory and were kept under mission protection to prevent their removal to camp. They received biblical instruction and training as housegirls and were a source of great satisfaction to the missionaries. But most were skilled in escaping missionary surveillance long enough for meetings with their boyfriends, and if pregnancy resulted, they fell from missionary grace. Since this was a frequent outcome, most were banished from the sanctuary of the dormitory and returned to camp, where once again they came under the control of Aboriginal power, in the form of the Law. As long as they remained in the "mission" arena, the girls were assured of a measure of protection from irate relatives of their boyfriends, but once banished from beneath its protective umbrella (with its overtones of "government law") they had to bow to Aboriginal will.

"Kids playin' up and runnin' around": The Contemporary Situation

Although relations between the Aborigines and missionaries at Jigalong were often tense and antagonistic and the Aborigines were happy to see them leave for good in 1979, the Christians had performed many administrative functions that the Aborigines realized were essential to the continued existence of the settlement. However, one of the functions that the Aborigines had not fully comprehended was the nature of the disciplinary role that the missionaries had performed. This was because it had been carried out almost entirely in the mission arena. The physical plant and entire mission area (i.e., not the camping areas) were regarded by the Aborigines as "whitefella business" and therefore as of little concern of theirs. They respected the rights of whites over "their" area, so if incidents occurred there among Aborigines, they were anxious to shift the locale to the camp area as quickly as possible, lest the whites take advantage of the interactional setting to interfere in Aboriginal business.

In the actual camp area, and in all matters concerned with their religious activities, the Aborigines considered themselves masters and brooked no outside interference in their internal affairs. Missionaries could intervene and stop fights among Aborigines in the mission area without violent Aboriginal objection. But their action never finished the matter, and once back in the camp the dispute continued. Further missionary attempts to stop fighting usually led to strong objections by the Aboriginal men, who would tell the missionaries to go back to the settlement (unless they ignored the presence of the missionaries in camp altogether). The Aborigines accepted the burden of missionary paternalism and control as long as it did not extend into the affairs of the camp or appear to threaten in any way the integrity of the Law.

Since the early 1970s and the advent of new government policies of Aboriginal self-management, the situation of the Jigalong Aborigines has changed dramatically. They have been required to take responsibility for more and more of the management of their community. The "whitefella business" formerly left to the missionaries to deal with is to an increasing extent Aboriginal business, or at least the business of the elected Aboriginal council. Houses, store, physical plant, and the like are now community property, the upkeep of which is council responsibility. The dormitory system was abandoned before the missionaries left, and school-children are now in their parents' care almost full-time, that is, apart from the few hours each weekday that they attend government school.

The white advisers and staff members have considerable *de facto* power and remain essential to the running of the community. In accordance with the new policies, however, they are supposed to remain inconspicuous and be as non-directive as possible, so as to encourage Aboriginal decision-making and initiative. Given the legacy of extreme paternalism and the complete exclusion of the Aborigines from decision-making in matters concerning government administration of their welfare, it has proved difficult for the Jigalong Aborigines to assume these new responsibilities and to exercise judgement in the field of what was formerly "whitefella business". The problem of controlling their children (which in reality is largely that of protecting property), like the more serious problem of the effects of alcohol-related problems and "delinquency", are alike in having no traditional precedents and in having been dealt with in the mission era by the whites. The Aborigines do not share the great concern of the local whites about some aspects of the discipline problem, such as vandalism and breaking and entering, but are primarily worried because the onus has been placed on *them* to apprehend and punish the offenders.

Aboriginal and white perceptions of the magnitude of "problems" are reversed in the case of teenage promiscuity, which the Aboriginals regard as more serious than vandalism because it often involves partners whose kin relationships forbid that kind of sexual intimacy. Casual liaisons among such people are not regarded seriously as a rule, but there are indications that some young couples would like to cohabit as man and wife, an unthinkable and potentially fatal desire in times past.

In sum, the children as a collectivity are perceived by their elders (and local white staff) as getting out of hand, or "playin' up". They pose a threat to property and propriety and are no longer therefore a mere laughing matter.

In the mission era, the Christians were successful in keeping the school-age children in line most of the time, and parents did not worry about their children's conduct in the mission arena, which was regarded by them as the whites' domain and responsibility. Given their permissive attitudes, the Aborigines were not anxious to play the disciplinarian role if they could avoid it. They were thus quite willing to have the missionaries assume this task. Having ignored the content of this role, the Aborigines would not have realized the extent to which it involved teaching children to conform to behavioural norms having no parallels in the pre-contact situation. Only in retrospect, and in the absence of external agents of social control, are the Aborigines made belatedly aware of the importance of this role. The children's conformity to the rules and expectations of the whites was an essential ingredient in their adaptation that was being masked from the Aboriginal adults because they had placed it principally under the rubric of "whitefella business" and thus excluded it from their social field of responsibility.

In the desert the behaviour of children rarely if ever achieved "problem" status. At the mission, however, the whites created and highlighted a notion of it as at times "a problem", one that required firm sanctions. In the matter of sexual activity, the bitter opposition of the missionaries was supported by the Aborigines, but for different reasons. Crimes against property were a post-contact phenomenon, and since it was invariably missionaries' or government property, the Aborigines were not particularly concerned. "Getting into mischief" frequently involved property of some kind, so it too was considered insignificant by the parents, whose mischief-making in their childhood in the desert was never a matter for great concern. The bands that formed the core of desert social life were such that the number of age-mates a child possessed was never very large. In a settled community of several hundred people, with a high birthrate, there are large peer-groups and play-groups, and they roam about the camp and settlement areas at will. Their play is largely unsupervised by adults, and there is no "policeman" role built into the society to deal with this kind of gathering. Today, these are the groups that are seen by adults to be running wild and getting into lots of trouble, such as vandalizing buildings and breaking and entering staff homes. Boys with slingshots have broken thousands of dollars' worth of windows in both camp and settlement areas, but neither the council nor the parents have taken concerted action to ban the weapons, despite repeated suggestions by white staff that they do so.

Even without any urging from the whites, the Aborigines realize that they now have a "problem": the children are apparently becoming laws unto themselves at Jigalong. The council and many individual Aborigines blame parents for their failure to control their children adequately, but parents remain reluctant to take on the mantle of disciplinarian. Adults rarely chastise the children of others, either, since this invariably provokes a strong negative response from the parents concerned and often leads to physical violence among the adults. Children are not easily intimidated by their elders; they flee when chastised and chased, but frequently resume whatever it was they were doing before adults intervened. The traditional stress placed on self-reliance and independence among children has carried over from the desert. Only at school and during the mission era was this stress tempered by measures to ensure conformity to rules made necessary by a completely different social context.

However much they may privately wish to interfere at times, white staff members know that such action contravenes current policy. "The mission" as a social field has become Aboriginal business, but the Aborigines have stubbornly resisted the erosion of their old dichotomy. They would be relieved to have whites take on the task of disciplining children outside the camp environment, just as they would like whites to police and stem the inflow of alcohol into Jigalong. Instead, they are told by the white staff that, as Aboriginal business, these problems must be dealt with by the council and the community at large.

In the school environment, children are disciplined and encouraged to conform to behavioural norms dictated by their white teachers. But even here, changes in educational philosophy and policy have made the school atmosphere much more supportive and relaxed than before. Teachers now are on the whole much more tolerant of cultural differences and are reluctant to impose their will on the pupils through the threat or use of force. Parents therefore cannot turn to the teachers to fill the role that they remain reluctant to adopt.

To date, there has been a great deal of discussion, both in and out of the council, about the problem of controlling children. With each new crisis involving acts of delinquency by children, there is a fresh wave of determination to act decisively and punish the transgressors. Some teenagers accused of sexual activity have been beaten, and some offenders have been brought before public meetings in camp for chastisement. As in many other aspects of life, however, the gap between firmly expressed resolve and effective action is large, and the feeling that children are becoming increasingly out of control remains strong.

Old and New Laws, Dreaming, and Other Powers

Jigalong Aborigines who now harbour fond memories concerning aspects of the mission era are not yearning for a fresh infusion of fundamentalist theology. What they miss is the kind of paternalism that was unflinchingly applied in the social field of "the settlement" — that which absolved them of tasks they did not want, or feel any need, to assume. The present problem stems from several major sources: continuities in Aboriginal understandings about power and its locus as external to the self (cf. Munn 1970; Myers 1979); traditional attitudes to children, whose non-problematic status in the pre-contact society was transformed by the settlement situation and a new social field that demanded new rules; and a legacy of missionary paternalism that masked emerging problems and left Aborigines ill-prepared to assume necessary responsibilities associated with community self-management. It is not that the Aborigines have lacked the flexibility or imagination to adapt. Migration and the transition to a settled existence meant drastic alterations in their local organization and subsistence economy, and their post-contact experience has been one of continual adjustment and adaptation as they have successfully managed coexistence with whites while protecting the integrity of valued cultural forms brought with them from the desert. The altered circumstances demanded in many cases novel responses, and the Aborigines proved equal to the task. But in the case of the children, the disciplinarian role adopted by the missionaries obviated direct experience of a problem.

The Aboriginal elders, preoccupied with the forging of new unities between various groups that comprised the Aboriginal community, and the consolidation of the centrally important religious life, saw no threat in surrendering their children to the missionaries and the dormitory system. Their perception of "the mission" as the legitimate domain for the exercise of the power of whites led them to ignore much of what went on there, especially with respect to the content and rationale of the missionaries' role as disciplinarians. Over a period of more than two decades, they came to take for granted their children's conformity to the new law; in camp, of course, the old Law applied, and it gave children free rein.

Once the missionaries withdrew, however, parental expectations that their children would continue to behave as before in the settlement arena were not met. The "problem" of misbehaving children suddenly emerged and became theirs when the new administrative philosophies came into effect at Jigalong. Up to that point it is certain that the Aborigines were not aware that they had a problem with their children. As with other aspects of the contact situation, the paternalistic assumption by the whites of all responsibilities for what happened in "the mission" and all bureaucratic dealing between Jigalong and the outside society hid from Aboriginal awareness the emergence of difficulties that were absent in the desert. Since there was no tradition of missionary consultation with the Aborigines, there was no way for them to gain some perspective on the problems as they appeared and no opportunity for them to generate strategies to cope with them.

Today, the absence of the non-Aboriginal enforcer role and a prevailing Aboriginal reluctance to interfere with children's autonomy and their development of self-control prevent the Aborigines from acting to fill the gap left by the missionaries. Adults now feel the need to bring their children under control in the settlement environment where traditional attitudes to property are no longer appropriate and where the children constitute a much larger component of the society than in the desert. The population explosion that followed sedentarization and acceptance of Western medical treatment has produced a youthful community that had no parallel in size or demographic composition traditionally. So one part of the problem is the sheer weight of numbers favouring the young. Who is to effectively police these children out of school hours, and how this can be done without angering parents, remain unresolved dilemmas for the council. Although there has been some acceptance of Western birth-control practices at Jigalong, people are much more concerned about being overrun by dogs than by children, and in general they are delighted to have so many children to indulge and heap affection upon.

A major concern of the Jigalong adults is that today's children will grow up "in the Law". They hope that as adults the children will assume responsibility for the continuance of those valued behaviours and practices, particularly in relation to kinship and religion, that the Aborigines still see as essential to their cultural survival. They are therefore afraid to risk alienating their children lest the ensuing generation gap prove fatal to the Law. The Aborigines live simultaneously under both old and new laws, so children possess power that they never had traditionally — the power to abandon Aboriginal culture in favour of that of the whites, which is increasingly impinging on them and offers many attractions. Boys know nothing substantial of the powerful magnet of the secret-sacred life until the revelations begin with initiation in their sixteenth or seventeenth year. In the meantime, they are being schooled and wooed by a host of Western cultural elements, such as movies, music, trips to the city, all of which turn their horizon outward to the wider world rather than inward toward Aboriginal culture and its powerful secrets.

For concerned Aboriginal adults, then, the problem comes down to a matter of priorities. They fear the loss of younger people to the Law much more than they fear the consequences of children running wild and damaging property or breaking and entering. In the matter of sexual promiscuity among teenagers, the adults are torn between the desire to curtail such activity and the perceived need to take no firm steps in that direction lest they anger the offenders into open rebellion. This in turn could lead to the dreaded spectacle of wrongly related couples publicly proclaiming their resolve to remain together as man and wife. It is ironic that the same mission regime for which nostalgia is being felt by some Aborigines dedicated itself to the task of persuading children to reject their parents and the Law and adopt Christianity as their guiding light. Although the missionaries failed in this major objective, they nevertheless sowed the seeds for whatever resistance or rejection might later occur among the graduates of the dormitory. The successful transition back from dormitory life to camp that for so many years was made by the children again served to mask from the Aborigines that emergence of an unprecedented problem regarding competing ideologies. The children rejected Christianity right enough, but some harboured potentially dangerous notions about "free choice of spouse" and other aspects of the "whitefella law" that were perceived as desirable.

Nostalgia for the paternalism of the mission days may not be unique to the Aborigines of Jigalong. Recent reports of conversion to Christianity among communities in some other parts of the country suggest that Aborigines see in fundamentalist objections to drinking a possible solution to pressing problems connected with alcohol abuse. Their interest in Christianity may prove to be less focused on its theological content than on its coercive potential. It may well carry the possibility that once again external agents of power and control will step in — this time to prevent the Aborigines from destroying themselves.

Conclusion

The distinguished Australianist Professor Stanner recently chose as the title for his collected essays the words of an Aboriginal elder, "White man got no Dreaming", an apt summation of how many Aborigines see the essential difference between themselves and whites. The fundamental concept of the Dreaming and its primacy as the source of all life-sustaining power and knowledge for Aborigines stands in contrast to the power of whites, which desert Aborigines perceive as coming from somewhere else, perhaps from God, but certainly not from the Dreaming. From the perspective of the Jigalong Aborigines, the power of the whites comes from afar and has long been personified by policemen and government officials. They have striven to maintain a clear separation of the two manifestations of power, principally by assigning one to "the camp", as symbolizing Aboriginal culture and land, and the other to "the mission" as the social field of the whites, embodying everything that was not "of the Dreaming".

Just as the elders looked after the Law in their domain, so too should the whites look after their law in the domain of "the mission". The insistence of the missionaries that they remove the school-age children from camp to dormitory carried with it the metamessage that they assumed responsibility for looking after the children.[2] That the children would thus be subjected to, and dominated by, white people's power while in that situation was expected by the Aborigines and tolerated as an inevitable consequence of their children's incorporation into the domain of "whitefella business".

The accommodation worked out by the Aborigines worked remarkably well throughout the mission era and enabled them to maintain a healthy and vigorous Law in the settlement and kept the whites from seriously interfering in the internal affairs of the camp, where the dictates of the Dreaming Law predominate. The children in the dormitory were only temporarily lost to the power of the whites, and the conceptual and social isolation of the "camp" from the "mission" solved for the Aborigines some of the pressing problems of overlap between the old and new laws and between two different systems of power.

Elsewhere (Tonkinson 1978a) I have outlined the strategy adopted by the Aborigines to cope with attempts by whites in the post-mission era to achieve a unification of "camp" and "mission" by according to Aborigines for the first time a measure of power and responsibility derived from sources within the society of the whites. From the foregoing discussion it should be clear why the Aborigines would want to avoid such a symbiosis. They resisted it by expecting their elected councillors to handle all of what they still considered to be essentially "whitefella business". It was up to the councillors to decide what information could be usefully communicated to the camp domain, and to keep the rest confined in "the mission". The concerted attempts by whites to convert "whitefella business" to Aboriginal business and thus destroy the old compartmentalization of these distinct, and to a certain extent opposed, domains, has proved to be a major problem for the Aborigines at Jigalong. The other, related one is that of being given responsibility for the exercise of a measure of power deriving not from the Dreaming but from whites. As in the traditional society, mediation carries with it responsibility for looking after others, but the Aboriginal councillors know very little of the nature of this power and cannot apply it in the same ways that were used traditionally, because this power is not of the Dreaming. This lack of understanding, plus the paternalistic legacy, account for the continued heavy reliance of the Aborigines on their white advisers and for the large amount of *de facto* influence thus possessed by the latter.

As Myers points out in the previous chapter, councillors become trapped by the conflicting demands made of them. They are delegated to exercise new powers and therefore automatically assume in Aboriginal eyes a responsibility to look after the people, but there is "no agreement about what constitutes appropriate action, the common good, or even the 'society' itself". In the desert, there were no such problems, since the dictates of the Law provided acceptable guides to proper behaviour; both the sources and the methods of mediation of Dreaming powers were understood. In the contact situation there have been no attempts at syncretism of the two power realms; on the contrary, a clear separation has been consciously maintained, so the Aborigines see no adaptive lessons to be learned from their understandings of Dreaming power and therefore no wisdom in trying to apply principles drawn from one in the exercise of the other.

To the extent that the council system has succeeded at Jigalong, it has perpetuated a deep-seated separation of the two conceptual realms that in the contemporary situation of change necessitate some degree of fusion. If the Aborigines are to cope effectively with the pressures imposed by the outside world, it may be essential that they learn to use the new power that is gradually being made available to them. And to do this, they will have to accept much of what was formerly "whitefella business" as their own, and to evolve a system of allocation of white-derived power and responsibility that is acceptable to the community at large. Thus, with respect to the problem of children "playin' up", and that of uncontrolled influx of alcohol and unregulated drinking, the Aborigines will need to fill some coercive "policeman" roles in a way that has wholehearted community backing.

Given the biases against hierarchy and the fundamental opposition between generalized ascribed authority and the dictates of the kinship system, the problems confronting these desert Aborigines are major ones.

Because of the masking functions of paternalistic roles, the Jigalong Aborigines will probably encounter other emerging problems that they did not know they had. How effectively they can develop strategies to meet these new challenges may well depend on how effectively they can bring about a fusion of "camp" and "mission", and "whitefella" and *mardu* business. Should this occur, some of the strategies that worked so well over millennia of desert existence could be applied with equal force to their present circumstances. If they come to regard power as a unitary phenomenon, to place the power of the Dreaming inside that of the whites or conversely embrace the latter within their conception of a truly all-encompassing Dreaming, they will achieve the same kind of symbiosis that many Melanesians seem to have done in rationalizing their circumstances after contact with whites. If power is conceptualized as an undifferentiated force, something having common properties regardless of ultimate source, the Aborigines may be well on the way to achieving a new kind of accommodation, one more suited to the pressures that now beset them.

Notes

1. Fieldwork on which this paper is based was carried out at Jigalong and in the Western Desert proper on various occasions between 1963 and 1979. My thanks to Fred Myers for his many valuable comments on an earlier draft.
2. In the previous chapter Myers, whose Pintupi informants are culturally similar to the Aborigines at Jigalong, suggests that the concept of "looking after" or "holding" is a dominant symbol of Pintupi social life. Just as the elders mediate the power of the Dreaming in looking after their people and protecting the integrity of their social order, so too should local whites (who are likewise not sources but mediators of power) look after Aborigines in all matters pertaining to the impingement of alien society on Aborigines' lives.

References

Berndt, R., and Berndt, C. 1964. *The World of the First Australians.* Sydney: Ure Smith.
Munn, N. 1970. The Transformation of Subjects into Objects in Walbiri and Pitjantjatjara Myth. In *Australian Aboriginal Anthropology,* ed. R. M. Berndt. Perth: University of Western Australia Press.

Myers, F. 1979. Emotions and the Self: A Theory of Personhood and Political Order among Pintupi Aborigines. *Ethos* 7, no. 4: 343–70.

Stanner, W. E. H. 1958. The Dreaming. In *Reader in Comparative Religion,* ed. W. A. Lessa and E. Z. Vogt. New York: Harper and Row.

Tonkinson, R. 1974. *The Jigalong Mob.* Menlo Park, Cal.: Cummings.

————. 1978*a*. Aboriginal Community Autonomy: Myth and Reality. In *"Whitefella Business"*, ed. M. C. Howard. Philadelphia: Institute for the Study of Human Issues.

————. 1978*b*. *The Mardudjara Aborigines.* New York: Holt, Rinehart, and Winston.

The Torres Strait Islanders and the Pearling Industry: A Case of Internal Colonialism

JEREMY BECKETT

The Torrest Strait Islanders are Australia's Melanesian minority. Currently numbering some ten thousand, they are today found throughout the continent, but their homes are a score of islands that lie between Cape York and the southern coast of New Guinea.[1] The Islanders' first known contacts with Europeans occurred early in the seventeenth century, but they did not have to come to terms with a permanent white presence until the middle of the nineteenth. This was not the catastrophe for them that it was for so many mainland Aborigines. The Europeans came mainly to exploit the region's marine resources, and so had no occasion to displace indigenous communities or encroach upon traditional means of livelihood. They did, however, need labour, and Islanders wanted the goods that could be got by working. This exchange relationship provides the key to an understanding of post-contact Torres Strait society and of that society's relationship with the rest of Australia.

Although meshed into the mainland economy for more than a century, Torres Strait has remained an enclave of underdevelopment with its own distinctive structure. This has been due less to geographical isolation or cultural backwardness than to the nature of the marine industry and the place of the Islanders in it. The industry, which is to say pearling and trepanging, has always been marginal, able to survive only through access to cheap labour. Lacking any alternative, Islanders have worked for small wages; but this they could do only as long as they could supplement their earnings with sea food and garden produce. They were thus anchored to their communities, which became part of the industry's support structure.

Torres Strait is part of Queensland, and the state government's "native affairs" agency has been a powerful political force there.[2] Until recently, however, its activities consisted largely of maintaining and regulating the arrangement just described and the indigenous communities that lay at the back of it. In relation to the rest of Australia, the policy did perpetuate the Islanders' status as a distinct and culturally inferior minority and confined them to a little niche in the labour force where they neither competed nor combined with white workers.

Since the mid-1960s the marine industry has been in a depression from which it seems unlikely to recover. Meanwhile, a burgeoning mainland economy has drawn Islanders out of their isolation into the general labour force, while those left behind exist mainly on welfare payments and employment in government relief programmes. Their plight is a familiar one throughout the world, and its social repercussions have been far-reaching. This paper, however, focuses on the period when pearling was still the mainstay of Torres Strait.

A Theory of Internal Colonialism

Torres Strait during this period can usefully be viewed as an internal colony of Queensland and of Australia. This approach is not new, even in its application to Australia. In 1971 Rowley described northern Australia as colonial, pointing out the many similarities with Papua New Guinea (Rowley 1971, pp. 1–26); and recently Hartwig has argued the relevance of a more precisely defined model for an understanding of the Aboriginal situation (Hartwig 1978).[3] But the term has been widely used since the 1960s, to describe the plight of Indians in Central and North America, of the Celtic fringe in the British Isles, of Bretons in France, and of Chicanos in the United States.[4] Even when we leave aside those cases where the term is used simply to indicate the writer's ideological stance, we find little consistency. This is not the place for a review of the literature. I shall simply state my own conclusion that it is not usefully applied to racism as such, or to dispersed minorities such as the Afro-Americans. Minimally, I define an internal colony as a region or enclave which is exploited and controlled from without through a set of distinctive institutions. One of these institutions is a body of doctrines stating the difference between the colonized and the colonizers, typically in terms of ethnicity or race, but also by reference to religion or cultivation.

The form that colonialism takes will vary according to the prime motive for colonization, whether it be territorial control, the settlement of surplus population, the extraction of natural resources, or the exploitation of labour. This is of particular relevance to the relationship that develops between the metropolitan and pre-existing local economies. Harold Wolpe takes this relationship as critical in the formation of internal colonialism in South Africa, where the primary concern is with labour (Wolpe 1975). He argues that the "normal" tendency for capitalism to destroy other modes of production may be offset by a contrary tendency to preserve them, when they can be harnessed to the industrial machine. Thus South African capitalism can keep the wages of its Bantu workers low by leaving the reproduction of labour, the support of women and children, and of men when they are not in employment, to the subsistence economies of the homelands. The government's apartheid policy, then, maintains the articulation of the two modes of production.

Some Marxist and dependency theorists have doubted whether capitalism can exist for any time in articulation with other modes of production. Although these forms may persist, are they not transformed through their involvement with capitalism, so that the logic of their operation becomes subject to its laws of motion (see, e.g., Leys 1977)? This is certainly one possibility, as the following account suggests; but some of the "transitions" are unconscionably long drawn out. Part of the difficulty stems from the lack of agreement over the meanings to be given to *articulation* and mode of *production*: the picture changes as the emphasis shifts from relations of production to relations of exploitation or of exchange (cf. Foster-Carter 1978). Again, a good deal of ambiguity attends traditional forms of ownership when they are enjoyed during the pleasure of a colonial government. Since these problems cannot be explored here, I shall bypass them, simply suggesting that the articulation of productive processes is always worth investigating, particularly when one is capitalistic and the other derives from a pre- or non-capitalist economy. The critical question is whether this latter process can be said to operate independently of, or at least outside the command structure of, the former — albeit under its protection. Since these are questions of more and less, they are better discussed by reference to concrete instances.

Whatever the status of subsistence production, co-existing with capitalism, it seems clear that the articulation is unstable and in constant need of regulation. Classical formulations of the transition to capitalism stress the separation of the worker from his means of production, and the development of a proletariat that works without coercion and moves freely in the labour market.[5] A colonial order such as we have described must inhibit the realization of these tendencies without suppressing them completely. Thus the subsistence cultivator must have his land to return to, but not be so tied to it that he cannot be persuaded to leave it for periods of wage labour. In the same way he must have a need for money, but not so great that he will be unwilling to do without it when industry has no need for his labour. The regulation of this balance is one of the key functions of colonial administration.

Wolpe developed his model to deal with South Africa, where capitalism developed predominantly by means of its articulation with non-capitalist modes of production; and in a final footnote he leaves open the question "whether the notion of 'internal colonialism' has any proper application in conditions of racial discrimination where, however, the internal relations within the society are overwhelmingly capitalist in nature, that is where non-capitalist modes of production, if they exist at all, are marginal" (Wolpe 1975, pp. 244, 252). The Australian economy as a whole has not developed in this way; but in the north and centre certain industries, particularly cattle ranching and pearling, have depended upon indigenous labour which has been in part maintained by subsistence activities. Whether or not these conditions amount to internal colonialism in Wolpe's sense, it is clear that similar mechanisms are at work. However, it would be unwise to ignore certain differences, particularly in the functioning of government. For if some industries are relatively unimportant in a national economy, their interests may be subordinated to those of others more influential, and to reasons of state.

In northern Australia the cattlemen and pearlers had no big competitors, but they were not always in harmony with government. By the turn of the century all Australian governments except Tasmania had established special agencies to control the indigenous population. The principal achievement of the period was to isolate a large proportion of this population in isolated settlements where they would no longer be a nuisance to Europeans. The problem was to maintain these communities, since governments were unwilling to foot the bill and demanded that the inmates should be self-supporting. In some places there was opportunity for employment, but the demand was seasonal and uncertain and wages were well below what was required to reproduce the populations from which the labour came. Hunting and gathering might go some way towards filling the gap, but usually shelter and basic facilities, as well as rations and clothing for the indigent, had to be paid for from the public purse. As government servants with a job to do, and too little money to do it with, administrators sometimes came into conflict with local employers who defaulted on wages or paid below the agreed rate. In the anti-colonial climate of the period following the Second World War, the federal government was embarrassed to find its treatment of its native wards subject to international scrutiny. A general upgrading of programmes was not a matter of national priority, and ministers, ill-informed on local conditions, turned to senior administrators for advice in the formation of new policies. Queensland in particular had been noted for several forceful officials whose careers spanned numerous ministries and governments.

Torres Strait was remarkable for having a robust subsistence economy that worked in harness with the pearling industry for many years. However, it was also remarkable for a high level of government activity which could not be understood simply as a support service for the private sector. Consequently, internal colonialism was manifested in a peculiar form. I shall consider the region as a whole, with its seventeen indigenous communities focused on the commercial and industrial settlement at Thursday Island, but I shall be giving particular attention to Badu, which, more than any other, committed itself to commercial production.

The Marine Industry

Sydney-based trepang boats were reported in Torres Strait as early as 1846 (MacGillivray 1852, p. 308), but from 1868[6] until recently pearl shell has been the staple of the industry, with gold-lip mother-of-pearl and trochus as the most important varieties.[7] Both have been luxury products for alluring but fickle overseas markets. Trepang, otherwise known as *beche-de-mer,* went as a culinary delicacy to the Chinese market, which closed at the outbreak of war in the Far East. Pearl shell, used mainly for ornaments and buttons, has had a worldwide market; this, however, has been controlled by a few big dealers, first in London and later in New York. Though organized in an association, the Torres Strait master pearlers have had no control over prices, and so have been subject to market manipulations as well as the vagaries of fashion. They have also been limited in their capacity to expand by the availability of shell; one year's overfishing results in shortage for several years after. Bach, the historian of the industry, wrote in its last phase, "The economy of the industry is precarious, with a record of recurrent financial crises over the last forty years" (Bach 1961, p. 107). Pearling has had its prosperous times, but the reward for capital and labour has always been uncertain.

Enterprises ranged from small, locally based operators to well-known metropolitan firms such as Burns Philp. Any tendency toward consolidation was offset by the excessive efficiency of large concerns — resulting in overfishing — and on the other hand the ease with which a small operator could start up. Just enough capital was needed to buy, fit out, and provision a sail-boat, usually a lugger or cutter, big enough to accommodate ten to twenty men. Diving equipment was needed for gold-lip, which was mostly below seven fathoms, beyond the reach of skin divers. Trepang and trochus were found at lesser depths, and all that one needed was a few dinghies to carry the divers from the lugger to the reef. In short, pearling and trepanging were labour-intensive industries, with wages the major cost and the critical factor in determining profit margins. The recruitment and organization of labour were thus of paramount importance.

Veterans of the industry, white and black, all insist that the skipper's ability was critical: "Better a good skipper with a bad crew than a bad skipper with a good crew." He had to be familiar with tides, currents, and winds and had to know where the fish was most abundant and most easily got. He needed also to be able to keep up the pace of work for weeks at a stretch, to reduce tensions among polyglot crews living under cramped noisome conditions, and to keep in check the resentments of men who, particularly in the early days, had been subject to gross abuse.[8]

The owners of the boats rarely took charge themselves. They preferred to avoid the squalid conditions, the poor diet, and the weeks of monotony; still more the dangerous and debilitating deep-water diving. Fortunately the owners could find able and reliable skippers at relatively low cost. In the 1870s, when the price of shell was still high, whites were attracted to the work in which a skipper-diver could make as much as five hundred pounds in a year (Somerset Magistrate's Letter Book, 3 April 1875). But as shell became scarcer and prices fell, employers looked to Asia and the Pacific Islands for workers ready to accept less money. The skippers and divers of the 1880s were Rotumans and New Caledonians, Malays and Manilamen, until in the 1890s the Japanese arrived, ready to undercut and outwork them all. In 1907, in the wake of the White Australia legislation, a royal commission investigated the feasibility of replacing alien workers with Europeans, as had been done in the sugar industry (*Queensland Parliamentary Papers*, 1908, p. lxi). But it was clear that no white man who could earn £8 a month as a coastal seaman would risk life and health for £8 17s, which was the going rate for a diver (ibid., p. lxiv).[9] The masters insisted they could not pay more, and the Queensland government did not take up the commission's proposal for a subsidy (ibid.). As a result, the Torres Strait pearlers and trepangers, along with their colleagues in Western Australia and Darwin, remained exempt from the provisions of the White Australia policy right up to the outbreak of war with Japan. They were not allowed to resume when the war ended; but the labour, though local, was still cheap and coloured. Islanders now filled the gap, not white men.

The 1907 commission recognized that if white men could not be got to work as skipper-divers, there was no way they would work as deck hands and skin divers at the going rate of one to two pounds a month. These jobs could be given to Islanders, Aborigines, and Papuans, who, it allowed, had "natural rights to employment", as well as being tractable (ibid., p. lxix). The first boats to work in Torres Strait had come already manned by Pacific Islanders; other "kanakas" made their own way up from the Queensland canefields and even from Sydney.[10] But an industry liable to sudden booms needed to be able to expand its labour force at short notice. The indigenous populations of the region could be made into a convenient labour reserve if they could be broken in. At first they proved unwilling to work for prolonged periods, and if kidnapped tended either to abscond or to succumb to exotic diseases. But with time they acquired immunity and became inured to remaining at sea for months on end. Moreover, they could be paid less than the more sophisticated Asians and Pacific Islanders. From the beginning of the century up to the outbreak of war in 1941 they made up more than half of the industry's labour force, with the Islanders constituting around 20 per cent.

Whether foreign or local, the workers were supported only while they were working, and there was little for their wives and children, still less for the communities from which they were recruited. In other words, the reproduction of labour was left to the subsistence economies of Torres Strait and of the countries of Asia and the South Pacific, which thus became subordinated to the marine industry.

The Torres Strait marine industry did not become a basis for any kind of diversification. There being few other exploitable resources, profits were either ploughed back or invested in more promising fields elsewhere.[11] The industry may be said to have carried Torres Strait to the threshold of the Australian economy and then left it there. After the initial developments of the 1870s and 1880s it could neither expand nor diversify. Even this stunted development depended on continuing supplies of cheap labour. The labour supply itself depended on the back-up support of subsistence economies; and once foreign labour was excluded the indigenous communities were largely responsible for the organization of labour as well.

The Islanders

On the eve of colonization, around the middle of last century, there were between three thousand and four thousand Islanders distributed over twenty islands.[12] They lived by hunting turtle and dugong, by fishing, and either gathering or cultivating vegetable foods. The relative importance of these activities varied from one zone to another according to the resources available and the size of the island in relation to population. In the western islands men busied themselves with hunting the great sea mammals, while the women fished and gathered wild roots and berries; there was little or no gardening. By contrast, the small, fertile, densely populated eastern islands rarely saw dugong and got their turtle mostly during one season. Both men and women devoted themselves to gardening and some fishing. The tiny central islands provided little vegetable food, either wild or cultivated; their inhabitants spent their time catching turtle and fish, part of which they traded with the cultivating peoples to the east.

Social organization was broadly the same throughout the islands and neighbouring New Guinea. Social relations were phrased in the idiom of kinship, with a patrilineal emphasis in the recruitment of residential and ritual groups. Economic activities dispersed and fragmented society. In the eastern islands men gardened with their wives and unmarried daughters, or alone. Elsewhere women gathered wild foods and caught fish alone or in small groups. Some co-operation was required to handle the big canoes that were used for hunting and trading, but the number never exceeded ten. This tendency to dispersal was offset by a rich ritual life that periodically brought together the people of a community, and sometimes of several communities.

Pearlers and trepangers were the first foreigners to gain a foothold in the Islands. They found the Islanders eager for trade goods such as iron tools and cloth, and ready to work at least for short periods to get them. But if workers were unwilling they were sometimes kidnapped, as were women to serve as prostitutes on the boats. Attempts at resistance only served to demonstrate the foreigners' superiority, so that when the London Missionary Society arrived in 1871 it met little opposition and may have been welcomed as a protection against the rest (London Missionary Society Reports, Sept. 1876). Within a decade the LMS had won the adherence of the majority of Islanders and begun the work of turning them into black replicas of the Victorian "respectable working class".[13] The Queensland government had completed its annexation of the islands by 1879, but lacking the means of administering them it was content to leave the missionaries to guide the "chiefs" it had appointed.

Armed with secular as well as religious powers, the missionaries set up their own petty theocracies, overturning the old religion and closely regulating individual conduct. However, their congregational structure gave ample opportunity for the older men to participate in church activities, gaining status and a little authority as elders and deacons. Since the resident pastors were mostly Polynesians and the Islanders had little direct contact with Europeans, the result of this reconstruction bore more resemblance to the Christianized communities of the South Pacific.

The missionaries regarded most of the pearliers and trepangers as a "bad influence" and would probably have preferred not to let their flocks stray out of their sight; but they could scarcely stifle the demand for trade goods, and indeed money was required to support the life-style they were introducing. Before long they were encouraging communities to compete in the generosity of their donations to the mission and in, church building. Most of this money came from the wages of the young, unmarried men, who were most in demand with employers and most easily spared from their communiites, being otherwise unproductive and a potent threat to sexual morality. The young men had their own incentive. Foreign workers in search of local wives had introduced marriage payments in the form of cash and manufactured goods: Islanders had to match them or miss out (Haddon 1908, p. 115).

It was, then, the young men who signed on for the boats, spending ten months of the year away from home, while their fathers stayed back to guard the morals of their wives and advance themselves in the mission hierarchy. Combining their traditional authority as parents with their new authority as church leaders, they effectively nullified the young men's economic importance and succeeding in controlling most of the money they brought back. Having right of veto over marriage, they delayed the event so that they could enjoy the work of their sons a little longer and hold out for a good price for their daughters.

The older, married men continued in subsistence production gardening and fishing in the company of their wives and daughters, and hunting with their age mates. However, towards the end of the nineteenth century they were buying small boats and working neighbouring reefs for shell or trepang. This seems to have reflected the growing demand for cash goods, including flour and rice, but did not amount to a complete abandonment of the subsistence production. Fish, dugong, and turtle could still be caught on the way back from the working grounds. Not surprisingly, this arrangement proved more attractive to the hunting peoples of central and western Torres Strait than to the horticulturalists of the east.

The one difficulty with this arrangement was that it failed to provide for the "hungry time" during the nor'-west monsoon. The climatic conditions that caused a dearth of wild and cultivated foods and made hunting and fishing difficult also brought commercial fishing to a standstill. Flour, rice, and canned goods could tide the people over, but money often ran out before the end of the season. Per capita cash income was still low, and there were other calls on it, to support the church and to finance ceremonial feasts and marriage payments. Clearly, then, more effort had to be put into commercial production.

To meet the problem, two missionaries formed a non-profit-making company, Papuan Industries, in 1904. Its beginnings are described as follows: "Revd. F. W. Walker, preaching at one of their church services, had reproached the Islanders for their apparent indolence. He pointed out the great wealth of marine produce at their very doors, the proceeds of which, if collected, would provide for the seasonal 'hungry times'. He was afterwards approached by a deputation of the people who explained that they had no money with which to buy fishing boats large enough to work profitably (Blackley 1961, p. 265). For the next twenty-five years Papuan Industries lent Islanders the money to buy boats, selling their produce and marketing trade goods at fair prices.[14] After a few years the Queensland government went into partnership, taking over the company when its founders retired in 1930. Long before this date, it had taken effective control of what came to be called the "company boats".

Government Policy

This governmental intervention repays further analysis. At the level of policy it was consistent with the statewide extension and consolidation of control over the indigenous population. By 1890 it had acquired the means for administering the islands and begun establishing teacher magistrates in the larger communities. This precipitated a struggle with the LMS theocracy, which ended with the society's withdrawal in 1914. An Aborigines Protection Act was passed in 1897, but the government resident, the Honourable John Douglas, who had maintained his own paternalistic regime since 1886, considered that the Islanders were not in need of it (Douglas 1899).[15] But when he died in 1904 the incoming chief protector had them declared Aborigines for the purpose of the act.[16]

The White Australia agitation was at its height during these years, and working-class fear of cheap labour was being expressed in terms of virulent racism.[17] The Aborigines were scarcely a labour threat, but they were included in the general opprobrium, as an offence to white sensibility and morality. They could not be deported, like the kanakas and Chinese, but they could be kept out of the way, "for their own good" as well as for that of the white majority. From this emerged a policy of protective segregation whereby Aborigines would be confined on settlements and have as little outside contact as possible. The practice might better be described as arrested segregation, for there was never enough money to institutionalize everyone. Nor could the settlements be made self-sufficient, so that it was necessary to hire out the best workers to pastoralists who, in any case, needed their labour. Since the government would have to provide if the worker was not paid or if he squandered his earnings, it had its own reasons for supervising employment and holding Aboriginal earnings. Under the tight controls that emerged, the government did not so much teach the Aborigines thrift as practice it on their behalf.

Islanders came under this regime after 1904. The commercial and administrative settlement on Thursday Island could not be rid of the Japanese; but Islanders and Aborigines were to be kept out as much as possible, and the surviving Pacific Islanders to be settled elsewhere. The Torres Strait communities were to be made self-supporting, with the aid of the company boat system, but the masters were to be allowed to hire the best workers under government supervision.

The Islanders would not constitute an economic liability as long as the hungry time could be provided for; but they must be closely regulated if they were to be a reserve of cheap labour for the marine industry. They must, of course, have a need for money so that they would be ready to work when required. However, while some communities, notably in the eastern islands, clung to the old ways, the majority had a very lively appreciation of money. The problem was rather to check it so that they would not demand higher wages or refuse to return to their gardens when the masters did not need them. In 1898 Haddon remarked that the Mabuiag Islanders were living on flour and rice, leaving their gardens untended (Haddon 1901, pp. 121–22): a few years later, during an economic downturn, the government was ordering them to resume planting.[18]

The government's control over the Islanders' money also enabled it to keep a brake on consumption, simply by giving or withholding approval for each purpose.[19] Its monopoly of retail trade worked to the same end, effectively limiting purchases to necessities such as foodstuff, clothing, and tobacco. (Alcohol was strictly forbidden now.) Finally it was able to subtract a proportion of each man's wages, at one point as high as 20 per cent, to be held in an Island Fund against hard times (London Missionary Society Correspondence, 18 Aug. 1913).

The company boats served the two purposes of providing small incomes for those who could not get work in the private sector, while drawing into the labour force those who still clung to the old life. It also trained those who were still too young to go onto the masters' boats. The purchase price of the boats was to be subtracted from earnings, so that the scheme should not be a charge on the Australian taxpayer.

The scheme was not a complete success and caused intermittent conflict between the Islanders and the government. The boats, for the most part small cutters, were not equipped with diving equipment and so were marginal enterprises when compared with the masters' well-equipped luggers. As a consequence, their earnings were small and not always enough to cover running costs. The teacher-magistrates complained of time wasted on hunting expeditions and visits to other islands for religious festivals, and they employed the heavy sanctions that were now at their disposal. The Islanders, who made the mistake of beliving that the boats, once paid off, were theirs to use as they pleased, gave up in disgust and had to be forced back to work.[20]

The government nevertheless persisted with the scheme, expanding its fleet to take advantage of the post-war boom and persuading the men to divert their efforts from trepang and mother-of-pearl to trochus shell, which currently commanded a good price. In 1924, twenty-eight boats earned more than twenty thousand pounds; and with wages on the masters' boats raised to between £3 and £4 10s a month, the communities were fully self-supporting, if not well-to-do.[21] The number at work also increased, from 358 in 1921, when the population was about three thousand, to 587 in 1923; and it continued upwards through the 1930s. This was partly due to population increase, but mainly due to the expansion of the company boat fleet, which gave employment to the older married men and the less fit.

The relative prosperity of the 1920s, during which Islanders increased their dependence on store commodities, came to an abrupt end with the Great Depression of the 1930s. The masters retrenched; the company boats worked on, but average per capita earnings for the year totalled only eight pounds. The resentment that this aroused was not soothed by improving prices, and in 1936 the Islanders went on strike for four months.[22] The private sector of the industry was unaffected. The grievances seem to have been various. The chief protector of the time supposed that the men wanted to handle their own money (Bleakley 1961, p. 270). Veterans of the strike cite the wretched pay, and the seeming lack of correspondence between effort and reward. Evidently officials did not bother to explain the complex system of deductions for debts incurred in earlier years, current running costs, and various community and contingency funds. Some workers simply supposed that they were being robbed.[23] On the masters' boats they were assured of a minimum wage, and earnings were generally higher. This was partly because the masters took only the best workers, but the unfavourable comparison remained.

The government was able to bring the Islanders into line with a show of force but knew it would face trouble again before long if earnings did not improve. The only solution was to increase productivity, and the only way of doing this was to build up a cadre of skippers who could step up the old, easy-going pace of work.

The Islanders had produced little in the way of leadership up to this point. Authority had not been much developed in the traditional society, and what there was had disappeared during the missionary reconstruction. The church leaders confined themselves to parish matters, and the local government councillors, who had replaced the old chiefs, were overshadowed by the government teacher-magistrates. As in other parts of Melanesia, ambitious individuals strove to aggrandize themselves only to be cut down by an egalitarianism that had been reinforced by the Islanders' lowly position in the colonial order.[24] The old-style company boat skippers were at most *primus inter pares*, elected by community or crew, and regularly replaced, perhaps "to give someone else a chance", perhaps because they had antagonized the men. Many chose not to take the slightly larger share of the boat's earnings to which the system entitled them. Discussing such matters in later years, Islanders all agree that a boat could not do well when "everyone boss". In that case, it worked at the pace of the slowest worker, arriving late at the working grounds and coming back early, on one pretext or another. To work boat and crew at full capacity, and to get ahead of running costs, a "tough skipper" was needed.

During the 1920s a few tough skippers had emerged, mainly from among the half-caste descendants of Pacific Island seamen, but their authority was personal. Only in Badu, in western Torres Strait, did the skipper's authority become institutionalized, largely owing to the achievement of Tanu Nona.

Tanu Nona was born in Saibai Island in 1900, the son of a Saibai woman and a Samoan seaman. His parents settled in Badu soon after, and there he was raised along with his seven brothers and three sisters. He began with no particular advantages. His father was evidently a stern man and ambitious for his sons, but without wealth or influence. Tanu had to make his own way and, according to his own account, lost no time in doing so.

I got my first boat from Mr Luffman [a master pearlier] in 1918. Then when I was nineteen I got the Coral Sea. I was going up to New Guinea to work out from Samarai, but my mother wanted me to stop and I took over as skipper of the island cutter, I've been a skipper ever since. Later the Poid people [a neighbouring community] made me captain of their lugger, the *Manu*. The government set me to race [i.e., compete] with Douglas Pitt from Darnley Island. In six weeks I got ten ton of trochus; Douglas Pitt only got five. That's how Badu got the *Wakaid*, the biggest lugger in Torres Strait. For six years we kept the cup [awarded by the government for the winning boat], until competition was cancelled.[25]

The *Wakaid*'s success was not easily won.

We stayed out sometimes for ten months on the coast, from Cape York to Gladstone [i.e., along the north Queensland coast]. You must have a strong captain to make those boys work. If they not get much shell I not let them into the dinghy to eat dinner, midday. They got to eat their piece of damper [bread] standing on the reef. Some skippers work only half day, six in the morning till dinner time, then sail on to the next reef night-time. Making the crew work is the main thing. Also knowing the tides. But you must make those boys finish the reef. Bad skippers leave some shell behind.

The government was quick to recognize Tanu's ability and to advance him. The competition, designed to take advantage of inter-island rivalries, probably strengthened his hold over the crew, and, when he won, enhanced his reputation. The *Wakaid* would have been an added source of pride and, because of its size, an asset in subsequent competitions. Nevertheless, the success was essentially Tanu's, and he is the one credited with "teaching Badu to work". No doubt his forceful, not to say aggressive, personality was an important factor in transforming the old easy-going routine, but he was also able to take advantage of an unusual circumstance within the community. Towards the end of the 1920s the community resolved to replace its decaying wooden church with a cement building. Tanu, already elected a local government councillor, now became a church-warden and director of the project. He began by decreeing that every able-bodied man should work full-time on the boats, giving up a portion of his earnings for the project. He next overrode the rule that a man might only work on the boat belonging to his tribe, henceforth taking into his crew the best workers whatever their affiliation: "I thought it silly that a good man couldn't work with others because he didn't belong to their tribe, and might have to work with other men who were no good. That was how *Wakaid* got all the best men."

With the benefit of hindsight we can regard these minor innovations as the opening moves in a process that was to transform Buda and have important implications for other communities. However, it is unlikely that even Tanu could see so far ahead. In the meantime the innovations could be justified in terms of established community values, principally the erection of a handsome new church that rivalled the Thursday Island cathedral for size. If the young men came home with more money than ever before, their mothers and fathers and the church leaders were the main beneficiaries. Tanu, then, remained a community as well as an economic leader, with wide popular support.

As if often the case with innovators, Tanu's relationship to the community was ambiguous (Press 1969). Though Badu bred he was not Badu born, and while he had acquired fictive kin and affines there he had no true kin. Again, as a "South Sea half-caste", he could lay some claim to superiority over "Torres Strait natives" according to the prevailing ethnic stratification.[26] Finally, while nominally an appointee of the community, he was developing an unusually close relationship with the government, which was rumoured to pay him a secret retainer over and above his skipper's share. This relationship was strengthened by his refusal to join the 1936 strike, and his subsequent reward, the *Wakaid,* now to be worked as a family boat.

Normal life was interrupted in 1941 with the outbreak of war in the Pacific. Torres Strait became a field of military operations, though not of hostilities, and almost every able-bodied Islander served alongside white soldiers as members of a special volunteer contingent. Their contacts with the white troops were a radical departure from what they had known hitherto. At the outbreak of war they had been more cut off from the rest of Australia than they were at the turn of the century, their only contacts being with whites who were in authority over them. They now found themselves included in a new camaraderie and hearing ideas that challenged what they had learned in church and schoolroom. Having served "King and country", they thought they would be entitled to a "new deal" promised Australian servicemen when the war ended. The Islanders supposed this would mean "freedom": the end of government supervision and segregation, and "full pay". As one veteran explained to me, years later, "We all came out the army with swelled heads."

In the new climate, the Queensland government found it difficult to restore the pre-war regime.[27] However, boom conditions in the pearling industry, following four years of inactivity, eased its task and enabled it to offer certain concessions without making any structural change. Taking advantage of the Australia-wide anti-Japanese feeling, the government insisted that the Islanders could and should provide the industry with all its manpower, including skippers and divers as well as crew.[28] It also negotiated a new wage agreement which brought the basic rate to a little over 50 per cent of the national basic wage, with bonus incentives, and higher rates for divers and skippers. The latter could now hope to earn as much as white workers.

The government had been negotiating wage agreements with the masters since 1904, as part of its statutory control over native employment. In 1907 Protector Costin had suggested that the Islanders were "worth" two pounds a month, though "of course they have very inflated ideas of their own value" (*Queensland Parliamentary Papers* 1908, p. 60). In fact, he was going along with established practice which rated Islanders below Asians and Kanakas, but above Papuans and Aborigines. His successors arranged increases from time to time, sometimes in response to shifts in living costs, sometimes in response to fluctuations in the industry. The employers, of course, insisted that increases were beyond their ability to pay, and more than the Islanders were "worth". But while these assertions can be taken with a grain of salt, it must also be recognized that the industry was predicated upon cheap labour and had to compete with cheap labour producers such as the Philippines and the Cook Islands.

The gains made in the post-war boom years were soon swallowed up by inflation, and though the rates increased from time to time, there was a decline in real terms and a widening gap between earnings in Torres Strait and those on the mainland. After two years of feverish activity, the markets were glutted and shell was once again hard to find. The number of boats and men at work declined, then picked up, reaching a post-war peak in 1950/51, slumping in the next year, partially recovering in 1956/57, then falling away, this time for good. In 1960 an economist observed that the industry seemed less viable every year (Bach 1961, p. 113), and within a few months competition from plastics had dealt it a mortal blow.

Trends within the government fleet were similar to those in the private sector. During the boom it acquired forty boats, which the Islanders were quickly able to pay off from their wartime savings and post-war gratuities. But increasing stringencies forced one enterprise after another out of the race. The Island boats were left far behind when the master pearlers mechanized their fleet with engines and compressors. The government had to follow suit, but this meant a rise in running costs, so that more boats fell into debt. The government now adopted the policy of reducing its overall commitment and concentrating its boats in the hands of those who could run them most efficiently. By 1957 the fleet had dwindled to twenty-two, and by 1961 to fifteen, eight of them run by Badu's Nona company, which left some islands with no boat at all. By the mid-1960s the six Nona boats were the only ones still working.

All these changes had important implications for the communities, both social and economic. The government boats had always worked out from their home islands; now the masters' boats often did so. This meant supplies of dugong and turtle at the end of each working spell, which might be every four weeks if the work was mother-of-pearl. With 600–700 kg of meat to supplement the fish and crops produced by those who stayed ashore, the income from the subsistence sector was considerable.[29] As Badu's fleet grew, so did its subsistence production, but at the expense of other islands which became increasingly hard up.

There were other changes in the organization of work. When Island skippers took over the masters' boats, they brought with them the traditional norms that had already been adapted to work on the government boats. Most of the latter were owned by family companies like the Nonas. If additional labour were needed, the skipper mobilized his own kinship and affinal connections. Master boat skippers recruited in the same way. Initially recruitment was mainly confined to the skipper's community, but as some communities lost their boats while Badu, specifically the Nonas, acquired more, it became necessary to recruit outside and even outside the kinship circle.

As I noted earlier, the Nona company came into being after the 1936 strike, when the government made over to them the big lugger *Wakaid,* under Tanu, but it was not long before the company expanded and they had boats of their own. The boats were lost during the war, but the company resumed work in 1946 with two new ones. Once again the Nona family, which now included grown-up sons of the older brothers, began by working together, hiving off as new boats became available. However, the expansion was too slow for some, who left to work for master pearlers. Most members of the family had the chance to prove themselves as skippers, either in the government or the private sectors, and while some failed, five of the brothers and four among the rising generation won solid reputations. However, Tanu continued to get the largest catch.

The company's quick expansion may have aided its survival. Other family companies, on Badu and elsewhere, foundered on internal rivalries ("everyone wanted to be boss"); whereas ambitious Nonas found an outlet before tensions reached danger point. Only the younger members worked under Tanu for any length of time, and even they sustained the hope of eventual advancement.

As well as skippering his own boat, Tanu acted as company head. He interfered little in the day-to-day routines of the other skippers, but advised the government on how the money was to be allocated. The younger skippers, particularly, had little idea of how their earnings were computed. He also had a say in who should take charge of the boats. This was an area of considerable uncertainty, for the rights of company members remained undefined. In 1958 Tanu told me that he intended to divide the fleet among the branches of the family: one lugger to his most successful brother; one for two younger brothers; one to the family of a brother now dead. Three luggers belonged to him, but one of these should go to the family of his eldest brother, who had retired. This left out of account three brothers who were working for master pearlers, and who only benefited in the family's collective expenditures on weddings and memorials to the dead. They might, perhaps have been accommodated in further expansion, but in the event there was no further expansion. Moreover, the family of the deceased brother failed to make a success of their venture and lost the boat to another branch. The son of Tanu's eldest brother resigned his command after some years, but was not replaced: the interest of this branch also lapsed. With the decline in pearling from the late 1960s, the number of Nona boats began to decline. After 1971 there were only two boats, skippered by two of Tanu's sons.

The company could run on in this uncertain manner because legally it was the government, not the Nonas, who owned the boats. In earlier reports the government spoke of Islanders working off the price of their boats, becoming in some sense owners, thought still under government supervision. Later reports make no such reference, and it would seem that the government was the real owner, although Tanu played an important part in management and was well paid for his services.

The Nonas trained skippers both for their own boats and the pearling companies. Masters and officials took Tanu's recommendations seriously, and were not often disappointed. Badu skippers had a clear sense of authority, in sharp contrast to the indecisive leaders characteristic of other communities. Tanu's harsh regime of the 1930s remained their legendary charter, but it was no longer a direct model, since few now worked trochus. Mother-of-pearl fishing required tight discipline while the divers were down, but not long hours of gruelling work or prolonged absence from home. Diving could only be done for a few hours each day, and for about three weeks in the month. Nevertheless, the "hard work" ethic persisted: skippers left for the working grounds before the water was clear and stayed out until it was too dirty for diving. They stayed neither for church service nor festival. Anyone who showed signs of lingering was said to be tied to his wife's apron strings. These standards were ultimately sanctioned by financial incentives and the risk of losing one's boat. But they were also maintained by the competitiveness among skippers, which ensured that any falling short would be noticed and commented upon. The Nonas were particularly jealous of their family reputation and they all lived in fear of a rebuke from Tanu. The situation in Badu, with a dozen or more skippers at work, was quite different from that in other communities where there might only be one or two.

Throughout Torres Strait there was tension between skippers and their men, who always had some sense of being exploited. These feelings were not absent on the Badu boats, but were offset by other considerations. Divers, certainly, had something to gain by subscribing to the Nona regime. Skippers knew the value of a skilled man and showed appreciation in various ways. Although the Nonas generally preferred their own kinsmen, they did occasionally give other men recommendations that got them master boats. However, the divers' commitment was tempered by the realization that it was the Nonas, and not the ordinary Baduans, who gained from their labours.

Ordinary crew enjoyed the camaraderie of boat life but got little in the way of prestige or money, and they bore the brunt of the senior workers' tensions. Skippers had no hesitation in punching a youth who was disobedient, and occasionally threw someone overboard. It is worth noting that they were all big men. For these abuses there was no redress. The Island council was unsympathetic, being made up of Nonas, and the government referred complaints back to the council. Even parents might withhold support, for it was the custom for poorer families to ingratiate themselves with a skipper by sending a son to work under him. In return for this favour they could ask for a free passage to Thursday Island and expect generous shares of turtle and dugong caught by the boats on their way home from the working grounds. The old company boats had shared the meat out equally among the tribe; latter-day skippers gave out meat or withheld it as they saw fit. A poor family, committed to a wedding or funerary feast, was wholly dependent on the generosity of a skipper for these festive foods.

The foregoing account is indicative of the changes taking place in Badu as a result of its commitment to pearling. The economic structure was also the power structure in a direct sense. An elected council would have found it hard to control the skippers, but in fact there had been no contest since 1947 when the government dismissed incumbents who were hostile to it and the Nonas. Thereafter, Tanu held office for life and secured the election of members of his family unopposed on his nomination.

The composition of the community, which now numbered about five hundred, had itself changed. There were relatively few people over forty, because many of the older generation had removed to Thursday Island, either to take up jobs ashore or get away from the Nonas, or because the Nonas had expelled them. But the skippers needed more young men than Badu could provide, and went recruiting around neighbouring islands which no longer had boats of their own. The Nonas' kin ties with Saibai proved useful here, as did their affinal connections with several other communities. Those who became their regular associates and proteges soon settled on Badu, swelling the ranks of their supporters. To accommodate them the council abolished traditional land tenure, taking upon itself the right to allocate house and garden plots.[30]

The Nonas and their cronies became increasingly differentiated from the "village people". Their control of subsistence as well as cash production was reflected in their lifestyle. They occupied spacious modern houses on high land, back from the village, and maintained large households that included poor relations and hangers-on who helped around the place and ran errands. The largest share of dugong and turtle meat went to them, and they maintained large gardens, worked by their boat crews during "dirty water time". With all these resources, their wedding and funerary feasts were the most lavish in Torres Strait.

Kinship remained the prevailing idiom of social relations, but people were also beginning to speak of "skipper class" and "crew class", and to regard the young Nonas as having better life chances. These young men were leaders among their peers and seemed to be able to get away with misdemeanours that would have landed the others in gaol. They married into the more important families in Torres Strait and showed a marked preference for wives with Pacific Island or Asian ancestry over "Torres Strait natives".

As the "skipper class" rose in wealth and power, traditional forms of interdependence among ordinary Baduans dwindled in importance. Young people abandoned their parental homes for the more convivial and abundant households of their skippers, looking to them as marriage sponsors rather than their impoverished kinsfolk. The church, which had once provided the main source of prestige for older men, was now left to the women to run, with Tanu and a brother making occasional major decisions. Religious festivals were still celebrated in the traditional way, but they were not always well attended and the dancing was often perfunctory. The real conviviality went on up at the big houses above the village, where one went only by invitation.

While Badu was becoming fully committed to pearling, reducing subsistence production to a subsidiary activity, other communities were continuing in the old way. They sent their young men to work on the Nonas' boats, or those of the white pearlers, and themselves stayed at home to make gardens and fish. Saibai, now without luggers, revived the old canoe trade with Papua. Although now getting an additional income from social service benefits, their incomes were well below what they had come to regard as their right as a result of the wartime experience. Even if they were to go to sea themselves, their earnings would not bring them appreciably closer to their goal. One heard such mutterings even in Badu, but the Nonas had a quick way with malcontents; elsewhere, however, protest was overt. To add to the problem, population was increasing while industry remained stagnant. The government expanded its building and welfare programmes, providing work for some four hundred, but it could not afford to expand indefinitely, or to take up all the surplus labour, despite the low rates of pay.[31]

The burgeoning economy and favourable labour market of northern Australia offered a safety valve for Torres Strait unemployment, but also posed a threat to the regional wage structure. Up to the outbreak of war, the government had confined Islanders to their reserves. After the war it allowed them to settle and work on Thursday Island, but the few available jobs were soon taken up and the demand for employment was nowhere near satisfied. In 1947 a small party of Islanders went south to cut cane. The experiment was a success and was repeated in subsequent years. At the end of each season, some of the cane-cutters found other jobs and stayed behind. Presently their numbers were augmented by young Islanders who had absconded from trochus boats at north Queensland ports.

Although by 1960 there were probably no more than five hundred Islanders living on the mainland, their presence there had a profound effect on the situation in Torres Strait. They were mainly concentrated in railway fettling, an occupation unattractive to whites, but which did not have discriminatory rates for coloured workers. With overtime payments, a man could earn five to six times what he got at home, and the money was his to spend as he pleased, for the government did not extend its controls to the mainland. Islanders were soon in demand as first-class tropical workers (a marked change from Torres Strait, where they were always told they were lazy). News of life on the mainland filtered back, increasing the restlessness of pearling workers, and of government employees whose wages were geared to those in the industry.

Further emigration was obviously a solution to unemployment, but if not controlled it could also deprive the pearling industry and the government of their labour supply. The government solution was to delegate the decision to Island councils. Tanu was able to block emigration not only from Badu but from all the islands supplying him with labour, on the ground that Islanders were not yet ready to live without government protection.

In 1960, however, the industry suffered a permanent reverse. Plastics emerged as a cheaper competitor to shell in such fields as button manufacture. The trochus market collapsed and the demand for mother-of-pearl fell sharply. The industry was saved from extinction by the establishment of pearl culture stations, requiring supplies of live shell, but overall demand was still down and unlikely to expand. In 1960 eight government boats and five European-owned boats had worked out of Badu, in 1967 the numbers were six and two. With the population increasing, jobs declining, and mainland employers ready to fly Islanders to construction camps in the Northern Territory and Western Australia, it was no longer possible for councils to say no. Some Baduans settled on the mainland; others alternated spells home and away. But those at home could be more selective about whom they worked for. At the end of the year skippers could be seen treating their men to drinks in the hope of recruiting them again for the next season. It was said that one particularly rough skipper had been forced out because he could no longer get crew.

At the time of writing there are still a few luggers at work, one or two commanded by Nonas, but the crews are Papuan. Many of the Islanders who remain are either pensioners or employees, earning mainland rates of pay in various federal and state government programmes. A number of Baduans work on their own, cray fishing, using federal-funded boats and freezers. The Nona company is defunct, and most of the younger generations are working on the mainland. Among the surviving brothers there has been discord over the undistributed assets of the family business. Tanu is the only one to have invested his savings, in Brisbane real estate, and it is assumed that this will pass to his many children.

The Nonas domination has declined with their economic power. People are no longer dependent on them for meat, employment or transportation. Tanu, old and infirm, retired from political life in 1976 with an OBE. He died in 1980. The Queensland government has allowed his position as western island representative to pass to one of his sons, but the family no longer controls the Badu council.

Conclusions

In this paper I took as my point of departure a model of internal colonialism based on the articulation of capitalism with non-capitalistic modes of production. The rationale for this articulation is the reproduction of labour for industry through a continuing subsistence sector rather than through wages. The role of government is to maintain this articulation which, I have suggested, is inherently unstable.

In Torres Strait the cheap labour reserve for the region's marine industry was for many years maintained by subsistence activities such as hunting, fishing and gardening. The Queensland government's function was to regulate this system. Having assumed responsibility for the Islanders, it had a duty to make them self-supporting so that they would not become a charge on the state, but its policies were generally consistent with the pearlers' interests. Segregation stopped Islanders going to the mainland to fill the gap left by repatriated kanakas, ensuring a reserve of good quality labour for the marine industry. The control of wages, of Islanders' earnings and of retail trade, all served to blunt the demand for more money: at the same time local officials saw to it that Islanders went to work when they were needed. The company boat system accommodated the demand for employment which the private sector could not meet. In this endeavour the administration encountered a good deal of difficulty, and it looks as though making the scheme a success became a career commitment for certain officials, even an end in itself.

The various island communities varied a good deal in their responses, with Badu and Murray providing the sharpest contrasts. On Murray Island commercial and subsistence production were virtually antithetical, separating the men from the boys in a literal sense. The place of a man was in his garden and in community affairs, obtaining his cash needs through control of his unmarried sons. Thus a skipper was an anomalous figure, a man without a garden and without a voice in community affairs, always subject to his land-based peers. In this case it makes some sense to speak of two modes of production, even though the land the people gardened belonged, legally speaking, to the Crown.

Badu's outstanding success in pearling can partly be attributed to its successful co-ordination with turtle and dugong hunting. Since the pearling lugger was used for both operations, pearling remained the dominant activity and the skipper controlled both meat and money. This provided a sound base for the institutionalization of his authority and its extension into community affairs. In these circumstances it makes rather less sense to speak of two modes of production.

As Badu skippers took over the organization of production, they worked through indigenous institutions. Crews worked not just for wages but to build churches or to advance their island's prestige. Their relationship with the skipper was expressed as an exchange between kin, obscuring the element of exploitation and the increasing inequality. Having an ambiguous status in the community, the Nonas were able to manipulate these forms while transforming them into instruments of capitalism.

Around the turn of the century, Islanders occupied an inferior position in the labour force *vis-à-vis* Asians and Pacific Islanders as well as whites. With the elimination of foreign labour after 1945 they were able to become skippers and divers. However, almost all the top-notch skippers were part Asian or Pacific Islanders, perhaps because the notion of foreigners being superior survived. This brought into existence a small elite who, like the Nonas, could earn as least as much as unskilled whites, and who enjoyed a much higher standard of living than other Islanders. Despite its class-like character, this elite was not an extension of mainland stratification but a colonial token, having no currency outside Torres Strait. Its control of capital was tenuous at law and effective only under the peculiar conditions prevailing within the region. Similarly, the control of labour, on which it was primarily dependent, was achieved through the manipulation of kinship and communal ties. It is significant that a sizeable part of the Nonas' wealth went in lavish wedding and funerary celebrations which validated their status among their own people, but not among whites. In short, the elite was more firmly tied to Torres Strait than humbler Islanders, and it quickly moved into alliance with the government when the colonial structure came under threat.

We have seen that the colonial regime came under severe strain after

1945 as a result of the rupturing of isolation, a revolutionary rise in expectations under conditions of stagnation, and a burgeoning population. The opening up of Thursday Island and of a new range of government jobs went only a short distance towards solving the problem; and boat companies, skippers, and local government councils became increasingly subject to conflicting pressures. Cracks began to appear in the facade of kinship loyalty and communal solidarity.

The opening up of the mainland labour market provided a short-term solution to the problems of unemployment, economic frustration, and political disaffection, but at the cost of undermining the colonial system. Those who remained became increasingly unwilling to work for small wages or to accept the discrimination between black and white workers. Once Torres Strait workers had made their name elsewhere, the colonial economy's need for a labour monopoly came into direct contradiction with the mainstream economy's need for a free labour flow.

Commonwealth government welfare payments, such as child endowment and pensions for the old and invalided, further complicated the picture after 1943. In the quasi-urban conditions of Thursday Island they were an indispensable subsidy to wages that were seriously inadequate, given the impossibility of subsistence production. On islands like Badu, they similarly subsidized wages, marginally reducing dependence on gardening and fishing. On Murray Island, by contrast, they relieved some men of the necessity of going to work. However, lest it be supposed that these people were irredeemably committed to home and garden, it should be remembered that they were the first to work on the mainland, and were largely responsible for the good reputation of Torres Strait workers. Now that a number are employed on Murray at standard wages, gardening has been drastically reduced.

Over the last decade there has been a substantial input of government funds for education, housing, health, and economic uplift. With the decline of the marine industry, Torres Strait leaders have been increasingly concerned with competing for these prizes, and the old pearling elite are being replaced by new men with better education and wider horizons. Long anchored to their boats and their communities, the Nonas and others like them had neither the time nor the inclination for travel and education. Tanu is now dead, and although one of his sons occupies a position of importance, the family is dispersed and the Badu chairmanship has passed to someone else.

Colonialism as I have defined it exists only as a dead shell in the Strait and as a memory for those Islanders — more than half — who live in the towns and cities of the mainland. The racist and cultural notions that sustained colonialism during its heyday are still alive, though now transmuted into the more benign ethnicity, at least in official statements. Indeed, the Islanders are trying to reassert their distinct identity in relation to Aborigines as a means of deflecting colour discrimination and competing for government funds. In the same way they have retained and transplanted colonial institutions such as the church and the feasting complex as a means of coping with rapid change. But these are merely the colonial heritage, not the thing itself. Having gained freedom of movement and effective separation from their lands and their fishing grounds, they have joined the ranks of Australia's unskilled workers and are sharing with them the experience of unemployment and the battle for welfare funds.

Notes

1. This paper is a revised version of an article published under the same title in *Aboriginal History* 1 (1977). The writer worked in Torres Strait for twenty-four months from 1958 to 1961 as a research scholar of the Australian National University, returning in 1967 and 1976 under the auspices of the University of Sydney.
    For further data on hunting, see Nietschmann 1976.
2. The agency has gone under many names, including the Chief Protector's Department, the Sub-Department of Native Affairs, the Department of Aboriginal and Islander Affairs, and now the Department of Aboriginal and Islander Advancement.
3. Hartwig applies to the Australian case the model of Harold Wolpe, which is discussed below.
4. The first writers to make extended use of the notion are the Mexicans Gonzalez Casanova (1965) and Stavenhagen (1965). For a recent application of their ideas, see Barrera 1980. Following a rather different approach, Hechter has applied the term to the Celtic fringe of the British Isles (1974), and his followers to other parts of Western Europe (*Ethnic and Racial Studies* 2, no. 3 [1979]). For yet other uses of the term, see Bee and Ginderich 1977 and Wolpe 1975, whose ideas are discussed below.
5. As Taussig notes (1977), these perceptions are to be found in the writings of both Marx and Weber.
6. Captain Banner established a pearl-shell station on Warrior Island in 1868, which seems to have been the first in the strait.
7. Black-lip mother-of-pear and green snail shell have also been taken at times. Pearls provided a welcome bonus, but they occurred too irregularly and unpredictably to provide a basis for the industry.
8. In the early years the Pacific Islanders had often been blackbirded, and Aborigines were shanghaied during the present century. For an account of labour abuse in Torres Strait, see Evans 1972.
9. A report of the Northern Australian Development Committee, published in 1946, observed: "For many years, pearl shell fishing was a most hazardous occupation. One of the risks to which the whole crew was exposed was that of beri-beri, owing to the necessity for using preserved food with no fresh fruit or vegetables; another common hazard among the divers was that of divers' paralysis, a result of too rapid changes of pressure. Many men died of

these diseases. The rough and ready life also took its toll. Living quarters were cramped and uncomfortable, the life was utterly monotonous, there was little provision for living while on shore. It was taken for granted that luggers' crews usually spent the last days of their lives as physical wrecks." The report adds there was now more skill in the treatment of the bends, although fatalities still occurred from time to time.

10. The Somerset Magistrates' Letter Book for 1872–1877 contains a number of references to crews recruited in various parts of the Pacific. From these sources and from the recollections of the descendants of Pacific Islanders born in Torres Strait, it seems that the majority came from Rotuma, Samoa, and Niue and from various islands in the Solomon and New Hebrides groups.

11. During the early years of the century, several coconut plantations were established, but there seems to have been little or no copra production. For a few years after the Second World War, wolfram was mined on Moa Island. Otherwise the only resource has been fish, which to date has been exploited only on a small scale. For an analysis of the Torres Strait economy and its prospects, see Treadgold 1974.

12. This assessment, based on a number of sources, is discussed in Beckett 1972, which summarizes the available data on indigenous Torres Strait. The primary source is the six-volume work edited by Haddon (1904–1935).

13. For an account of the London Missionary Society in Torres Strait, see Beckett 1978.

14. The 1897 Queensland Parliamentary Commission report indicated that Walker was helping Islanders to buy before the establishment of Papuan Industries. However, the LMS would not allow its missionaries to engage in trade. Walker was obliged to resign his position, but stayed on after the LMS withdrew in 1915 (LMS correspondence, 13 Sept. 1896; see also Austin 1972).

15. See also Chief Protector of Aborigines Report for 1904.

16. See *Queensland Parliamentary Debates*, 1938; p. 408.

17. The best account of this period is to be found in Evans, Saunders, and Cronin 1975.

18. See Chief Protector of Aborigines Report for 1910; p. 20.

19. The LMS missionary O. T. Harris recorded in a letter of protest to the Queensland home secretary that the Thursday Island protector had refused to allow an Islander to buy an iron roof for his father, because others would want to do the same thing, and there was no knowing where this kind of thing would end (correspondence of the LMS, 18 Aug. 1913).

20. See Chief Protector of Aborigines reports for 1910 (p. 20) and 1914 (p. 12).

21. See Aboriginals' Department reports for 1925 et seq.

22. See Aboriginals' Department reports for 1935–36.

23. This was alleged in the Communist press, which took up the Islanders' cause (*Workers Weekly*, 21 Jan. and 21 Feb. 1936). The *Brisbane Telegraph* of 8 January 1936 reports a statement by the responsible minister to the effect that the Islanders "were contributing something towards the support of Aboriginals on the Mainland". Just what they were contributing and how was never made clear.

24. For a discussion of egalitarianism, see Beckett 1972.

25. Interview with Tanu Nona, August 1959.

26. Pacific Islanders married to local women were allowed to remain after their fellows had been deported. However, they were faced with the choice of becoming Aborigines under the terms of the act or removing to the St Pauls or Hammond Island missions, where conditions were much the same as on the reserves. Their status nevertheless remained anomalous, and after 1945

their half-caste descendants were allowed to vote, take alcohol, and travel as they pleased. These rights were still denied to half-castes living on the reserves.
27. See Sub-Department of Native Affairs reports for 1946–47.
28. Ibid.
29. Nietschmann (personal communication, 1977) found that a sample of forty-two dugong averaged 254.7 kg of butchered meat; a sample of fifty-four turtle averaged 131.1 kg. Badu luggers regularly brought back one or two dugong and several turtles each month and would go out for more if there was a feast. With eight luggers working, Badu was well supplied with meat. For further data on hunting, see Nietschmann 1976.
30. It should be added that there was ample residential and gardening land. The change was made in order that those without hereditary rights should not be beholden to Baduan owners. See also Haddon 1904, pp. 294–91.
31. Reports of the Chief Protector and of the Aboriginals' Department indicate that the Islander population rose from 2,368 in 1913 to 3,765 in 1938. In 1948 the stated figure was 5,000 and in 1960 7,250. Estimates by Caldwell, Duncan, and Tait (1975), based on the Commonwealth census, are considerably lower but record similar rates of growth.

References

Austin, Tony. 1972. F. W. Walker and Papuan Industries Lt. *Journal of the Papua and New Guinea Society* 6, no. 1: 38–62.
Bach, John. 1961. The Political Economy of Pearlshelling. *Economic History Review* 14, no. 1: 105–14.
Barrera, Mario. 1980. *Race and Class in the Southwest: a Theory of Racial Equality.* Indiana: Notre Dame University Press.
Beckett, Jeremy. 1971. Rivalry, Competition and Conflict among Christian Melanesians. In *Anthropology in Oceania,* ed. L. R. Hiatt and C. Jayawardena. Sydney: Angus and Robertson.
——— . 1972. The Torres Strait Islanders. In *Bridge and Barrier: the Natural and Cultural History of Torres Strait,* ed. Donald Walker. Canberra: Australian National University.
——— . 1978. Mission, Church and Sect: Three Types of Religious Commitment in the Torres Strait Islands. In *Mission, Church and Sect in Oceania,* ed. J. A. Boutlier et al. Ann Arbor: University of Michigan Press.
Bee, Robert, and Ronald Ginderich. 1977. Colonialism, Classes and Ethnic Identity: Native Americans and National Political Economy. *Studies in Comparative International Development* 13.
Bleakley, J. W. 1961. *The Aborigines of Australia.* Brisbane: Jacaranda.
Caldwell, J. C., Helen Duncan, and Maree Tait. 1975. *The Demographic Report. (The Torres Strait Islanders,* v. 4.) Canberra: Australian National Univeristy.
Douglas, John. 1899. The Islands and Inhabitants of Torres Strait. *Queensland Geographical Journal.* n.s. 15 (1899–1900): 25–40.
Evans, Gaynor. 1971. Thursday Island 1878–1914: A Plural Society. BA (Hons) thesis, University of Queensland.
Evans, Raymond, Kay Saunders, and Kathryn Cronin. 1975. *Exclusion, Exploitation and Extermination: Race Relations in Colonial Queensland.* Sydney: Australia and New Zealand Book Company.

Foster-Carter, Aidan. 1978. The Modes of Production Controversy. *New Left Review* 107: 47–77.

Gonzalez Casanova, Pablo. 1965. Internal Colonialism and National Development. *Studies in Comparative International Development* 1: 27–37.

Haddon, A. C. 1901. *Headhunters, Black, White and Brown.* London.

——— . ed. 1904. *Reports of the Cambridge Anthropological Expedition to Torres Straits.* Vol. 5 Cambridge: Cambridge University Press.

——— . 1908. Vol. 6.

——— . 1935. Vol. 1.

Hartwig, M. C. 1978. The Theory of Internal Colonialism – the Australian Case. ANZAAS paper, 1976. In *Essays in the Political Economic of Australian Capitalism,* ed. E. G. Wheelwright and K. Buckley. Sydney: ANZ Book Co.

Hechter, Michael. 1974. *Internal Colonialism: The Celtic Fringe in British National Development 1536–1966.* London: Routledge.

Leys, Colin, 1977. Underdevelopment and Dependency: Critical Notes. *Journal of Contemporary Asia* 7.

London Missionary Society. Reports and Correspondence, New Guinea boxes. Microfilm. National Library of Australia, Canberra.

MacGillivray, John. 1852. *Narrative of the Voyage of H.M.S. Rattlesnake . . .* 2 vols. London: Boone.

Nietschmann, Bernard. 1976. Torres Strait Island Hunters and Environment. Seminar paper, Department of Human Geography, Australian National University.

Press, Irwin. 1969. Ambiguity and Innovation: Implications for the Genesis of the Culture Broker. *American Anthropologist* 71, no. 2: 205–17.

Queensland Parliamentary Papers. 1908. Report of the Royal Commission Appointed to Inquire into the Working of the Pearl-shell and Beche-de-Mer Industries, etc. *QPP* 1908, vol. 2, p. 395.

Rowley, C. D. 1971. *The Remote Aborigines.* Ringwood, Vic.: Penguin.

Somerset Magistrates' Letter Book, 1872–1877. Oxley Library, Brisbane, MS.

Stavenhagen, Rodolfo. 1965. Classes, Colonialism and Acculturation. *Studies in Comparative International Development* 1: 53–77.

Taussing, Michael. 1977. The Genesis of Capitalism amongst a South American Peasantry: Devils Labor and the Baptism of Money. *Comparative Studies in Society and History* 19, no. 2: 130–55.

Treadgold, M. L. 1974. *The Economy of the Torres Strait Area: A Social Accounting Study.* Vol. 2 of *The Torres Strait Islanders.* Canberra: Australian National University.

Wolf, Eric. 1957. Closed Corporate Peasant Communities in Meso-America and Central Java. *Southwestern Journal of Anthropology* 13, no. 1: 1–18.

Wolpe, Harold. 1975. The Theory of Internal Colonialism: the South African case. In *Beyond the Sociology of Development . . .* ed. Ivar Oxal, Tony Barnett, and David Booth. London: Routledge.

Aboriginal Brokerage and Political Development in South-Western Australia

MICHAEL C. HOWARD

In recent years, the Australian federal government and the various state governments have been actively trying to improve conditions for the Australian Aborigines. Most governmental action has taken place through legislative reform or through the support of welfare and development-oriented programmes. Despite some success in these undertakings, the net result has been the creation of an Aboriginal elite, consisting largely of Aborigines who serve as cultural brokers for their administrative patrons. Governmental activities have done little to benefit the majority of Aborigines, either politically or economically. The existing socio-economic system, of which Aboriginal brokers are an integral part, has served primarily to block Aboriginal bids for power and drain Aboriginal society of its intellectual resources by co-opting the better educated and more articulate Aborigines and incorporating them in a structure that functions to *control* Aborigines. The government has thus created a rather subtle structure of indirect rule.

The "changes" that the Australian government has introduced on behalf of the south-western Aborigines in particular have only superficially altered their structural position in relation to the rest of Australian society. After decades of governmental planning, these people remain an underdeveloped, relatively powerless segment of the population; the policies implemented to "help" them have only served to maintain their low status. Aboriginal brokers, operating within what is termed the "inter-ethnic political field", have played a significant role in ensuring the continuity of Aboriginal powerlessness.

Frank (1967) has pointed to an aspect of underdevelopment that seems to be exemplified in the case of Australian Aborigines: that although there is continual change, things all too often remain the same. Despite this continuity, however, such underdeveloped situations should not be seen as static. Structures of inequality and dependency come into being in the course of time and once created must be sustained by the groups whose interests they serve. Underdevelopment must be seen as a dynamic social and economic process subject to the demands of continual reproduction. The maintenance of underdevelopment is not always a simple matter, and structures change and break down through conflicts generated by various combinations of internal and external factors. Frank notes that there are critical periods in the history of underdeveloped societies when significant structural changes are possible. Even radical change, however, does not imply an end to dependence or exploitation. Much reform is mere sham, and even when substantial change does occur, new structures of exploitation and domination during post-reform periods commonly evolve (e.g., see Zaldivar 1974). Even after revolutionary upheavals, the traditional elite or basic structure of underdevelopment may perservere and emerge in new (or perhaps not so new) guise.

The process by which structures of underdevelopment and domination are maintained through crisis periods is perhaps one of the more important questions in development studies. It is only when such processes are understood that realistic programmes can be devised to alter existing conditions. The discussion below focuses upon one such crisis period in Aboriginal affairs; the reformist era initiated by the brief ascendancy of the Australian Labor Party in the mid-1970s. It is my contention that despite considerable activity in the political and economic arenas, the political and economic position of south-western Aborigines did not substantially improve during this period.

The Setting[1]

The south-western portion of Western Australia is at present inhabited by over eight thousand persons of Aboriginal descent and by approximately 750,000 non-Aborigines. Most of the Aborigines living in the area are part of the ethnic sub-category of Nyungar or Nyoongah. The social organization and cultural system of the area was severely disrupted by European colonization and conquest during the nineteenth century. Hunting and gathering became increasingly difficult and less desirable as a means of subsistence as European settlement spread. By the latter part of the nineteenth century, such economic pursuits were for the most part replaced by hand-outs or European-related employment on a sporadic basis (see Biskup 1973), although some Nyoongah retained at least a partial foraging adaptation into the twentieth century.

The settlers' attitudes toward Aborigines assured them an unenviable position in colonial society. The feelings of whites towards Aborigines varied, from the extremes of advocating their extermination to hoping for their eventual assimilation. Few saw much value in Aboriginal culture or were willing to treat Aboriginals as equals. Initially, some of the more liberal-minded settlers had hopes of quickly being able to "civilize" the Aborigines, but by the middle of the nineteenth century very few of these liberals still held such views. By this time it appeared to many whites that the Aborigines were a "dying race". Problems began to emerge (from the white perspective) toward the end of the century when it became apparent that the Aborigines were not going to make matters so simple.

Depopulation in the south-west was considerable. From an estimated population of over 6,000 living in the region before contact, the total Aboriginal population had decreased to about 1,400 by 1901, and of these only some 850 were categorized as "full-bloods". During the last decades of the nineteenth century, while the Aboriginal population was growing smaller, there was a dramatic increase in the non-Aboriginal population after gold was discovered in the eastern part of Western Australia. Changes in the size and composition of the white population had significant repercussions for Aborigines. They were now hopelessly outnumbered, and there remained almost no sanctuary from the incursions of the white man. Although the number of full-bloods in the south-west has continued to decline throughout the twentieth century, there has been a steady increase in the part-Aboriginal population.

A few part-Aborigines were able to take advantage of the buoyant economy of Western Australia during the late nineteenth century. These persons formed an upper strata of Nyoongah society, but their ascendancy in absolute terms was short-lived. By the First World War their socio-economic status was little better than that of other Nyoongah. The period 1890–1914 also witnessed growing anti-Aboriginal feelings in the south-west. The Aborigines were considered an embarrassment to such a modern society, and as their number began to show signs of increasing, they were viewed by some as a potential competitive source of cheap labour.

The endeavours of trade unionists and other interest groups led to an onslaught of ever more repressive legislation that was passed with the immediate aims of getting persons of Aboriginal descent out of sight and of providing stricter supervision of them (see Biskup 1973; Rowley 1970). The first major step toward government control of the Nyoongah, although instituted with relatively good intentions, was the establishment of the Aborigines Protection Board in 1890. The Aboriginal Acts of 1905 and 1936, as well as other pieces of legislation, institutionalized anti-Aboriginal feelings, eroded what rights they had possessed, and gave government officials considerable power over Aborigines. This included the forcible placement of many Nyoongah on native settlements, which resembled prisons, and the denial of adequate schooling, health care, and other services that the government afforded white Australians. Aboriginal prospects for employment, besides the most menial, low-status positions, virtually disappeared. The 1936 act, as noted by Paul Hasluck, gave the Aborigines a "legal status that has more in common with that of a born idiot than any other class of British subject" (Hasluck 1942, pp. 160–61). At the same time, differential treatment of Nyoongah according to their "colour" and their behaviour toward whites, acted in a manner favouring social stratification and discouraging ethnic solidarity. This differential treatment helped to create an Aboriginal elite which owed its precarious position (for the most part only marginally better than that of other Aborigines) to the good will of a few white patrons – in particular the Aboriginal protector (Howard 1980).

During the Second World War, Aborigines in the south-west were able to avail themselves of labour shortages in the civilian sector of the economy and to contravene existing restrictive regulations. At this time many Aborigines began to move to Perth, initiating a trend that has continued up to the present (Makin 1970; Howard 1975). The post-war period witnessed a renewal of interest on the part of whites in "civilizing" Aborigines. This led to a lessening (but not the disappearance) of overt bureaucratic control of Aborigines' lives and to new opportunities in employment and education.

Despite recent social and economic advances by some Nyoongahs, their situation remains very unsatisfactory. In rural areas many Nyoongah continue to live in overcrowded and run-down dwellings on Aboriginal reserves. Employment opportunities have been limited primarily to seasonal farm work and a handful of full-time jobs on road maintenance, on the railway, or for shire councils (the latter resulting from federal government subsidies). Income for many Aborigines comes from various forms of welfare payment, and a large percentage of rural Aborigines are heavily dependent upon welfare services. Ethnic relations in country towns vary greatly, and in a few instances the situation has improved. Elsewhere, however, relations have deteriorated as the old forms of paternalism have broken down. Formal education of Aborigines has shown little progress since the opening of schools to Aborigines in the 1950s (McKeich 1971).[2]

Possibilities for employment in Perth, although greater than in the country, are very restricted. The kinds of work that are available to Aborigines are generally unappealing, since Aborigines are subjected to on-the-job discrimination, isolation from fellow Aborigines, low wages, and other poor working conditions. There are exceptions to this, but not many; as in rural areas, welfare payments are a major source of income for urban-dwelling Aborigines.

Aboriginal political and legal rights have gradually been restored or granted in a formal sense, but *de facto* discrepancies remain. Aborigines continue to rely heavily upon government assistance in order to maintain even a minimal level of subsistence. Many Nyoongah live within a "welfare environment" that has left them subject to bureaucratic manipulation and has severely compromised their personal and social autonomy. Such manipulation by government employees has, of course, been carried out with the stated aim of developing Aborigines into socially and culturally acceptable Australians, who, it is hoped, will be better able to fend for themselves in the wider society. Unfortunately, stated aim and reality appear to have little in common, and the welfare system is structured in such a way as to work against achieving its public aims. The welfare machinery functions more as a mechanism of control and domination than as the means of Aboriginal salvation, and niches for brokers have developed in such a way as to support this system.

The Development of Aboriginal Politics in the South-west

A Diachronic Perspective

The data on traditional south-western Aboriginal politics and government are far from being adequate and are often contradictory. Nevertheless, it is possible to provide a general description of the political situation. Traditional mechanisms of social control were both formal and informal, and a corpus of "Law" was enforced, in part, by holders of certain offices. The principal offices were those of elder and curer; their roles appear not to have been too different from thos found elsewhere in Aboriginal Australia. There were councils, of the "community-in-council" (Kuper 1971) and more select varieties, although little is known concerning their internal dynamics. There were leaders, but individual power was restricted by a combination of ecological and socio-cultural factors. Inter-group relations beyond the immediate endogamous unit were not very common. Members of different groups did come into contact occasionally on an individual or group basis (e.g., at periodic gatherings held for purposes of trade and discussion of Law matters), but whether or not intercultural brokerage activities were very significant or institutionalized is difficult to surmise.

European contact and settlement changed the political situation in the south-west dramatically. Initially there was what may be labelled the frontier period. For Aborigines it was a time of experimentation and adjustment; many sought to incorporate what they saw as advantageous features of the new settler society into their own, while trying to avoid severe societal disruption. For a while this experimentation was possible to varying degrees, and except in a few areas of concentrated European settlement, south-western Aborigines were afforded a fair degree of autonomy, so long as they did not cause trouble for the whites. For the settlers it was also a period of experimentation and of trying to incorporate the Aborigines within their own European culture. Especially important in the present context are the attempts made by the whites to mould Aborigines into "proper" primitives through the imposition of such concepts as *tribe* and *chief*. This initial failure to understand Aboriginal society on its own terms laid the basis for much of what was to come in the development of white-Aboriginal relations. The white attitude was to some extent determined by the exigencies of colonial administration, which required not only that there be chiefs and the like for interactive purposes, but also that they be assessed according to how they helped or retarded colonial development. Hence, there arose a demarcation between "good" and "bad" leaders — status being assigned on the basis of criteria independent of political considerations internal to Aboriginal society.

The second period was that of more formalized, structural encapsulation of Aborigines within Australian society. To some extent it was a period in which the settlers' earlier ideas about Aborigines were translated into administrative structures. This period may be divided into an initial stage (1850s to 1890s) characterized by indirect rule, and a later one (1890s to 1940s) exhibiting more institutionalized and direct administrative control of Aborigines. Exclusion and control of Aborigines from Australian society was stressed during both of these eras; this encouraged the development of socio-cultural brokerage on a more formal basis than previously. In the first stage, such brokerage was affected through the offices of king, native constable, and the relatively ineffectual white protector. Increased non-Aboriginal settlement and related factors led to the development of the second stage and to the concentration of patronage and brokerage activities in the office of the chief protector. Aboriginal brokerage niches created during the early stage became less significant. The decline in the importance of Aborignal brokers led a few of those Aborigines, who would otherwise probably have become brokers, to try to assert themselves as independent Aboriginal leaders. However, they failed to gain Aboriginal support because of their marginality to Nyoongah society; they similarly failed to gain recognition from whites because of their radical posture (see Howard 1975).

The period of direct bureaucratic control and encapsulation reached its peak in the late 1930s. Further development in this direction was halted by the Second World War, which undermined the efficiency of administrative management and resulted in a liberalization of white attitudes toward Aborigines. Instability in the administration of Aboriginal affairs and wartime conditions led to a brief florescence of independent Aboriginal political activity. It was not long, however, before bureaucratic control was reasserted, though in a somewhat different fashion than previously had been the case.

The post-war period — a period of bureaucratic manipulation — has been something of a hybrid of the two stages of the previous period. Administrative direction of Aboriginal affairs has remained in modified form; its primary mode of operation has been through particular Aborigines and Aboriginal-related organizations. The post-war period may be divided according to government policies towards Aborigines: "assimilation" (1940s to 1960s) and "self-determination" (late 1960s to the present): although the differences between these two eras in a political and administrative sense are not as great as one might assume. Continuity of government personnel in the administration of Aboriginal affairs contributed to the continuity of policy.

During the assimilationist era, white administrators manipulated Aboriginal politics through a few Aboriginal-related voluntary organizations. By centralizing inter-ethnic political activities in these organizations, the state governments' Department of Native Welfare was able to re-establish control of Aboriginal affairs after the war and was able to halt the development of an independent, Aboriginal political field. Whites assumes management of Aboriginal affairs by consolidating the disparate organizations that had emerged after the war into a single body, the Native Welfare Council. The department was able to regulate this council and, through it, was able to weed out people with ideas inimical to its own aims. A few Aborigines were motivated by whites to express themselves politically by participating in voluntary organizations. The Aborigines who were involved in the principal voluntary organization, the Coolbaroo League, were subsequently pushed out of the league by the Aboriginal employees of the department. The league was then deemed sufficiently secure as an arm of bureaucratic policy; it was subsequently used to administer a local Aboriginal settlement (see Wilson 1958). The league thus became established as an Aboriginal front for the department, while it claimed legitimacy as an Aboriginal political body. Problems with this organization (its members demanded to be paid for their work) eventually led to a merger with the Native Welfare Council; the resulting organization (which would later become the Aboriginal Advancement Council) was internally dominated by whites. One of the most important outcomes of the assimilationst era, then, was the establishment of formally constituted, welfare-oriented voluntary organizations, which became the only means through which

Aboriginal activists could achieve recognition by non-Aborigines.

The impetus of the campaign (conducted primarily by whites) for Aboriginal citizenship (granted in 1967), led to the transformation of assimilationist policies into policies advocating Aboriginal self-determination. As in the immediate post-war period, this resulted in an upsurge of Aboriginal-related political activity and a broadening of the inter-ethnic political field, along with a loosening of direct departmental supervision. Political action, however, was still channelled through welfare-related, formally constituted voluntary organizations (*para-bureaucratic* is perhaps a better term), established along lines acceptable to whites. Most Aborigines operating within this field (and their number was small) appear to have shared with whites the assumption that this form of organization was the correct and legitimate one for Aborigines, or at least that it was the only type that would be recognized by the dominant society. Attempts to establish more autonomous Aboriginal organizations (e.g., the Black Power movement) were poorly supported by Aborigines and unable to survive as bureaucratic control was reasserted. Politically motivated Aborigines thus had two options: they could either form new voluntary organizations or attempt to gain control of the older ones.

Direct bureaucratic management of Aboriginal organizations was established in 1972, after the Labor Party victory in the federal election. Relatively large sums of money were made available to Aborigines by the federal government. This money, however, was channelled through the local Aboriginal department, which was loath to give money to groups who were not appropriately constituted, or to individuals not affiliated with acceptable organizations. This influx of money virtually eliminated independent volunteerism, and through such financial control the bureaucracy was able to direct more easily the path of Aboriginal development as it saw fit.

A development potentially disruptive to the department's new hegemony was the creation of the National Aboriginal Consultative Committee by the federal government (see Howard 1977). The state bureaucracy was able, however, at least temporarily to neutralize the activities of the Perth delegate by aligning itself behind those Aborigines who had come to owe their political status (and often their employment) to continued acceptance of the legitimacy of voluntary organizations as representative political bodies. These Aborigines, who saw the NACC as a threat, were assisted in their efforts to neutralize the threat by the federal department's luke-warm support for the NACC, as its delegates began to demand actual power in Aboriginal affairs.

At present it appears as though Aboriginal self-determination efforts in the Perth area are being directed by the Department of Aboriginal

Affairs/Aboriginal Affairs Planning Authority (new titles for the Department of Native Welfare), through a small group of Aborigines who are in a dependent relationship with that department. Although these individuals are given some opportunities for freedom of action and political manoeuvring, their activities must conform to the rules of the game laid down by whites and must present no great threat to continued dominance by non-Aborigines. Perhaps one of the most striking aspects of the post-war period of Aboriginal politics has been the chameleon-like ability of the variously named Aboriginal department to maintain its control over the field despite changes in the overall arena.

Continuity in Change

Since the period of initial contact and conquest, there have existed two discernible political fields in Aboriginal politics in the south-west: the intra-ethnic and inter-enthnic. From an Aboriginal perspective, each of these fields has been predicated through the adoption of differing personal political strategies. On the one hand there have been people who, either through choice or lack of perceived option, have sought relative autonomy from the wider society — or more specifically, from those white agencies designed to control Aborigines. Aborigines who have chosen this approach place high value upon such things as intra-Aboriginal sociability (and the security if affords), socio-economic equality, and reciprocity expressed through the medium of kinship. The power one individual is able to assert over others within this sphere is relatively limited as a result of internal factors favouring democratization and external ones such as limited access to economic resources. Those adhering to the above strategy tend to be highly integrated into what may be termed "mainstream" Nyoongah society. An important feature of Aborigines following this strategy is that they view most government agencies and agents as a threat to their well-being. They interact with such non-Aborigines when they must, but try to limit relations as much as possible. This does not imply that these persons do not desire change, for most do want greater control over their own lives and an improved standard of living, but they perceive the role of the government in promoting these things as ambiguous at best.

The strategy pursued by other Aborigines is to seek economic gain or political power by working within the political structure made available to them by whites — as cultural brokers. Accrual of power for Aboriginal brokers tends to be limited in comparison to that attained by whites, although brokers may gain more power over other Aborigines than is possible in the intra-ethnic sphere. The increased power of this group results primarily from their acceptability to whites rather than to Aborigines. One of the main differences between those active in this field and those in the intra-ethnic one is that cultural brokers exhibit a strong desire to gain, either for themselves or for other Aborigines, material items and social status that are closely in accord with the goals of most members of the dominant society. Such individuals are frequently marginal to local Aboriginal society, because they are set apart by either their prior social status or by their desire to achieve, and might be categorized as entrepreneurs.

While socio-cultural marginality has not been necessary for success or entry into the inter-ethnic field, it has been a decided advantage to Aboriginal brokers. This is principally because the social and behavioural requirements of intra-Aboriginal relations conflict with those demanded of Aborigines by whites. Aborigines who are less marginal socially than brokers but who nonetheless adhere to some of the relevant socio-economic goals of the wider society find themselves becoming progressively marginal to Nyoongah society as they are pressured to conform to the expectations of whites and as they become socialized to politics within the field. Primarily because of its integration into the domain of the white bureaucracy, the inter-ethnic field over the past few decades has been divorced from "mainstream" Nyoongah society. Socialization of Aborigines draws them more tightly into the relatively closed, remote realm of the Aboriginal department and takes them away from the Aboriginal world.

The potential for development afforded by action within the context of the inter-ethnic field must be considered in analysis of the Aboriginal political situation. It will be argued that there is, in fact, very little scope for beneficial change within this inter-ethinic field. The superficiality of the limited development that does occur is evidenced in the emphasis on "concreteness" by the actors: upon buildings, formal organizations, on things that can be readily quantified or put into annual reports and newspaper articles. Such "concrete achievement" is only a facade of development, since the basic structural relations blocking actual development are retained or modified to suit changing conditions. Aborigines acting within this context, like their white counterparts, become immersed in day-to-day manoeuvring, losing sight of core issues and generally accepting the "definition of the situation" as it is dictated by those in power. Aborigines have struggled to gain control of voluntary organizations, accepting this as a way to power, while actually losing power and autonomy in the process. They quarrel among themselves over the goods that are artifically limited (by the local Aboriginal department), but never question how or why the goods are limited (by the white bureaucracy, according to its own aims). In short, instead of providing an avenue for Aboriginal advancement, the inter-ethnic field has functioned as a structure of indirect rule. Instead of giving Aborigines a greater degree of political autonomy, it has set low ceilings to advancement for persons of Aboriginal descent and has given only a little power to a few of them. It has ensured that the Nyoongah are *net losers* of power and autonomy. It would seem that, although there have been minor changes in recent years, there has been considerable continuity in the basic structure of Aboriginal politics.

Aboriginal Brokers[3]

Historical Antecedents

The differential incorporation of south-western Aborigines and the progressive encapsulation of their politics during the nineteenth century created niches for patronage and brokerage. From the outset, whites have served as cultural brokers in the south-west. In the nineteenth century few whites were knowledgeable about Aborigines, and those who were sometimes served as cultural brokers for other whites. Many settlers, however, preferred to rely upon their own presumed "expertise" in dealing with Aborigines, an expertise based largely upon racial stereotypes and misinformation. A person's actual knowledge of Aborigines did not necessarily affect his standing as an expert or broker. In such situations it is difficult for clients to evaluate the means by which a broker operates among those of the other culture or the degree to which the broker's claims of reliability can be trusted, particularly when the client's own views are at considerable variance with the actual situation. It is often more important that the client is fed information that supports his world view. In the south-west, this situation is made possible by the overwhelming power of white clients and brokers over Aborigines — the whites simply do not have to understand Aborigines. This is not the case for Aborigines, who because of their status are more dependent upon accurate information for advancement or survival. But as with whites, they are usually unable to judge the validity of the message that the broker transmits and thus are dependent upon his good will and ability to transmit messages accurately.

Whites frequently served simultaneously as both patrons and brokers for Aborigines. As patrons they were generally ineffectual beyond mildly easing the Aborigines' plight. Many of these patron-brokers existed on the fringes of white society. With a few exceptions (e.g.,

John Forrest), those in power demonstrated little sympathy for Aborigines and even less willingness to alter structural impediments to Aboriginal advancement. With the introduction of an Aboriginal-related bureaucracy in the late nineteenth century, the role of "Aboriginal expert" became increasingly formalized and came to be monopolized by members of the Aboriginal department. Independent white "experts" had to keep in mind the wishes of the department, because of its power in Aboriginal affairs and its ability to deny them access to Aborigines or just to make things generally difficult for them. Only very recently has this niche broadened and become more independent of bureaucratic control. Those acting as brokers have thus been very susceptible to the pressures of bureaucratic goals and politics. This means that all white brokerage and expertise has been effectively concentrated in the hands of those wanting to maintain the present status of the Aborigines in relation to the Aboriginal department and white society. Rather than serving as advocates of the Aborigines in white society, brokers generally serve as advocates of the dominant society, who are attempting to mould Aboriginal society in a way acceptable to non-Aborigines.

The patronage and brokerage niches available to Aborigines during the nineteenth century were fairly limited. Nonetheless, a desire to gain access to the spoils available from white society, coupled with a more general need to mediate inter-ethnic relations, did encourage some Aborigines to attempt to fill such niches as they became available. Patronage within the intra-Aboriginal context occurred, if only to a very limited extent. The potentialities for this form of patronage, however, were restricted by the lack of "first order resources" (Boissevain 1974) available within the ethnic unit, and were also limited by the constraints, such as norms of kinship reciprocity, presented within the internal socio-cultural milieu. The possibility of Aboriginal patronage in the inter-ethnic sphere was even more remote. Whites alone were able to distribute "primary" resources like hand-outs and employment.

Postions as cultural brokers were available to Aborigines; their clients included both whites and Aborigines. The native constables and kings performed relatively institutionalized brokerage roles. For the whites, these office-bearers were necessary to the pursuance of a policy of indirect rule, while for Aborigines they were at times useful in mollifying the effects of white rule (although frequently just the opposite was true) and in providing limited access to the dominant society. It was from among those Aborigines who had a reasonable command of English, who were involved in inter-ethnic exchanges for personal or economic profit, that whites selected kings and other office-holders. This can be seen as an attempt to reward those who had been "good", in the belief that it might set an example for others to follow.

Although individual inter-ethnic Aboriginal brokers were not always able to acquire or maintain a monopoly over the flow of information in a given situation, there were factors that did promote their nodality in exchanges. For whites it was easier to deal through a few Aborigines who had been acculturated to non-Aboriginal ways. Not only were these individuals more willing to interact with whites than were other Aborigines, but having too many Aborigines "hanging about" might in fact lessen the person's standing in white society. It was important not to become too closely identified with Aborigines.

Because of the asymmetrical loci of power, considerations related to white preferences were of more significance in restricting niches for Aborigines than factors relating to Aboriginal opinions or concerns. Thus, even though other Aborigines might not consider a person a suitable broker, or afford him much status within Aboriginal society, they might make use of him because of his social ties with whites. Until the latter part of the 1890s, the more tradition-oriented south-western Aborigines had infrequent need of such brokerage. For those attempting to achieve at least a modicum of assimilation into white society, however, patronage and brokerage were of more significance.

The particular nature of inter-ethnic brokerage and the resultant communication structure encouraged whites to see or promote Aboriginal brokers as leaders (Howard 1978). Aboriginal "leadership" came to be closely identified with persons who were viewed as playing a leading part in encouraging fellow Aborigines to act in ways acceptable to whites. Such "leadership" existed alongside, and at times overlapped with, leadership as it was recognized by Aborigines. The structure of intra-Aboriginal leadership evident at this time, which in some ways was a continuation of the pre-contact situation, and which still persists, was one of leadership within very narrow bounds (i.e., close kin) and with limited power. It was through Aboriginal brokers, promoted by whites as leaders, that an effort was made to create something of a "head" (or "mask") for the acephalous south-western Aboriginal society, although it was to be a head with little power, since this was retained by whites, and a head that remained fairly disjointed from its body.

The importance of patronage and brokerage for Aborigines increased as white society (and white bureaucracy) came to be of more relevance in their everyday lives. Toward the end of the century, Aboriginal brokerage positions were generally held by the "better-class", part-Aborigines. The latter were persons who had managed to achieve some success and a limited respectability in the white world, often through the assistance of white patrons.

By the First World War, the situation of better-class Nyoongahs had deteriorated considerably, and the overall mode of incorporation of south-western Aborigines had become harsher and more strictly controlled by white administrators. In the native settlements, control of Aborigines was assisted by Aborigines from the north who worked closely with the police. The overall scope for Aboriginal brokerage came to be very limited as Nyoongahs concentrated on building defences, and white society became primarily concerned with Aboriginal removal. Brokerage activities did not cease entirely, but the niches for more institutionalized brokerage were eliminated.

Conditions after the Second World War (e.g., the assimilationist policy and return to indirect rule) created potential brokerage niches for entrepreneurial Aborigines possessing the requisite resources. The cultural brokers who filled these niches could, at the same time, be promoted by white patrons as Aboriginal leaders. The intent appears to have been for these persons to demonstrate to both Aborigines and whites that there were Aborigines capable of behaving like whites, and that these individuals were actively involved in affairs affecting Aborigines. To add to the status of these brokers, they were assigned the title of leader or spokesman, titles that replaced earlier designations of chief and king but which represented little difference in power or substance. For the most part, brokers were expected to be satisfied with those spoils granted them by their patrons (such as jobs). At some time in the unspecified future, when they would be deemed sufficiently responsible to administer Aboriginal affairs and when they could be counted on to make the "right" choices, they would become "real" leaders.

Communication between whites, especially when they are government employees, and Nyoongahs generally has been difficult; the liberalism of those in Aboriginal-related bureaucratic posts or those active in a more voluntary capacity after the Second World War has done little to alleviate this situation. Aboriginal responses to the queries and actions of those in administrative positions, and often to other whites as well, have tended to be of two types: (a) those aimed at manipulating the situation to get the most out of it, and (b) those aimed at stopping communication. As in the pre-war period, Aborigines who adopt the former approach, who may actually seek out cross-cultural communication for such ends, are usually the ones serving as cultural brokers for non-Aborigines. Government administrators generally depend on these persons for so-called grass-roots information regarding the feelings and activities of the Aborigines under their "care and guidance".

It is not surprising that white patrons tended (and for the most part continue) to give most credulity to those brokers who provide them with information fitting most closely with their own preconceptions, rather than giving it to brokers who aid them in the search for some scientific or socio-cultural truth. Behaviour and life style, as in the previous century, have emerged as important criteria for support by whites of Aboriginal "leaders" or brokers (Howard 1978). These Aboriginal brokers assist their patrons in maintaining communication with Aboriginal people (or at least an Aboriginal person). But they may also distort situations to suit their own ends, sustaining their niche and maximizing their personal gain. A pattern that emerged during the decades following the Second World War (there is evidence of it before the war as well) is for whites concerned with inter-ethnic relations to find Aborigines who fit with their image of what an ideal Aboriginal should be. These ideal clients feed their patrons reassuring information; they are supported because they represent the "real" voice of the Aboriginal people. Thus, the patron becomes the voice of the Aboriginal people through the medium of an Aboriginal client who has sought their patronage. In cases where Aborigines have had sufficiently influential patrons, they might be proclaimed to be Aboriginal leaders.

The niches available for aspiring brokers in the inter-ethnic political field and the possible spoils have been quite circumscribed until very recently. Since the 1890s, patronage for Aborigines was primarily focused on the office and personage of the protector (later the commissioner for the Aboriginal department). After the Second World War, promotion of Aboriginal leadership and political activities was kept within narrow bounds, and the patronage of the commissioner of native welfare remained a significant consideration in most inter-ethnic political activities.

During the early post-war period, the commissioner of native welfare attempted to support Aboriginal brokers who were relatively well connected with the local Aboriginal community, with the hope of enhancing assimilation. At this time, the department itself was only beginning to hire Aborigines to fill a few minor posts. Those persons hired by the department tended to be outsiders by Nyoongah standards, coming from other parts of Western Australia. The late 1950s witnessed a change in inter-ethnic Aboriginal brokerage/leadership. Persons of Aboriginal descent who were more acceptable by bureaucratic and white standards (i.e., those employed by the Department of Native Welfare) than the older leaders, entered into competition with the latter for occupancy of the leader/broker niche. Most of these newer leaders had very little influence among other Aborigines. At this time there was an important shift in emphasis by white patrons, from encouraging influential Aborigines to act in ways felt to further Aboriginal assimilation, to promoting the efforts of relatively acculturated persons who were not necessarily influential among local Aborigines. Even minimal consideration of a person's standing in local Aboriginal society was abandoned as a criterion for bestowing leader/ broker status on an Aborigine, and the new leader/brokers were, for the most part, quite marginal to Nyoongah society. This state of affairs continued into the 1960s, as the leader/broker niche was consolidated within a single voluntary organization (the Native Welfare Council/ Aboriginal Advancement Council).

Contemporary Brokers

There have been several changes in the nature of Aboriginal brokerage during the last few years. Although it is difficult to arrive at satisfactory figures (see Howard 1975), it would appear as though the number of Aborigines involved in brokerage activities, in what may be termed a professional or semi-professional capacity, has increased since the mid-1960s. This has resulted mainly because of changing white (i.e., government) attitudes and policies toward Aborigines, and the creation of a larger number of institutionalized positions for brokers. It is also significant that a larger pool of relatively well-educated and accul-turated Aborigines was able to avail itself of these opportunities. Aborigines born during or soon after the Second World War, who were subject to less harsh conditions than older Aborigines, were becoming old enough to take part in such affairs. These persons had greater expectations regarding employment and wages than did the older generation; their goals were difficult to realize except by becoming professional brokers. Upwardly mobile Aborigines were presented with few options other than becoming part of the structure of indirect rule. The number of these positions available, however, is limited by how many of these jobs the government is willing to create or sub-sidize, and by the number of them that Aborigines can wrest from whites. Because of the perceived desirability of these positions and the lack of solidarity among many of those competing for them, political struggles among Aborigines within the inter-ethnic field have intensi-fied. Relevant to all of these factors, of course, are power considera-tions, the Aborigines' lack of it in relation to whites, who dictate the availability and nature of spoils, and those aspects of Aboriginal culture and mode of incorporation into the wider society that militate against greater ethnic unity and more comprehensive political mobilization.

A desire to assist fellow Nyoongahs, for the most part selectively applied, is not uncommon among Aborigines living in Perth. In the majority of cases this is directed by socio-cultural norms of intra-ethnic reciprocity. For those Aborigines who are more fully acculturated into the wider society (e.g., Nyoongahs and non-Nyoongahs living in the city who would be classed as "better-class"), this pattern of normative behaviour has either broken down or never existed. When such persons are motivated to "do something for Aborigines", for whatever reason, this usually takes the form prevalent in white society (e.g., voluntary or welfare work for the "less fortunate" in a formally institutionalized context).

For individuals who are relatively well-integrated into Nyoongah society, who desire to transcend intra-ethnic, normative expectations and do more for their people, few options are available. Because the loci of power and spoils are primarily external to Aboriginal society, these persons are attracted to political activities within the inter-ethnic field. As they find themselves progressively caught up in activities related to the field and become socialized into its ways, it becomes difficult for them to retain sight of their original goal. "To help the Aboriginal people" comes to be translated into continual political manoeuvring to gain access to the spoils available from the more powerful whites, and strategic considerations become more and more geared to white expectations and desires. This development can be seen through analysis of Aboriginal attendance at meetings of voluntary organizations. Because this is viewed as a possible way to get something done, politically motivated Aborigines begin to attend an occasional meeting of one or two of the organizations. Few stay at this level for long and either quit to search for an alternative method or make the transition to full-time involvement. Once the latter course is chosen (the extent of free or conscious choice here is sometimes minimal), it is common for the individual to become inundated with meetings to attend and work to do, which becomes increasingly related to the internal concerns of inter-ethnic politics. The individuals involved are given a sense of being a part of important undertakings, but fail to develop a valid perspective of the nature of the arena and the implications of their activities.

A few brokers seek to avoid political involvement, trying to restrict their activities to the welfare sphere. But in a situation where almost all activities and positions are viewed by others as part of the political field, "neutrality" is difficult, and eventually they are forced either to give up their position or to enter the political fray. To some extent it is possible to avoid political involvement by taking a job with a government agency, where employment is more secure than with para-bureaucratic organizations. Some Aborigines, of course, seek to use their government position as a political base (which, although secure, is also constricting), but others find it a way by which they may remain involved in welfare work and thus support indirect rule while avoiding or minimizing association with inter-ethnic politics.

Positions available for Aborigines in the state bureaucracy have never been numerous, although within the past few years there have been a few more opportunities. Until very recently the Department of Native Welfare was the only government department that offered any hope of employment for Aborigines, and only a handful of these government jobs were available in the Perth area.[4] Virtually all of the Aborigines working for the department in the metropolitan Perth area may be classified either as better-class Nyoongahs who have only tenuous ties to local Aboriginal society or as "outsiders" (Aborigines from other areas of the country). Among those holding senior positions, many began their careers with the department during the early post-war period. The power of Aborigines within the bureaucracy is quite limited, and for the most part they have very little influence on policy decisions. From the perspective of their brokerage activities, the social isolation of Aboriginal bureaucrats has been enhanced by their affiliation with a government department. This isolation is compounded by the fact that Aboriginal employees of the department must work in offices that are not frequented by Aborigines. The clash between the values and expectations of the bureaucratic milieu and those of the Aboriginal milieu and the stigma attached by Aborigines to government affiliation have also contributed to the isolation of the Aboriginal elite from other Aborigines and to a greater cleavage between the inter- and intra-ethnic political fields.

During the early 1970s, the characteristics of the bureaucratic brokerage niche available to Aborigines were altered in two ways. At a local level brokerage niches became less restrictive for those Aborigines demonstrating a relatively high degree of acculturation, because of the creation of new positions for Aboriginal liaison officers in a greater number of voluntary organizations and in other government departments (i.e., the Department of Community Welfare and Public Health). This development represented little improvement, however, in opening the niche to a wider spectrum of Aborigines. Instead, it further isolated a few of the elite and marginal Aborigines and provided additional jobs for a group that was already fairly well off.

The second alteration in the character of the bureaucratic brokerage niche came with the entry of the Commonwealth government into the local Aboriginal arena on a more substantial and formal basis. After the Aboriginal department in Western Australia was integrated into the federal Aboriginal bureaucratic structure in 1974, a few senior Aborigines in the state department were promoted and transferred to Canberra. Rather than moving Aborigines into more significant positions in the state administration, giving them some degree of power in the local branch of the department, they were sent to Canberra, where they assumed low positions in the administrative hierarchy and were rendered relatively powerless. For other local brokers, the entry of Canberra into the arena added greater complexity to inter-ethnic politics, and some were drawn into what may be designated the national-level Aboriginal political field (see the chapter by Jones and Hill-Barnett).

Important to an analysis of Aboriginal brokerage in the context of Aboriginal politics is the extent to which persons in this role are able to attain power within the political arena. This involves the broker's ability to convert his "second-order" resources into "first-order" ones (Boissevain 1974).[5] Aborigines had virtually no opportunities to achieve such conversions until the late 1960s. More recently, some brokers have, to a limited extent, acquired power by virtue of their ability to translate the support of influential whites into government grants and to transform these into spoils (i.e., jobs) to be distributed among other Aborigines. Such persons are often those proclaimed to be leaders by whites. In a real sense, their power is quite circumscribed. Aborigines in brokerage positions continue to be largely dependent upon the good will of white bureaucrats. To enter the inter-ethnic political field requires that one relinquish autonomy in the hope of gaining power, but the nature of the field and the sources of power make it impossible for Aborigines adopting this strategy to obtain more than minimal power.

Aboriginal brokers sometimes attempt to use a variety of power sources to achieve their ends, but such actions often prove risky and difficult. They may employ such strategies as trying to bring pressure to bear on recalcitrant local bureaucrats through appeals to Canberra, to various politicians, or to the media, or they may search for alternative sources of whatever they desire (usually money). This assumes, however, systematic interrelationships which frequently do not exist. An Aboriginal broker may seek support in Canberra in order to force local bureaucrats to act favourably towards his requests for money, only to find this move of little use. Resistance in the Perth office (where meddling by those in Canberra is looked upon rather unfavourably), may become less overt (e.g., the request may be temporarily lost, or the office may agree to act on it and then do nothing) but not necessarily less effective in stopping the submission from being acted upon favourably. Although expansion and greater complexity within the inter-ethnic arena have resulted in greater scope for manoeuvrability by Aborigines, potential obstacles have emerged which require considerable knowledge of the arena to overcome. This has worked to the disadvantage of those not well integrated with the bureaucratic milieu, and has made it easier for white administrators to maintain control over Aboriginal affairs despite their rhetoric of self-determination for Aborigines.

Brokers and Aboriginal Incorporation

It has been argued that most of the persons acting as Aboriginal middle-men (under various designations) do not perform such a role, although their position is ostensibly a bridging one.[6] In fact, they operate mainly within a closed political field which excludes widespread or significant Aboriginal participation and in which a range of socio-cultural factors and the nature of inter-ethnic power relations make the actual performance of the brokerage role insignificant. The Aboriginal political entrepreneurs who fill the brokerage positions are unable to perform effectively as middlemen, either because of their status in local Aboriginal society or because the requisites of inter-ethnic political action progressively make fulfilment of the role difficult as the actors become integrated into the white-dominated political field. The inter-ethnic field thus serves to redirect or control political actions by Aborigines which might threaten the *status quo*. Government policies within the field also have served to enhance Aboriginal social stratification, creating an elite which shares the values of white administrators.

The inter-ethnic political field is part of a structure of indirect rule, and participation in it by Aboriginal brokers is of questionable benefit to Aboriginal political development. Acting within the confines of this field, the Aboriginal brokers add an element of legitimacy to a mechanism of control and manipulation operated by non-Aboriginal administrators. It is important to recognize, however, that Aborigines and whites active in the inter-ethnic field do not view the situation from this perspective. Rather, they tend to see themselves as being at the forefront of Aboriginal development efforts. It is probable that recognition of the true function of the inter-ethnic political structure would cause at least some of those now active in the field to alter their strategies, but there are numerous factors working against this, and the defection of a few Aborigines would have little effect on the continuance of the basic structure.

Continuity in the system of political domination has been possible during the 1970s primarily because the principal rules and prevailing ideologies have changed very little from those established in earlier periods. Thus, although the quantity available to Aborigines has increased, spoils are still controlled by whites and distributed in such a way as to promote dependency. This has occurred at a time when there are perhaps greater economic opportunities for Aborigines in Australian society than ever before. However, these opportunities represent a threat to volunteers and professionals involved in Aboriginal welfare work, as the possibility of Aboriginal autonomy becomes imminent.

By using existing patron-client links with Aboriginal brokers, and by encouraging better-class Aborigines to enter into similar kinds of relationships, whites have been able to influence the direction of Aboriginal "advancement" in such a way as to ensure that elite Aborigines remain dependent upon white patronage. This is accomplished by encouraging Aborigines to seek employment within the welfare structure, and by retaining white control of what is widely recognized as the only legitimate political field.

For those Aborigines who are successful in the welfare sphere, there are rewards by way of income and status. These persons are able to attend meetings throughout Australia and overseas, they are often provided with cars at government expense, and they are allowed to interact with upper-class whites and with high government officials. This sudden access to hobnobbing with the elites is bound to be heady stuff for members of a group only recently recognized as Australian citizens. For the Aboriginal broker, there is clearly much to be gained from white patronage. They are even allowed to believe that they are helping the Aboriginal people. From a broader perspective, however, they are promoting the very system which for years has deprived Aborigines of true political power and economic viability. In fact, it can be argued that brokers are not only helping to deprive other Aborigines of power but are also furthering Aboriginal underdevelopment by removing resources from Nyoongah society. This occurs when their skills and income are withdrawn from Aboriginal society, where they would have been subject to normative expectations to share these resources. The skills of Aboriginal brokers are instead utilized by the dominant whites for white ends; their incomes are devoted entirely to their efforts to advance in the white man's world.[7]

Aboriginal participation in the inter-ethnic political field has helped to sustain the illusion that voluntary organizations and the like represent legitimate Aboriginal political bodies acting on behalf of the entire local Aboriginal population. A facade of political participation and advancement is thus supported, allowing whites to maintain control over Aboriginal politics. For Nyoongahs, this represents a net political and economic loss, since they are no longer seen by others to be subject to discrimination.

Brokerage and Underdevelopment

The above analysis has demonstrated that patronage and brokerage play a vital role in maintaining the low socio-political status of south-western Aborigines. This perspective is not shared by most whites involved in Aboriginal affairs; understandably, they do not want to see themselves as agents of Aboriginal repression. Their views are more in accordance with ideas found in much of the traditional literature on development, which portray middlemen or brokers as agents of desirable change. This perspective has recently been criticized by a few authors, who have found that brokers often serve to promote underdevelopment rather than economic and political progress. Long (1975, pp. 273-74) has suggested that studies of patronage and brokerage are of considerable importance in refining macro-level theories of underdevelopment, since they provide insights about the "on the ground" dynamics of exploitation and domination. So far, however, there are relatively few studies that focus upon this aspect of brokerage (see Salzman 1974; Galt 1974; Gonzalez 1972; Guasti 1977).

The actor orientation and underlying narrow functionalist perspective of many brokerage studies has led to their stressing the reciprocal nature of relations between brokers and their patrons or clients, while ignoring the implications of brokerage in regard to power differences between the respective social groups. As has been shown with Aboriginal brokers, particular actors may gain from patron-client interchanges, and reciprocity may be a significant feature at the level of dyadic exchange, but for most members of the less powerful unit, the activities of such persons can be far from beneficial. As the present study has demonstrated, and as Wolf (1956, p. 1076) and Adams (1975, pp. 51-52) have pointed out, brokers tend to represent the interests of the more powerful.

Clearly, brokerage must be viewed as affecting and as being affected by power relations between groups, and no study of middlemen or brokers can ignore this aspect of social life. The importance of this may be seen, for example, in regard to the broker's role in bridging gaps between groups. At one level it is important to determine whether or not brokerage activities favour closing or maintaining gaps; it is apparent that this is affected by the nature of power relations between groups and by the broker's desire to maximize his own position (see Paine 1974, p. 26). At another level (and this is easily the most critical part of any analysis of brokerage), there is the question of how the broker's activities influence relations between groups in broad social, economic, and political terms. In the case of dominated peoples, this requires attention to their mode of incorporation into the encompassing structure of control. Maintaining gaps can be an important defensive mechanism for societies attempting to halt further external encroachment (see Nash 1971; Howard 1976a). Under such circumstances, brokers whose activities maintain gaps may be of value to the society. Unfortunately, it is not always a simple matter to determine the net effect of these actions. In the case of south-western

Aborigines, it could be argued that Aboriginal brokers, by fostering an illusion of integration, are assisting the Nyoongah by helping to limit direct government control of Aborigines. It must also be recognized, however, that their activities impede any real political development for Aborigines, and from this perspective it is difficult to see their existence as beneficial to the Nyoongah.

Notes

1. Traditional south-western Aboriginal society is discussed at length in Howard 1976*b* (see also Howard 1979). Many of the situations presented in this chapter are examined at greater length in Howard 1975.
2. Education for Aborigines at higher levels may in fact further Aboriginal underdevelopment. For example, a programme established for Aboriginal students at one tertiary institution in Perth channels them into being trained as welfare workers instead of in some area which might help to improve the Aboriginal condition. In fact, this is the only major programme of higher education available to Aborigines in the state.
3. Biographical treatment of individual Aboriginal broker/leaders is provided in Howard 1975.
4. There were six Aborigines working in the head office of the Aboriginal department in Perth in 1973: less than one-fifth of the total number of persons employed there.
5. Such a conversion would not necessarily lead to an improved status for most Aborigines. In all likelihood it would simply mean replacing the whites who are now in dominant positions with Aborigines, with little change in the basic structure. It would, of course, enhance the legitimacy of the structure.
6. This situation raises an issue concerning the nature of brokerage which is not adequately treated in the literature, but which is of relevance to the basic definitional question, concerning the materials used in building analytical constructs or models. In particular, it points to the need to distinguish brokerage as an ideological construct of the ethnologist from brokerage as an ideological construct of the actor; and brokerage as ideology from brokerage as praxis.
7. In some ways this development parallels the process of "internationalization" discussed by Cardoso and Faletto (1970) and Sunkel (1971) in regard to current patterns of external control of the Latin American economy. Cardoso's concept of "dependent development" (Cardoso 1977*a*, 1977*b*) is also of relevance in the present context, particularly his discussion of the role of elites. This aspect of Aboriginal underdevelopment will be explored at length in a forthcoming paper.

References

Adams, Richard N. 1975. *Energy and Structure.* Austin: University of Texas Press.
Biskup, Peter. 1973. *Not Slaves Not Citizens: The Aboriginal Problem in Western Australia 1898–1954.* Brisbane. University of Queensland Press.

Boissevain, Jeremy. 1974. *Friends of Friends: Networks, Manipulators and Coalitions.* Oxford: Blackwell.

Cardoso, Fernando H. 1977*a*. Current Theses on Latin American Development and Dependency: A Critique. *Boletin de Estudios Latinoamericanos y del Caribe* 22: 53–64.

————. 1977*b*. The Consumption of Dependency Theory in the United States. *Latin American Research Review* 12, no. 3: 7–24.

Cardoso, Fernando H., and Enzo Faletto. 1970. *Dependencia y desarrollo en America Latina.* Mexico City: Siglo Veintiuno Editores, S.A.

Frank, Andre Gunder. 1967. *Capitalism and Underdevelopment in Latin America.* New York: Monthly Review Press.

Galt, Anthony. 1974. Rethinking Patron-Client Relationships. *Anthropological Quarterly* 47: 182–201.

Gonzalez, Nancie L. 1972. Patron-Client Relationships at the International Level. In *Structure and Process in Latin America,* ed. Arnold Strickon and Sidney Greenfield. Albuquerque: University of New Mexico Press.

Guasti, Laura. 1977. Peru: Clientism and Internal Control. In *Friends, Followers and Factions,* ed. Steffen W. Schmidt et al. Berkeley: University of California Press.

Hasluck, Paul. 1942. *Black Australians: A Survey of Native Policy in Western Australia, 1829–1897.* Melbourne: Melbourne University Press.

Howard, Michael C. 1975. Nyoongah Politics: Aboriginal Politics in the South-West of Western Australia. Ph.D. dissertation, University of Western Australia.

————. 1976*a*. Review of *Koro: Economic Development and Social Change in Fiji,* by R. F. Watters. *Anthropological Forum* 4, no. 1: 116–17.

————. 1976*b*. Aboriginal Ethnography in the Southwest of Australia. MS.

————. 1977. Aboriginal Political Change in an Urban Setting: The N.A.C.C. Election in Perth. In *Aboriginal Change,* ed. Ronald M. Berndt. Canberra: Australian Institute of Aboriginal Studies.

————. 1978. Aboriginal "Leadership" in the Southwest of Western Australia. In *"Whitefella Business": Aborigines in Australian Politics,* ed. Michael C. Howard. Philadelphia: Institute for the Study of Human Issues.

————. 1979. Aboriginal Society in Southwestern Australia. In *Aborigines in the West,* ed. Ronald M. Berndt. Nedlands: University of Western Australia Press.

————. 1980. Migration and Inequality: The Sociocultural Significance of Aboriginal Internment in Southwestern Native Settlements. *Anthropological Forum* 4, nos. 3–4: 292–307.

Kuper, Adam. 1971. Council Structure and Decision-making. In *Councils in Action,* ed. A. Richards and Adam Kuper. Cambridge: Cambridge University Press.

Long, Norman. 1975. Structural Dependency, Modes of Production and Economic Brokerage in Rural Peru. In *Beyond the Sociology of Development,* ed. Ivar Oxaal et al. London: Routledge and Kegan Paul.

Makin, C. F. 1970. A Socio-Economic Anthropological Survey of People of Aboriginal Descent in the Metropolitan Region of Perth, Western Australia. Ph.D. dissertation, University of Western Australia.

McKeich, Robert. 1971. Problems of Part-Aboriginal Education with Special Reference to the South-West Region of Western Australia. Ph.D. dissertation, University of Western Australia.

Nash, Manning. 1971. The Impact of Mid-Nineteenth Century and Economic Change upon the Indians of Middle America. In *Race and Class in Latin America,* ed. Magnus Mörner. New York: Columbia University Press.

Paine, Robert. 1974. *Second Thoughts about Barth's Models.* London: Royal Anthropological Institute.

Rowley, Charles. 1970. *Outcasts in White Australia.* Canberra: Australian National University Press.

Salzman, Philip C. 1974. Tribal Chiefs as Middlemen: The Politics of Encapsulation in the Middle East. *Anthropological Quarterly* 47: 203–10.

Sunkel, O. 1971. Capitalismo transnacional y desintegracion nacional. *El Trimestre Economico,* April–June.

Wilson, John. 1958. Cooraradale. B.A. (Hons.) thesis, University of Western Australia.

Wolf, Eric. 1956. Aspects of Group Relations in Complex Societies. *American Anthropologist* 58: 1065–78.

Zaldivar, Ramon. 1974. Agrarian Reform and Military Reformism in Peru. In *Agrarian Reform and Agrarian Reformism,* ed. David Lehmann. London: Faber.

Aboriginal Power and Self-Determination in Adelaide

JAMES C. PIERSON

The history of the discriminatory treatment of Australian Aborigines is well documented, as are numerous problems and prejudices confronting many members of the Aboriginal population.[1] One recent study contends that most contemporary Aborigines are disadvantaged in almost all areas of life, indicating a need for comprehensive changes in Aboriginal opportunities and relevant governmental policies (Broom and Jones 1973). The general status of Aborigines is also indicated by the absence of attention to them in volumes devoted to discussions of "class, status and power in Australia" (Encel 1970), "opportunity and attainment in Australia" (Broom and Jones 1977), and "power and hegemony in Australian life" (Connell 1977) except to note their general exclusion from the areas under consideration. Yet a national Australian public opinion poll conducted in 1974 projects from its sample that 19 per cent of the population over sixteen years of age consider that Aborigines suffer "not at all" from "unjust treatment" (McNair 1975, p. 75). The fact that 78 per cent of the population consider that Aborigines suffer from such treatment either "a little" or "a lot" is noteworthy (3 per cent had no opinion), but its importance diminishes in light of the consideration that almost one-fifth of the population do not perceive any particular problems in Aboriginal treatment and opportunities.

The bases of such attitudes may be a lack of knowledge of the living conditions of many Aborigines, a backlash against recent governmental expenditures for Aborigines (Pittock 1975), or simply apathy. Whichever, since the attitudes and awareness within the general population play important roles in the lives and opportunities of members of any minority group, the figures indicate that the contemporary situations of Aborigines require considerable change if they are to attain any sort of equality.

Equality for minority groups in contemporary complex societies is often discussed within the context of "power", referring to the extent to which members of a particular group have access to the social, educational, economic, political, and other socio-cultural opportunities available to other groups within the larger society. Power, in this context, also refers to the opportunities of the former to make and put into effect decisions that govern their daily lives and futures. A consideration of the potential for "Aboriginal power" is therefore important to an understanding of the contemporary situations and futures of Aborigines throughout Australia. This paper examines these topics in a specific time and place by presenting what is essentially a historical perspective with an emphasis on a relatively recent period (the late 1960s and early 1970s) in Adelaide.

The paper focuses generally on the individual aspirations, various group goals, adaptations, and potentials of Aborigines in Adelaide in the early 1970s. The ethnographic data on which it is based was obtained between September 1969 and February 1971. This time is one of particular importance in the development of Aboriginal "power", or at least movements seeking it, at the national level as well as in Adelaide and the rest of South Australia.

Between one-fourth and one-third of the Aborigines in South Australia live in the Adelaide area. Despite general exclusion from many opportunities within the larger society, these "urban Aborigines" remain closer in physical, economic, and socio-cultural terms to power, influence, and participation in the institutions of the larger society than do Aborigines in other parts of the state. A specific focus of the paper is therefore on the political, economic, and social opportunities and adaptations among these urban Aborigines. These adaptations and the current situations of urban Aborigines are the results of the history of Aboriginal-white contact and the treatment of Aborigines by governmental policies, agencies, and representatives. The general perspective, therefore, also includes some reference to situations in other parts of South Australia; in many ways, the opportunities and activities of the urban residents affect the lives of Aborigines in the rest of the state.

A recent discussion of potentially fruitful foci for urban anthropological research gives considerable importance to the examination of "adaptive strategies" in the attempts of "ethnic, racial, or other populations to achieve power, security, or status within specific cities" (Fox 1977, p. 158). This statement suggests the importance of an examination of the contextual setting in an analysis of a group's urban adaptations; it also implies that such adaptations and the mechanisms developed to achieve them are significant components of real and potential ethnic group power and self-determination. The following discussion is organized around a similar viewpoint, giving attention to historical and socio-cultural data in considering such strategies and their real and potential results for Aborigines in Adelaide.

Variations within the Aboriginal urban population are surveyed below to illustrate different attitudes, interests, backgrounds, and influence. Although the power being discussed refers to Aborigines as a group within the larger society, the differential influence of persons within the Aboriginal urban population is also considered. General developments within the larger society and Aboriginal adaptations to them are examined and analyzed below to suggest future possibilities and to explain past and contemporary situations. Political developments that often give the South Australian government a progressive reputation for its administration of "Aboriginal affairs", for example, are discussed to suggest their actual and potential contributions to Aboriginal independence and self-determination.

Ethnic pride and identity are being expanded and redefined within the Adelaide Aboriginal population (Pierson 1977a). It is the conclusion of several recent anthropological studies that such ethnicity plays a generally positive role or gives a competitive advantage in the adaptations of members of ethnic groups to new political, economic, and socio-cultural situations (such as an urban environment) or in achieving more self-determined and self-defined participation within a complex society (e.g., Cohen 1974; Despres 1975, Bennett 1975; De Vos and Romanucci-Ross 1975). The general and specific foci referred to above therefore incorporate a consideration of the positive and/or negative effects of such processes of ethnicity within the context of the development and potential of Aboriginal power in Adelaide and South Australia.

The ethnographic materials presented below consider Aboriginal ethnicity in such structural contexts as kinship, social networks, and voluntary associations as well as in the socio-cultural contexts in which these relationships may be relevant. The goal is to examine the contributions or, possibly, the barriers expanding ethnicity may create for Adelaide Aborigines in their attempts to gain access to social, political, economic, and educational advantages within the larger society. If such increased participation is accomplished at the expense of certain relationships *within* the Aboriginal social community, it should be considered that the gains may not outweigh the costs.

Aboriginal Backgrounds

Aborigines comprise a small percentage of the Adelaide population, as do Aborigines in Australia generally. Even the most liberal estimates place persons of Aboriginal descent at less than 1 per cent of the total population of Australia; the most reliable estimates for South Australia

— approximately ten thousand Aborigines (Gale 1967, p. 28) compared with a population of 1,091,875, exclusive of "full-blooded Aboriginals", in 1966 (Commonwealth Bureau of Census and Statistics, South Australian Office 1969, p. 100) — are roughly the same. The *Adelaide* Aboriginal population in the early 1970s, however, was between two thousand and three thousand people (Gale 1972; Pierson 1972),[2] making Aborigines less than half of 1 per cent of the total urban population (based on figures from Commonwealth Bureau of Census and Statistics 1972, p. 135). The concomitant lack of Aboriginal influence in political matters is compounded by residential patterns in the Adelaide area. As a small population with a low frequency of registered and participating voters, Adelaide Aborigines attract little attention from state or national politicians; the scattered locations of Aboriginal households, resulting from conscious governmental attempts to avoid concentrations as well as actual availability, give Aborigines no influence as a voting bloc even in local elections.[3]

The minority status of Adelaide Aborigines is also generally explicit in economic, social, and educational situations and opportunities (Pierson 1972). Aboriginal participation in certain institutions of the larger society is primarily negative. Adelaide Aborigines, for example, tend to be arrested and prosecuted at a much higher rate than their numbers and behaviour warrant. Their experiences during arrest and trial are frequently different from those of non-Aborigines in similar situations and often lead to gaol sentences because of a lack of adequate representation (Pierson 1972; Eggleston 1976). Even when certain opportunities do arise, such as financial assistance to attend secondary or tertiary schools, earlier experiences and general pessimism about the eventual results of an investment of considerable time and effort tend to make them readily accessible to very few people. Few examples of Aboriginal successes in European educational and economic terms exist for the local Aboriginal community, and many of the successes that have occurred have been achieved at the expense of the person's close ties within the Aboriginal community. Gale (1972) in fact suggests that Aborigines reared and educated apart from their Aboriginal families and social networks are more likely than other Aborigines in Adelaide to have opportunities in the larger society. Criticisms of this conclusion (e.g., Ryan 1973) ignore the fact that Gale is not suggesting that this should continue; she is simply observing that institutionally reared Aborigines in Adelaide have access to educational and subsequent employment opportunities that most other Aborigines do not. The costs, as Ryan suggests, are immense in terms of personal trauma and socio-cultural identity and interaction. The "power" achieved by a few individuals in such situations, in other words, is often achieved (without original choice or assent in almost every case) at considerable social expense and almost entirely within white terms, conditions, and decisions.

The situations of most other Adelaide Aborigines are quite varied; it is therefore useful to consider briefly the general composition and backgrounds of the local Aboriginal population. Some older Aborigines have lived in Adelaide for more than three decades; most of their children have never lived outside the city for any extended time. Most other adults, however, have become permanent Adelaide residents since the end of the Second World War, particularly within the past two decades. Aborigines have moved to Adelaide from several different general areas, but two near-by government reserves (each about 160 kilometres from the city) account for as many as half of the Aborigines in the city (Gale 1964, 1972). Rural reserve settlements near the coastal areas of the western port of the state account for additional urban residents, and the isolated interior regions of the state have contributed some individuals and families. The Northern Territory is the only other notable source of direct or indirect origin, and many of these people have come for special reasons, including educational training, medical treatment, and legal proceedings such as imprisonment and removal from families as wards of the state. Only a small percentage of the Northern Territory residents remain in Adelaide permanently, but many of those who have done so occupy special positions (as institutionally reared people) within the local Aboriginal social community.

Differences in background are recognized within the population and are significant in certain contexts of personal and organizational interactions. Since the Aboriginal population is dispersed with only general concentrations in the urban area, these relationships become important in defining the nature of the structure and organization of the ethnic community. The differences tend to emphasize not only the background but also the distance an urban resident is from his or her close kin. It should be emphasized, however, that these distinctions are made on the basis of general area of origin, such as a specific reserve, rather than on the basis of distinct traditional cultural characteristics or specific tribal membership. Adelaide Aborigines throughout the past several decades have manifested no cultural characteristics that descend directly from a specific traditional culture (Inglis 1961; Gale 1964; Pierson 1972). Persons whose origins link them directly to near-by reserves have never had extensive contact with any elements of traditional culture — even language — because missionization (the reserves originated as missions in the past century) brought together members of different tribal and language groupings and effectively eliminated separate traditional cultural components several decades ago. Persons from more distant reserve or rural areas in South Australia may have experienced certain features of a traditional culture, but time and space preclude any real continuity. The same is true for former Northern Territory residents, a number of whom were removed as children from tribal situations and never returned.[4]

In effect, these different origins aid in the definition of one's relationships to kinsmen and the extent of interaction with them. Kin relationships are important resources among Adelaide Aborigines, although most people are unaware of traditional kin categories or their significance. The idiom of kinship, in fact, can generally be viewed as one of the few resource bases available to *most* urban Aborigines in a system in which Aborigines are denied many of the opportunities available to non-Aborigines. For persons from the near-by reserve areas, generations of common existence on the reserve and continuing contact with some relatives and other reserve residents made close ties possible and functional. Kin relationships remain important to Aborigines from other areas as well. An individual's emphasis on kin ties may be, in fact, much greater than appears to be geographically feasible. Both spatially near and spatially distant kinsmen can provide an individual with significant adaptive advantages in the city. Some advantages are material ones, such as accommodation and food; others are social or psychological.

The kinsmen of some Aborigines are in the city or comparatively near by and can be relied upon for direct material assistance. The kinsmen can be regarded as continuing social contacts which occasionally become economically important. Other persons' kinsmen are geographically distant, but they may still provide emotional and psychological support. Personal characteristics and opportunities and the development of relationships with other Aborigines in the city may lessen the need for reliance on any of these resources for some Aborigines, but the *ties* nevertheless remain important within the context of the urban area.

Contextual Background: Adelaide and South Australia

Adelaide is important in a number of ways. It is the political and administrative centre for the entire state and population of South Australia and is also the administrative centre for the educational system of the Northern Territory. South Australia's and central Australia's only universities and teachers' colleges are in the Adelaide area. Adelaide serves the same area as an industrial and commercial centre, with major appliance and automobile manufacturers supplying the rest of the continent as well. Near-by agricultural and garden regions produce fruits and vegetables, and the major wine producing area in Australia is only eighty kilometres from the city. Grain crops are grown in outlying areas. Its coastal location makes Adelaide a fishing base and port city as well, establishing direct links to other parts of coastal Australia and the rest of the world. Even the sheep and cattle station owners of the distant outback of the state usually depend on Adelaide and its contacts as a market place.

Considering these and other resources, it is not surprising that the general population of Adelaide increased from 728,279 in 1966 to 809,466 in 1971 (Commonwealth Bureau of Census and Statistics 1972, p. 135). The Aborigines who migrate to Adelaide regularly cite perceived opportunities in one or more of these areas, in addition to social and leisure-time activities, as crucial factors in the decision to move to the city (Gale 1972; Pierson 1972). The opportunities, nevertheless, are rarely readily accessible to an Aborigine. The most important reasons lie not simply in the urban situation, but also in certain historical, political, and economic characteristics and barriers at the state level. A major variable in this sense is the state government unit responsible for the administration of "Aboriginal affairs". This unit, the Department of Aboriginal Affairs, was amalgamated with the Department of Social Welfare in mid-1970 for "bureaucratic reasons". The amalgamation was, in part, a recognition that a significant proportion of the Aboriginal population of the state no longer lives in rural or reserve areas and that social services should be available to these people as well. The unit, whether separate or part of a larger bureaucracy, is the manifestation at any given time of the state's attempts to fulfil the national government's directive decades ago to provide for the "assimilation" of Aborigines into the general Australian way of life. The South Australian responses over the years may be considered protective and necessary by departmental officials, but they have also tended to be restrictive and discriminatory in many cases, as will be indicated below.

South Australian Laws Affecting Aboriginal Self–Determination

Policies affecting South Australian Aborigines have changed numerous times during the past half-century. A major change occurred when the state introduced an Aboriginal Affairs Act in 1962 to repeal the existing Aborigines Act of 1934 and 1939. The Department of Aboriginal Affairs was established by the new act to carry out its directives; it is now part of a larger department but has a separate staff. This unit is responsible for administering the educational, housing, health, and general welfare needs of the state's Aboriginal population. Its organization, however, generally limits assistance to rural Aborigines, especially those on the eight government reserves, the three missions operated by church organizations under agreements with the department, or in rural welfare districts.

The new act in 1962 did introduce some significant changes, such as easing restrictions against selling alcoholic beverages to Aborigines in selected areas of the state. The South Australian Licensing Act, 1932 and 1960, outlawed the sale of liquor to an Aborigine without a card issued by the old Aborigines' Protection Board, the predecessor to the Department of Aboriginal Affairs, to "reliable" Aborigines certifying his or her exemption from such prohibitions. The new act eliminates the necessity of a card for identification as an "exempt Aborigine" and also eases some other restrictions regarding Aborigines and alcohol. It is nevertheless considered necessary by the government to retain many other restrictions. It remains an offence, for example, to supply alcohol to "Aborigines or persons with Aboriginal blood" in certain areas, generally on or near reserves and missions. A prohibition also remains against the possession of liquor on reserves and missions by any Aborigine. These regulations have been eased somewhat, unofficially, but few attempts have been made to east restrictions *on* an Aboriginal settlement.[5]

Other discriminatory regulations also were removed as a result of the Aboriginal Affairs Act of 1962, including one that outlawed "consorting" between whites and Aborigines (i.e., usually interpreted as being with an Aborigine in a public place). The new act thus eliminated or altered some laws, but it also established a "permit system" that requires most individuals to possess a permit issued by the director of the Department of Aboriginal Affairs for admission to an Aboriginal reserve.[6] The system may have been intended primarily to keep "undesirables" off of isolated reserves, but it can also legally limit the freedom of persons of Aboriginal descent to visit friends or relatives on reserves. An amendment to the new act in 1967 provided for the formation of reserve councils with Aboriginal membership, and these are usually able to grant permission for short visits. On some reserves, especially those closest to Adelaide, these councils are also allowed some range in governing other daily reserve activities.

Before the "amalgamation", the Department of Aboriginal Affairs was headed by a director appointed by the state governor on the advice of the state parliament. (The amalgamation essentially created another administrative position above the director to supervise both units.) There was also a ministry for Aboriginal Affairs (now part of the ministry of Community Welfare) in the cabinet of the state premier, with varying emphases placed on the position according to the attitudes and priorities of the current premier. The minister's duties include the management of reserves and the general supervision of Aboriginal welfare in the state. In these matters, the director and staff of the Department of Aboriginal Affairs are both the minister's advisers and his delegates for action. The minister's position is important, however, because he controls the government's expenditures for Aboriginal Affairs.

The Aboriginal Affairs Act also created an Aboriginal Affairs Board to "advise" the minister on the operation of the act and the general welfare of Aborigines in the state. The board includes a chairman and six members appointed by the chairman on the recommendation of the minister. Until late 1970 the board traditionally included three white members, supposedly possessing some useful expertise, and three Aboriginal members. In 1970 a fourth Aboriginal member was appointed to replace a resigning white, which finally created an Aboriginal majority. Previous white members have been persons with a professed interest in Aboriginal affairs, such as religious officials, but most have had little personal contact with a large number of Aborigines. Few Adelaide Aborigines in 1970 had heard of, much less met, the white board members.

The significance of these bureaucratic acts, agencies, and positions is that they influence and set limits on Aboriginal opportunities throughout the state. In all of their forms and activities, they have included, encouraged, or precipitated little Aboriginal influence. Appointments to the Aboriginal Affairs Board do allow the presentation of Aboriginal viewpoints and opinions, but specific items introduced for discussion by Aboriginal members are not always fully examined. When this happens to matters other Aborigines have requested the Aboriginal board members to consider, the latter are often accused of inactivity and lack of support for "their people", even though the situation is generally beyond their control. The result is often further frustration rather than Aboriginal input and influence.

Growing Aboriginal dissatisfaction with such matters and concern about the significance of the impending amalgamation led to a special meeting in Adelaide in early 1970 at which departmental representatives were reportedly going to advise local Aborigines on the functions and future plans of the department. The meeting actually provided little information beyond a summary of programmes that most of the people present were already well aware of. The meeting nevertheless indicated that the local bureaucrats were paying at least some attention to the protests of urban Aborigines, many of whom were actually only indirectly affected by the programmes that were discussed. The distribution of a lengthy statement from the director (who was not present) also clearly indicated the unit's main concerns. In a similar but more concise statement, the director had previously contended that the department's actions were based on acts of parliament, which therefore made it necessary to examine the state laws relating to the Aboriginal population to "understand" departmental policies. He listed four relevant areas of law:

1. The rights of Aborigines to recognition of their original ownership of the land. This is recognized through the Aboriginal Lands Trust Act;
2. The need to preserve historical records of Aboriginal man in South Australia, recorded in carvings and paintings on wood and stone and in other ways. This is recognized through the Preservation of Aboriginal and Historical Relics Act;
3. The need of Aborigines to receive guidance as they seek to adapt to the modern world, to receive assistance to develop either within their own communities or as part of the general Australian community. This assistance includes matters of health, education, employment and housing. This is provided through the Aboriginal Affairs Act;
4. The right of persons of all races to full citizenship and equality of treatment within the Australian community. The Prohibition of Discrimination Act protects this right. [Miller 1969, p. 13]

These areas of law are significant both to an understanding of departmental policies and to a consideration of the effects of these policies on Aboriginal rights and opportunities. Since the South Australian government was the first political unit in Australia to enact land rights or anti-discrimination bills specifically concerning Aborigines, the two relevant acts *and* their administration are particularly important in discussing real and potential Aboriginal rights and self-determination in the state. The Aboriginal Affairs Act, as discussed above, constantly affects Aborigines throughout the state in many ways. The Aboriginal and Historical Relics Act can be particularly important in publicly recognizing the importance of Aboriginal origins and identity; it thus has special symbolic significance for both Aborigines and whites. Because of these and other points, it is instructive to consider each area briefly, in order to examine the extent to which programmes in each area have contributed to or affected the growth of Aboriginal power and influence in both the state and the urban area.

Land Rights and Anti-Discrimination

The legislative acts respectively granting restricted Aboriginal land rights and prohibiting discrimination in public places are most profitably viewed in the same context because they resulted from the same governmental ideals. The Prohibition of Discrimination Act of 1966, which made it a punishable offence to refuse service or goods to persons on the basis of race, is phrased so generally that prosecutions are difficult. Whether or not it has been effective in expanding Aboriginal participation in public places is doubtful, even in the urban area. Its main effects are probably primarily symbolic ones as an attempt at the state level to legislate behavioural changes to promote Aboriginal social equality (Gale 1972, p. 66). It is, of course, very difficult to prove that services are delayed or refused "because" of race when other reasons, such as alleged inebriation or improper attire, can be stated. Such discriminatory acts therefore continued in the urban area long after the act was passed. Despite numerous discriminatory experiences and several complaints by both urban residents and visitors to the state attorney-general, only one case in the entire state had been brought to trial five years after the bill took effect.[7]

In addition to the Prohibition of Discrimination Act, the legislation that gives South Australia a positive reputation for recognizing Aboriginal rights is the Aboriginal Lands Trust Act of 1966. Land rights are often described as a major issue confronting Aboriginal Australia (e.g., Stevens 1970; Broom and Jones 1973), but most governmental and public attention to them has come within the past decade. The usual implication of such attention is that the recognition of land rights by whites and the state and Commonwealth governments will create Aboriginal economic independence, develop opportunities in rural areas, and precipitate changes that will be administered by the Aborigines themselves. When many Aborigines discuss land rights, however, they are referring to more than acquisition of existing reserves for development through further government planning. The quest for Aboriginal land rights includes a demand for the recognition that all of Australia was taken illegally from the original Australians by alien whites. Adequate recognition of land rights is considered by these Aborigines to include both monetry compensation and receipt of land and mineral rights.

The concept of the Lands Trust was formulated by a state Labor government in response to some of these points. Preliminary plans called for the establishment of mineral and oil rights on reserve lands in the form of a trust for Aborigines, although these rights on all land are legally established in the Crown. The attempt to establish these rights in trust ended when it was realized that the previous Liberal government had already made agreements with private companies for such rights on many reserve lands. The Lands Trust Act was still passed in a diluted form only by overcoming great parliamentary opposition. As it was finally passed, the act established a board with exclusively Aboriginal membership that can *recommend* that the government place certain reserve lands in trust for "the benefit of Aborigines". The eligible lands include unoccupied reserve lands, new areas made available by the state or Commonwealth, and occupied reserves offered to the Lands Trust through the action of the local Aboriginal Reserve Council. Action can then be taken only as a result of the recommendation of both houses of parliament. A lack of working capital presents another major problem to the Lands Trust, because financial assistance is available only through the same governmental channels.

The board established by the Lands Trust Act provides for as many as twelve members, all of whom must be of Aboriginal descent. Three members were selected at the inception of the trust; representatives of any occupied reserves taken into the trust will be added as land is acquired. The director of the Department of Aboriginal Affairs is named by the act to serve the trust as secretary.

The first acquisitions by the trust were unoccupied reserve lands, most of which seem to have little potential for economic development. The people and reserve council of one of the reserves near Adelaide joined with the trust board in November 1969 to request that the reserve land be invested in the trust. It was considered that this action may eventually provide aid, employment, and land development beneficial to current and future reserve residents. In mid-1970 the Lands Trust Board announced the beginning of a study by a management consultant firm to attempt to establish the most efficient methods of achieving such goals. It was announced earlier by the state governor, however, that a white man had been appointed as manager of the trust. The early lack of finances and the absence of communication between the manager and both governmental officials and the Aboriginal members of the board created immediate barriers. A general factionalism within the Adelaide Aboriginal community at the organizational level also made the trust a frequent target for criticism, because only one of the two local all-Aboriginal groups had a member on the original board.

The South Australian Lands Trust is important, nevertheless, because it does provide a legal mechanism for the eventual acquisition of land and associated rights. It did so before the issue became a topic of national, political, and public attention, largely as a result of the influence of the Labor Party premier and considerable work by local Aboriginal groups and some white sympathizers. It did not, however, immediately provide any lands other than the unused reserves areas. In effect, the much-heralded acquisition of "land rights" by South Australian Aborigines was slow to yield tangible (i.e., other than symbolic) results. In mid-1978, however, the premier announced plans to *guarantee* land and mining rights, including all access decisions, over 160,000 square kilometres of land in the north-west of the state to the area's Aboriginal population (Australian Information Service 1978, p. 3). Regardless of any anticipated mineral deposits, the rights themselves are unique in Australia, giving the Aborigines "more power than any other Aboriginal group in the country" (ibid.).

The South Australian government also passed the anti-discrimination bill before such issues became "popular" ones. The lack of prosecutions, the original problems with the Lands Trust Board, and the questionable utility of the unused reserve lands should not detract from the significant potential of these developments. Gale accurately points out that these acts, and possibly a few others, "attempted to encourage changes in policy rather than merely following what was already operating in practice" as had been done previously (Gale 1972, p. 66). Such changes may not have immediate social and economic effects, but they will likely bring longer lasting and more effective ones.

The Aboriginal Affairs Act

The third legislative act referred to in the director's statement is the Aboriginal Affairs Act, which has already been briefly discussed. In its provisions for the maintenance of Aboriginal "health, education, employment and housing", the act has been relevant primarily in rural areas. The adequacies or inadequacies of the department's programmes are a continual source of controversy, but they will be considered only briefly and more or less indirectly here. What is most important in the context of this paper is that Aborigines have had very little voice in the planning or operation of the department. In 1970, no Aborigines were employed by the department itself and only three were employed in related governmental positions. The only other potential Aboriginal input is through the Aboriginal Affairs Board, where the problems noted above often arise. A source of some optimism and also some original confusion within the Adelaide Aboriginal population was a survey of "Aboriginal opinion" begun in 1969. According to Fay Gale, whose earlier research indicated the need for such a survey, the general dissatisfaction with the existing "welfare structure" shown by the survey was a direct cause of the departmental amalgamation that occurred in 1970 (Gale 1972, p. 66).

The consideration of Aboriginal opinion is a positive step and may signal further Aboriginal contributions to important decisions. The general dissatisfaction indicated by the survey, however, is shown by several examples to be well founded. The facilities on most reserves, for example, have consistently been at best barely adequate. Even the reserves closest to Adelaide provide examples of the inadequate facilities for expanding populations. Significant population increases without expansion of facilities, in fact, may be seen as one of the major causes of Aboriginal migration to Adelaide from the two near-by reserves (Gale 1967, 1972; Pierson 1972, 1977a, 1977b). It becomes apparent in the urban setting that educational programmes in the reserve areas have been inadequate to enable most Aboriginal children to compete with children from other schools. This situation often causes the Aboriginal children to dislike school and leave it to seek employment as soon as possible. The available employment unfortunately is usually in unskilled and low-paid positions. The educational inadequacies of the reserve settings may therefore be seen as a direct barrier to potential Aboriginal opportunities, decreasing their choices for subsequent jobs, housing, and security.

Aborigines and Historical Relics

Public recognition of Aboriginal culture history may be primarily symbolic, but it is particularly important in a period in which Aboriginal ethnicity and pride are increasing as persons from a number of different backgrounds interact in the urban setting. The main manifestations of the relevant act in the late 1960s and early 1970s, however, seem also to symbolize that white Australians would be the final authorities in determining which aspects of the Aboriginal past to officially recognize as significant. A small but meaningful incident occurred in 1970, when one of the local Aboriginal organizations proposed the erection of a monyment on the west coast of the state to commemorate Aborigines killed by whites in a massacre in the late 1800s. The episode was briefly publicized when records of the event, which was part of a protracted dispute between white settlers and Aborigines, were uncovered. The Aboriginal group's proposal was criticized by several whites and one of the local newspapers which editorially suggested that it is better to forget the past and "make memorials to life, not death" (*Adelaide Advertiser*, 6 May 1970, p. 2). The fact that almost every Australian town has a war memorial to honour dead servicemen was not lost on local Aborigines, who considered themselves rebuked for suggesting something similar.

Aboriginal Adjustments: The Mechanisms for Aboriginal Power

The sections immediately above focus primarily on legal mechanisms that define Aboriginal opportunities and integration. Shortcomings or problems in each area have also been indicated, as has the demographic fact that as much as one-third of the state's Aboriginal population lives in the city, where many of the acts are superfluous or largely sumbolic. It is therefore important to consider the ways in which Adelaide Aborigines as a group, a series of groups (i.e., organizations), and individually are attempting to attain self-definition, self-determination, and some semblance of power.

A number of local Aborigines contend that they are "too busy to be bothered" with such issues as Aboriginal rights and power (Pierson 1972, p. 376). In effect, such statements imply that the individuals are too preoccupied with everyday attempts to cope with their lack of rights, opportunities, and power to be concerned with public declarations and demonstrations; they are simply more cognizant of personal survival than they are of the more abstract issues with which that survival might be correlated by an external analyst. The statements are also indicative of one of the major problems confronting any movement actively seeking Aboriginal self-determination and rights: there is no significant Aboriginal "middle-class" in Adelaide similar to the groups of "black business and profession men" in the urbanizing southern United States who were leaders and financial supporters of the movements during the early part of this century to overcome black oppression and attain participation in the institutions of the larger society (Brownell 1977, p. 140).[8] The opportunities for Aborigines to attain such positions are scarce, with Aboriginal business opportunities in the city almost non-existent.[9] In addition, some of the Aborigines who have been relatively successful in economic terms have few close ties with the general Aboriginal community. Financial support for the programmes in Adelaide thus depends on various organizational fund-raising projects or white sympathizers. The latter are an obvious source of potential conflict and problems within the population. Leaders and educationally and economically successful Aborigines with contacts in the Aboriginal community are not completely absent; certain situations often preclude their extensive influence, however, as is discussed below. The problems that remain for most urban residents in housing, education, employment, and social opportunities are being dealt with in a number of ways.

The question of what is occurring in Adelaide remains. The answer is a complex one which must focus on individuals, different types of individuals, and the informal and formal collections of people into groups and associations. At the individual level, people depend on the resources of close kin, close friends from the same rural background, and new acquaintances who are contacted in the social contexts readily available and accessible to an Aborigine in Adelaide. These contexts include the houses of kin or acquaintances, the two pubs in the Adelaide area that readily allow Aborigines to congregate, the weekend horse races, and the offices and numerous meetings and activities of various all-Aboriginal or "Aboriginally oriented" organizations. Most Aborigines in Adelaide, when they lack any basic resources, can usually depend on members of their social networks, which develop and expand in the urban area through a variety of contacts. For the most part, these contacts are concerned with basic adaptations and survival even when their primary functions are social ones. In certain respects, however, these relationships may also be the nucleus of formal inter-actions and activities that deal overtly with the abstractions mentioned above.

The category of "different types of individuals" used above refers primarily to persons from different backgrounds. Economic and/or educational success has been achieved by a number of Adelaide Abori-gines, for example, but it has frequently occurred at the expense of the peoples' relationships with most other Aborigines. Many early adult arrivals in the city found economic success and social acceptance by whites much more attainable if extended Aboriginal contacts were lessened or generally ignored. Some married whites and today may attempt to avoid identification with the general Aboriginal social community. This obviously affects their children's behaviour and contacts as well. The adults now between thirty and forty years of age who were reared in institutions in the urban area were generally denied contacts with Aborigines outside the institutions. Their current relationships with many local Aborigines still frequently reflect their "differences" and early isolation. Very importantly, however, almost all of these people are actively identifying with the Aboriginal com-munity and are attempting to overcome the problems their special backgrounds and statuses create within that community. A third category of people who have been economically successful also includes early arrivals in the city. These people are somewhat unique and sub-sequently few in number; several Aborigines have occupied permanent jobs with numerous promotions over several decades without ever losing contact with other local Aborigines. It is significant that the most obvious people in this category are not from near-by reserves; rather they are from rural cattle station backgrounds in the centre of the state. Their opportunities simply to learn skills and attain some self-confidence and experience in dealing with whites seem to have given them adaptive advantages over most persons from other backgrounds. Their relationships with other Aborigines in the urban setting have not suffered from their economic successes, as have those just mentioned, because the successes are seen as self-achieved ones and not the result of white contacts and influence.

In terms of opportunities and preoccupation with the abstractions of power, the most significant group of Aborigines consists primarily of the people who have been reared apart from their families. They, if they remain in Adelaide, have few if any Aboriginal kin in the area. In addition, they usually were reared in institutional homes, where it was mandatory to continue their educations far beyond the levels readily available to most other local Aborigines. They are therefore set apart in a number of ways from the general Aboriginal urban population. For these same reasons, they are usually the Aborigines considered most able and worthy by whites and are consulted, employed, discussed, and encouraged (and, in some cases, manipulated) by whites. Regardless of their own desires or goals, they are often seen by influential whites as "spokesmen" for the entire urban Aboriginal population. This attention is sometimes detrimental, because it creates another source of difference and antagonism with other Aborigines. In other cases it is potentially beneficial, because these people have the most direct access to "power", and the opportunity to share its benefits with other Aborigines often arises. The Adelaide Aboriginal community seems to be particularly unique in including a number of such people, almost all of whom attempt to use their positions in a positive way, regardless of the disagreements and disputes that may arise among them and with other Aborigines. People from this category have occupied influential positions in the state employment office and the national Office for Aboriginal Affairs. Some have also been appointed to the Lands Trust Board and the Aboriginal Affairs Board. Some people from other backgrounds also have obtained similar opportunities, largely through individual initiative or organizational membership or both. In all cases, however, a certain powerlessness is apparent, and criticism from other Aborigines is frequent. Yet financial, educational, employment, and housing programmes have begun to benefit some other Aborigines in the city and the rest of the state at least partly as a result of the presence of these people in important positions.

The context of white-dominated bureaucracies, however, inevitably limits the real power of an Aborigine regardless of his or her goals and background. The greatest potential for real Aboriginal self-determination at the present time therefore seems to be through Aboriginally controlled organizations that can function as both political and service groups, In Adelaide, such groups have influence and importance for both individual adaptations and group self-determination.

Aboriginal Associations and Aboriginal Self-Determination

Adelaide all-Aboriginal organizations have provided social services of particular adaptive significance (Pierson 1977b), as similar organizations have done in many other urban areas of the world (Anderson 1971; Gulick 1973; Kerri 1976). The organizations and their activities also provide important contexts of Aboriginal interaction and social network expansion. These Adelaide groups have been particularly effective in decreasing feelings of regional and personal differences, although such differences remain important in the complementary roles of the two major all-Aboriginal organizations in the city. The groups' effects go beyond such apparent roles, however; by providing access to jobs and information, the organizations lessen urban Aborigines' preoccupation with the basic requirements for survival and thus create a potential for the consideration of the more abstract causes and solutions of such problems. The educational functions of such groups, in fact, must be viewed as an important contribution to the more comprehensive Aboriginal exploitation of rights and opportunities among the services available within the larger society. Despite their urban bases, these organizations do not necessarily limit their programmes to the city. Near-by reserves are obviously affected to some extent, but the organizations are also effective as relatively large groups[10] in attracting public and political attention to issues concerning Aborigines throughout the state. These organizations have aided efforts to attract attention to the need for legislation on land rights and discrimination as well as to national constitutional referendums concerning Aborigines. The officials of the organizations are often consulted by governmental representatives and appointed to committees and boards dealing with rural issues.

This discussion and analysis of Aboriginal associations is not meant to suggest strict structural or functional similarities to ethnic associations in other urban areas of the world or even in other Australian cities. The generally positive adaptive roles of the Adelaide associations, however, are comparable to those in other urban situations analyzed

by anthropologists (cf. Anderson 1971; Gulick 1973; Kerri 1976).
It is important, nevertheless, that some analyses indicate a minimal
adaptive significance of ethnic-based voluntary associations in several
West African urban areas (Cohen 1969; Barnes and Peil 1977), a limited
if not limiting role of some organizations among blacks in Detroit
attempting to attain economic and political influence within the larger
society (Warren 1975), and generally little adaptive value attached to
voluntary associations in some situations (Kerri 1976). Negative interpretations of urban ethnic associations are in fact not new; Myrdal,
for example, long ago referred to ones among American blacks as
"pathological" reactions (Myrdal 1944; also cited in Warren 1975,
p. 70, Kerri 1977, p. 412). It is also possible that certain short-term
adaptive mechanisms, such as reliance on organizations like voluntary
associations or churches, may actually be adaptations to situations of
inferiority (cf. Mathews 1977 for a relevant discussion of "religion in
the Old South") rather than mechanisms of positive change.

Kerri, however, does discuss numerous important functions of
voluntary associations in many urban settings studied by anthropologists in both a cross-cultural review (Kerri 1976) and a discussion
of associations among blacks in United States cities (Kerrie 1977).
The latter emphasizes the importance of analyzing the associations
within their socio-cultural contexts (Kerri 1977, pp. 410–11, 416–17),
supporting Parkin's earlier suggestion that "we need to understand the
extent and nature of political functions performed by ethnic associations" in their respective settings (Parkin 1974, p. 144).

In effect, these studies and reviews collectively warn that the
presence of voluntary associations does not inevitably indicate that
they are important mechanisms of positive socio-cultural change.
Rather, they are responses to particular situations within both the
larger society and the smaller population unit and should be analyzed
as such. It is suggested, for example, that Aboriginal organizations in
Perth function more as a focal point of white attention and manipulation than as mechanisms of Aboriginal influence and self-determination
(Howard 1978a). Although white influence is by no means absent from
the Adelaide "all-Aboriginal" groups, the organizations seem to offer
considerable potential for and evidence of Aboriginal influence (Pierson
1977b), largely because of the ways in which the groups have evolved.

The Development of All-Aboriginal Groups in Adelaide

Groups concerned with some aspect of Aboriginal "progress" or
"advancement" or integration or possibly even power have proliferated

in Adelaide for almost five decades. Many have been short-lived, existing either for a very specific purpose or as a branch of another organization. Some white-dominated organizations persist even though they actually have very little direct contact with any Aborigines. A number of programmes have been initiated by other non-Aboriginal organizations for specific purposes, and some of these attempt to incorporate Aboriginal initiative. Organizations have appeared in recent years, for example, to provide Aborigines with legal advice and representation. The groups that are most important as indicators of Aboriginal attempts to achieve self-determination, however, are formally organized ones that limit voting and membership to persons of Aboriginal descent.

The origins of the Aborigines' Progress Association (APA) and the Council of Aboriginal Women of South Australia (CAWSA), the two all-Aboriginal groups that existed in Adelaide in the early 1970s, extend to an earlier group established and maintained by whites. This group, the Aborigines' Advancement League (AAL), originated in the 1930s and was the first significant group in Adelaide actually concerned with the human rights of Aborigines. Although obviously concerned with "Aboriginal advancement", the organization retained close ties over the course of time with governmental agencies. These ties and the general conservatism of the group created conflicts after Aborigines and a few activist whites became members in the late 1950s and early 1960s. The campaigns of these relatively new members for an all-Aboriginal community centre during 1963 and 1964 were repeatedly rejected by other members. Earlier suggestions of the desirability of an all-Aboriginal organization were pursued soon after, although some of the whites continued to pursue an active interest in the activities of the new group. In addition to the social functions carried out earlier by the "Aborigines' Activity Committee" of the original organization, the Aborigines Progress Association was established to contend with political influence, Aboriginal unification, and governmental and public actions affecting Aborigines. The membership grew to nearly fifty Aborigines, and scores more were affected by the group's programmes and activities. Within a few years, however, internal disputes developed over continuing white influence, financial affairs, and the specific nature of the programmes to be pursued. Accusations about the alleged disappearance of some money following a social function cemented a factionalism that resulted in 1968 in the formation of a second all-Aboriginal group (CAWSA), with membership limited to women. Not all of the women from the original group transferred to the new one, but there was a tendency for women from the near-by reserves to do so, especially if their affinal ties were also to local areas. In rare cases, a married couple was represented in the membership of both groups.

The APA continued its combination of social and political activities with occasional contributions of economic and social services. An attachment to a group concerned with Aboriginal education throughout the state and the sponsorship of an all-Aboriginal football club indicate the group's variety of concerns. A strong interest also remained in the establishment of an Aboriginal community centre. In effect, this group has consistently been seeking means and mechanisms to develop Aboriginal power, even if the phrase itself has been used only rarely and privately. Members of the organization generally avoided the use of the phrase in public in the late 1960s and early 1970s, as did Aborigines in most other parts of Australia, because of its connotations of violence for many white Australians (Pierson 1972, pp. 382–84). Nevertheless, APA members have consistently contended that Aborigines must work hard for such power, whatever its label, and that politically oriented activities are important preliminary steps.

CAWSA opened an office in central Adelaide soon after its formation to provide a variety of daily services, including basic advice on how to obtain assistance from governmental agencies. The obvious potential of the organization to reach urban residents not served by the government agencies led to some financial and other assistance from the Department of Aboriginal Affairs. Despite criticisms from non-members, this move was not necessarily a governmental attempt to control the organization; it was much more a recognition by the department of the contacts and efficiency of the group. Contributions from private sources created a degree of self-sufficiency and self-control that allowed the development of even more semblance of a truly all-Aboriginal organization, staffed and operated by and for Aborigines.

The two Adelaide organizations often seek the same general goals in different ways. It is in this respect that they remain largely complementary rather than competitive. The APA's continued interest in a community centre, for example, was never generally shared by CAWSA members. Yet in 1970, members of the two groups attempted to unite on a request to obtain state and national governmental financial assistance to establish such a centre in Adelaide. A demand for Aboriginal "unity" in such a request to indicate general interest and commitment was made by a governmental representative, and several meetings were held to indicate such unity. The eventual and tentative result was a preliminary office operated primarily by APA members, but also aided by the assistance and interest of CAWSA members and residents of the near-by reserves. These events began a slow but optimistic movement towards an Aboriginally controlled centre. The two groups and any factions originating from them will probably remain separate in most of their activities, but the centre movement seems to symbolize the increasing interest and involvement in more inclusive all-Aboriginal functions and institutions.

White influence, whether through individual manipulations or governmental resources and demands for unity, continues to affect the Adelaide organizations and many of their activities. Aboriginal organizations provide a visible target for non-Aborigines to pursue personal philosophies and interests, with the latter sometimes becoming vested. Similar situations at the national level in 1970, in fact, led to the separation of an all-Aboriginal splinter group from a national organization, which had long included both white and Aboriginal members. Yet it should be pointed out that groups limiting membership to persons of Aboriginal descent existed in Adelaide almost a decade before similar movements developed at the national level. In both cases, the first steps toward Aboriginal opportunities were attained with white assistance. Problems often arise when the whites, as individuals or members of an organization, are reluctant to give up their influence.[11]

Several events in Adelaide, such as the community centre movement, seem to indicate that such problems can be overcome. The Adelaide situation has slowly but definitely moved or evolved towards Aboriginal self-determination in areas such as the centre, while the resources and assistance of whites remain significant (frequently in a positive way) in others. Some whites fail to recognize that they are being subtly manipulated by the Aboriginal groups they believe they are "leading", because their vested interests keep them from effectively evaluating the situation.

Summary and Conclusion:
The Potential for Aboriginal Self-Determination

Factionalism, differences in philosophies and backgrounds, and internal disagreements play a role in defining the Aboriginal situation in Adelaide. The Aboriginal population, however, includes a significant number of people with the abilities, training, and contacts to exploit each opportunity. As such, a degree of real Aboriginal power seems to exist within the contexts of formal group activities as well as for certain individuals. The characteristics of Aboriginal ethnicity, ranging from informally expanded social networks to formal voluntary ethnic organizations, seem at least in the Adelaide area to increase positively the potential for Aboriginal power at both the individual and group levels.

This obviously does not mean that Aborigines in either South Australia or Adelaide itself have achieved full equality and self-determination within white Australian society. What the discussion above does seem to indicate, however, is that a number of factors have combined to provide the potential for such achievements, even if this has not yet been fulfilled to any great extent. The fact that Aboriginal power was even being discussed or considered in Adelaide and the rest of Australia in the late 1960s and early 1970s is itself significant. In some of the eastern states, where the phrase "Aboriginal power" was used more extensively than it was in Adelaide, the discussions may have been primarily the result of a diffusion of phrases and general rhetoric and goals from overseas. In Adelaide, however, it seems to have resulted from realistic considerations based on a number of historical and social factors (not the least of which are the relatively low profiles of many members of the local Aboriginal community).

Any Aboriginal power in Adelaide or South Australia will not be the result of large population figures and subsequent influence in political and economic matters. Rather it will be the result of specific characteristics and events within the Aboriginal social community and its urban and state contexts, a number of which have been discussed above. Whether one uses the phrase "Aboriginal power" or less impressive sounding ones such as "self-determination" or "self-definition", the discussion tends to imply an all-inclusive situation which incorporates all people and all situations. The circumstances of Aborigines in the context of Adelaide in the larger context of South Australia indicate that such generalizations are not appropriate, at least at the present time. A number of different components interact to provide considerable Aboriginal influence in certain situations, while such influence is only rudimentary or absent in others. In effect, there are both positive and negative factors affecting the acquisition of Aboriginal power and self-determination in Adelaide. Since such a general statement is similar to saying "yes and no" or "maybe" to some of the questions and considerations mentioned in the first part of this paper, salient points can be profitably reconsidered and summarized at this point.

First of all, Adelaide Aborigines (representative of Aborigines throughout the state) exist in historical, political, economic, and social contexts that define if not determine their access to basic resources and power. Reserve life, white domination, and limited opportunities characterize these contexts. Barriers to Aboriginal opportunities prevail, but some changes are indicated. Laws specifically concerned with Aborigines affect the past and often the present situations of the urban Aborigines and are obviously relevant to a consideration of Aboriginal self-determination. Some features of the general Aboriginal Affairs Act can be considered to be at least partly negatively discriminatory, although other parts of it are more positive than previous acts. Certain amendments are significant in creating or increasing Aboriginal influence in some decision-making processes. Other acts, while symbolically important, have been slow to precipitate real changes in behaviour. The Aboriginal Lands Trust Act, however, was an early step by the South Australian government to give at least some recognition to Aboriginal interests and began to take full effect in 1978. In several cases, the legislation gives further potential through legal mechanisms to Aboriginal self-determination in specific contexts.

Secondly, the lack of numerous basic resources and opportunities limits the interest of many Aborigines in the abstract consideration of Aboriginal power. A basic fact of life for Aborigines anywhere in South Australia is that, regardless of the legal chances begun in the late 1960s, it may take as long as one generation for any significant benefits to occur. The current generations of adults are often precluded from a number of economic opportunities because of the lack of educational and vocational training more than ten years ago. The search for and acquisition of adequate employment and other necessities of life in the city are the matters that preclude attention to such abstractions as Aboriginal rights and power. In many cases, it obviously becomes a vicious circle in which such "idealistic" matters are ignored because the lack of opportunities does not allow a significant number of people actually to seek additional ones. They are instead coping with the daily realities of the absence of such power. Nevertheless, their concerns for these realities are important components in eventually increasing Aboriginal self-determination. Numerous institutional mechanisms, for example, have developed or expanded in the urban setting to facilitate Aboriginal adaptations. Voluntary associations, the most inclusive of these, provide a direct link between overcoming the necessary preoccupation with the realities of scarce resources and attaining a realistic consideration of the abstractions of Aboriginal power by combining the diverse elements and characteristics of the Adelaide Aboriginal population. Despite problems with certain laws, the lack of application of other laws, lack of opportunity in many contexts, and paternalistic and manipulative whites, these organizations have evolved into effective institutions with numerous positive functions within the Aboriginal social community.

Thirdly, certain members of the Aboriginal population aid extensively in increasing the links between the Aboriginal community and the larger society. Although few in number and by no means constituting an Aboriginal "elite", these Aborigines have access to resources and contacts in the larger society that enable them to act effectively as "brokers" or "middle-men" for other members of the Aboriginal population. Many of these Aborigines' backgrounds preclude their full acceptance by all other members of the Aboriginal community, but they nevertheless retain an importance to Aborigines as a group if not to certain individuals. In effect, they have a sort of personal power that, combined with other factors, *may* eventually provide greater access to Aboriginal (i.e., group) power in the urban area.[12]

Fourth, both internal and external features of the local Aboriginal social community and their positive and negative effects must be considered in evaluating the potential for Aboriginal power and self-determination. In a negative sense, the contexts in which Aborigines have existed in the past have almost ensured a lack of opportunity in the present. The fears of some whites about "Aboriginal power" (based on their views of overseas situations) cause them to consider Aborigines who speak out on issues as "stirrers" or trouble-makers, and apathy often characterizes other whites' attitudes toward Aborigines. Factionalism and personality and background differences affect the internal unity of the local Aboriginal population, and white influence often increases these problems. Despite the generall disruptive actions of some whites, however, others have aided in less obtrusive ways. It is important that one such white was the premier of the state for most of the 1970s, including the time when the land rights and anti-discrimination acts were passed.

Finally, the diversity and complexity of the Adelaide situation should be apparent from the preceding discussion. Although Aboriginal power as a group characteristic remains only rudimentary, certain individuals do have access to numerous resources. The significant components of increasing power are contained within the state and the city and therefore seem independent of the success or failure of national Aboriginal rights movements despite some obvious relationships. From one perspective, however, it appears that the power is available to only a few individuals. Even for these few, the power, participation, and success often occur in situations that are defined and controlled by whites. Some contexts of Aboriginal influence appear superfluous, often dealing with situations far removed from the person's interests and experiences as an urban resident. From an alternative viewpoint that is based on a full consideration of all of the variables discussed above, it can be considered that the Aboriginal situation in Adelaide has slowly moved towards the acquisition of Aboriginal power in its most positive and constructive sense — participation in the larger society under conditions defined within the Aboriginal population with the decreasing influence of whites. The fact that even a few Aborigines have gained access to influence is positive as long as they retain ties within the Aboriginal social community.

It is in this context that increasing Aboriginal ethnicity seems to play one of its most important roles in Adelaide. Despite some sources of conflict, common feelings of being Aboriginal are tending to incorporate persons with a variety of resources to offer to the total Aboriginal urban population. Ethnicity as Aboriginal pride and its manifestations provides common points of interest and involvement even for most Aborigines who have had opportunities within the larger society. It creates a milieu for the interaction of these people with each other and with other Aborigines who can very profitably exploit such contacts and their subsequent resources. Some situations described above may strongly imply that intra-population factions and disputes preclude any beneficial effects from expanding Aboriginal ethnicity. Other evidence, however, indicates that differences in approach by the two formal organizations and differences in individual philosophies tend to function in complementary ways through various programmes which reach more people and subsequently expand the variety of resources and opportunities available to local Aborigines. Individuality and factionalism may be exploited by whites or even some Aborigines, but this exploitation is not necessarily one-sided. Some personal relationships become tenuous or expendable in the long term, but the resources still tend to benefit the Aboriginal population as a whole. Thus, by combining the contributions at the individual level from social networks and the social, economic, and political resources more readily accessible from the formal organizations, Aboriginal ethnicity in Adelaide seems to be playing primarily a positive role in achieving Aboriginal power and self-determination. The ethnicity subsequently focuses even more attention on considering and attaining what has been primarily abstract terminology. The realities rather than the consideration of abstractions remain the primary concern among Adelaide Aborigines, but optimism that Aboriginal self-determination will eventually become part of the reality does not seem unwarranted.

Acknowledgements

The research on which most of this paper is based was conducted during an eighteen-month period in 1969–71, and the data refer most specifically to that time period. The research was supported by National Institute of Health (NIMH) Research Training Fellowship 1 01 MH 43 743–02 (Cuan) and Research Training Grant 1 Tol 12046–01. I also wish to acknowledge the advice and encouragement of Norman E. Whitten, Jr., and Charles A. Valentine throughout the research, the assistance of Fay Gale, and the comments of Michael C. Howard on an earlier draft of this paper. The knowledge and patience of the Aboriginal people with whom I worked in Adelaide are also gratefully noted. Any errors or misinterpretations are, however, entirely my own.

Notes

1. Each of the volumes in the "Aborigines in Australian Society" series published by the Australian National University Press focuses on these topics. Among other relevant works are: Berndt 1969, 1971; Reay 1964; Stevens 1970, 1972; Sharp and Tatz 1966; Biskup 1973; Gale and Binnion 1975; Brown, Hirschfeld, and Smith 1974; Hiatt 1965; and Howard 1978c.

2. Higher estimates tend to include persons *temporarily* residing in the urban area, particularly for medical, legal, or educational reasons. Lower estimates exclude these people unless they remain after such purposes no longer exist.

3. The situation, of course, is not unique to Adelaide. Aborigines gained some political influence in the 1970s, but more as the focus of issues than as major voting blocs (cf. Broom and Jones 1973; Howard 1978c).

4. Several "part-Aboriginal" (i.e., also part-white) children from the Northern Territory were removed from their Aboriginal parents during the Second World War and placed in institutional homes in urban areas hundreds of kilometres away. The reasons for such removals are unclear, although the "safety" of the children from potential Japanese attacks was mentioned by authorities. The Aborigines affected by removal, some of whom have been unable to re-establish contact with relatives while others have done so only recently, consider the war simply provided an excuse for removal, since no "full-blooded" Aborigines were removed.

5. An experiment on Yalata mission on the state's west coast in the early 1970s allowed the strictly supervised sale of limited amounts of beer. Newer legislation, however, is designed to give Aborigines on the North-West Reserve in South Australia regulatory controls over liquor consumption and possession there as a part of general land rights (Australian Information Service 1978, p. 3).

6. Certain governmental representatives, members of the Aboriginal Affairs Board (if on official business) and a few other officials are the only exceptions.

7. The one case occurred in a country town after a publican refused to serve meals to two Aborigines who were in town to testify for the police in a murder case. One does not have to be a cynic to suggest that even this prosecution occurred for reasons other than those intended by the legislation.

8. Neither has there been a preliminary unifying force, central meeting ground, and general organizing influence such as religion (both as a system of belief and action and as a location) was among many blacks in the United States (cf. Mathews 1977; Jones 1971; Frazer 1963).

9. A discussion of economic opportunities for Adelaide Aborigines must refer to the acquisition of jobs and skills rather than to any sort of entrepreneurship. Opportunities for the latter are not supported by governmental programmes, and no independent businesses are operated in the city by persons of Aboriginal descent.

10. The combined membership of the two groups, if one includes only continuously active "dues-paying" members, would be approximately a hundred people. Activity groups and events, however, attract many times that number. An all-Aboriginal football club sponsored by one organization, for example, often includes about thirty Aborigines who are not members of the sponsoring group and attracts as many as a hundred supporters to its games and dances. The other organization conducts a weekly art class/social group that regularly attracts fifty to a hundred people, many of whom are

not association members. In other words, simple membership numbers do not adequately represent the groups' effects or strengths.

11. Ironically, the very loose affiliations of Adelaide organizations with the national ones seem to provide the former with a strength and self-sufficiency generally lacking in the latter. The Adelaide groups, for example, obtain almost no financial assistance from trade unions, which have been very active at the national level and in other urban areas and often expect considerable influence in return. The Adelaide groups generally owe very little to any one individual or group.

12. Richard Fox, in a summary of urban anthropological research that includes suggestions for future research, refers to such individuals as one of the most important links (for both participants and researchers) between an ethnic community and the larger society. These roles, however, as Howard (1978a, 1978b) indicates in the Perth area, may themselves in some cases be no more effective than influential members of the larger society allow them to be.

References

Anderson, Robert T. 1971. Voluntary Associations in History. *American Anthropologist* 73: 209–22.

Australian Information Service. 1978. *Australia Bulletin* 52 (21 August 1978).

Barnes, Sandra T., and Margaret Peil. 1977. Voluntary Association Membership in Five West African Cities. *Urban Anthropology* 6: 83–106.

Bennett, John W., ed. 1975. *The New Ethnicity: Perspectives from Ethnology.* Saint Paul: West.

Berndt, Ronald M., ed. 1969. *Thinking about Australian Aboriginal Welfare: With Particular Reference to Western Australia.* Perth: Department of Anthropology, University of Western Australia.

———. 1971. *A Question of Choice: An Australian Aboriginal Dilemma.* Nedlands: University of Western Australia Press.

Biskup, Peter. 1973. *Not Slaves Not Citizens: The Aboriginal Problem in Western Australia, 1898–1954.* New York: Crane, Russak.

Broom, Leonard, and F. Lancaster Jones. 1973. *A Blanket a Year.* Aborigines in Australian Society 10. Canberra: Australian National University Press.

———. 1977. *Opportunity and Attainment in Australia.* Stanford, Cal.: Stanford University Press.

Brown, Jill W., Roisin Hirschfeld, and Diane Smith. 1974. *Aboriginals and Islanders in Brisbane.* Australian Government Commission of Inquiry into Poverty. Canberra: Australian Government Publishing Service.

Brownell, Blaine A. 1977. The Urban South Comes of Age, 1900–1940. In *The City in Southern History: The Growth of Urban Civilization in the South,* ed. Blaine A. Brownell and David R. Goldfield. Port Washington, N.Y.: Kennikat Press.

Cohen, Abner. 1969. *Custom and Politics in Urban Africa: A Study of Hausa Migrants in Yoruba Towns.* Berkeley: University of California Press.

———. ed. 1974. *Urban Ethnicity.* Association of Social Anthropologists 12. London: Tavistock.

Commonwealth Bureau of Census and Statistics. 1972. *Official Yearbook of the Commonwealth of Australia, No. 58.* Canberra: Commonwealth Bureau of Census and Statistics.

212   James C. Pierson

Commonwealth Bureau of Census and Statistics, South Australian Office. 1969. *South Australian Yearbook, No. 4.* Adelaide: Government Printer.

Connell, R. W. 1977. *Ruling Class, Ruling Culture: Studies of Conflict, Power and Hegemony in Australian Life.* Cambridge: Cambridge University Press.

Despres, Leo, ed. 1975. *Ethnicity and Resource Competition in Plural Societies.* The Hague: Mouton.

De Vos, George, and Lola Romanucci-Ross, eds. 1975. *Ethnic Identity: Cultural Continuities and Change.* Palo Alto, Cal.: Mayfield.

Eggleston, Elizabeth. 1976. *Fear, Favour or Affection: Aborigines and the Criminal Law in Victoria, South Australia and Western Australia.* Aborigines in Australian Society 13. Canberra: Australian National University Press.

Encel, S. 1970. *Equality and Authority: A Study of Class, Status and Power in Australia.* London: Tavistock.

Fox, Richard G. 1977. *Urban Anthropology: Cities in Their Cultural Settings.* Englewood Cliffs, N.J.: Prentice-Hall.

Frazer, E. Franklin. 1963. *The Negro Church in America.* New York: Schocken Books.

Gale, Fay. 1964. *A Study of Assimilation.* Adelaide: Libraries Board of South Australia.

————. 1967. Patterns of Post-European Aboriginal Migration in South Australia. *Proceedings of the Royal Geographical Society of Australasia, South Australian Branch* 67: 21–37.

————. 1972. *Urban Aborigines.* Aborigines in Australian Society 8. Canberra: Australian National University Press.

Gale, Fay, and Joan Binnion. 1975. *Poverty Among Aboriginal Families in Adelaide.* Australian Government Commission of Inquiry into Poverty. Canberra: Australian Government Publishing Service.

Gulick, John. 1973. Urban Anthropology. In *Handbook of Social and Cultural Anthropology,* ed. John J. Honigmann. Chicago: Rand McNally.

Hiatt, L. R. 1965. Aborigines in the Australian Community. In *Australian Society: A Sociological Introduction,* ed. A. F. Davies and S. Encel. New York: Atherton Press.

Howard, Michael C. 1978a. Aboriginal "Leadership" in the South-West of Western Australia. In *"Whitefella Business": Aborigines in Australian Politics,* ed. Michael C. Howard. Philadelphia: Institute for the Study of Human Issues.

————. 1978b. Aboriginal Brokerage and Political Development in Southwestern Australia. Paper presented at Association of Social Anthropologists of Oceania meeting, Monterey, California, 1978.

————. ed. 1978c. *"Whitefella Business": Aborigines in Australian Politics.* Philadelphia: Institute for the Study of Human Issues.

Inglis, Judy. 1961. Aborigines in Adelaide. *Journal of the Polynesian Society* 70: 200–18.

Jones, Major J. 1971. *Black Awareness: A Theology of Hope.* Nashville: Abington Press.

Kerri, James N. 1976. Studying Voluntary Associations as Adaptive Mechanisms: A Review of Anthropological Perspectives. *Current Anthropology* 17: 23–47.

————. 1977. Urbanism, Voluntarism, and Afro-American Activism. *Journal of Anthropological Research* 33: 400–20.

Mathews, Donald G. 1977. *Religion in the Old South.* Chicago: University of Chicago Press.

McNair, Ian. 1975. A Profile of Australians: Some Characteristics and Attitudes. *Australian Quarterly* 47, no. 4: 66–77.

Millar, C. J. 1969. Aboriginal Affairs in South Australia. In *The Aborigines of*

South Australia: Their Background and Future Prospects, ed. J. W. Warburton. Publication no. 19. Adelaide: University of Adelaide Department of Adult Education.

Myrdal, Gunnar, et al. 1944. *An American Dilemma: The Negro Problem and Modern Democracy.* New York: Harper and Row.

Parkin, David. 1974. Congregational and Interpersonal Ideologies in Political Ethnicity. In *Urban Ethnicity,* ed. Abner Cohen. Association of Social Anthropologists 12. London: Tavistock.

Pierson, James C. 1972. Aboriginality in Adelaide: Urban Resources and Adaptations. Ph.D. dissertation, Department of Anthropology, Washington University, St Louis.

———. 1977a. Aboriginality in Adelaide: An Urban Context of Australian Aboriginal Ethnicity. *Urban Anthropology* 6: 307–27.

———. 1977b. Voluntary Organizations and Australian Aboriginal Urban Adaptations in Adelaide. *Oceania* 48: 46–58.

Pittock, A. Barrie. 1975. Politics and Race in Australia. In *Politics of Race: Comparative Studies,* ed. Donald G. Baker. Lexington, Mass.: Lexington Books.

Reay, Marie, ed. 1964. *Aborigines Now.* Sydney: Angus and Robertson.

Ryan, Lyndall. 1973. Recent Works on Aborigines. *Politics* 8: 384–86.

Sharp, Ian G., and Colin M. Tatz, eds. 1966. *Aborigines in the Economy: Employment, Wages and Training.* Brisbane: Jacaranda.

Stevens, Frank. 1970. Aborigines. In *Australian Society: A Sociological Introduction,* second edition, ed. A. F. Davies and S. Encel. Melbourne: Cheshire.

———. ed. 1972. *Racism: The Australian Experience.* Volume 2: *Black Versus White.* New York: Taplinger.

Warren, Donald I. 1975. *Black Neighbourhoods: An Assessment of Community Power.* Ann Arbor: University of Michigan Press.

The Political Context of Ethnogenesis: An Australian Example

DELMOS J. JONES AND
JACQUETTA HILL-BURNETT

Discussion of ethnicity is at present a major preoccupation of social scientists, including anthropologists, sociologists, and political scientists (see Said and Simmons 1976, Iris and Shama 1977, and Francis 1976).[1] Although many social scientists view ethnicity as one of the most important phenomena in the world today, there is little agreement on just what constitutes the phenomenon (Silverman 1976, p. 628, Bell 1974). Silverman suggests that a range of different types of situations are being lumped under discussions of ethnicity. While Handleman claims that current anthropological study of ethnicity "stresses the 'group' aspect of ethnicity, and the social factors which define the boundaries of the ethnic *group* in terms of principles of inclusion and exclusion of membership" (Handleman 1977, p. 187), others criticize the view that the ethnic group is an objective entity with a clearly identifiable membership. Those critics would abandon the concept of "ethnic group" (Silverman 1976, p. 130). The position taken in this essay is closer to the latter than to the former. We do not give up the idea of groups or of organizations based on ethnic dimensions, but we are suspicious of suggestions that an entire population, defined as an ethnic group, can constitute a group in any definitive sense that the term *group* is understood.

The term *group* is used both to refer to a population with some known or imputed characteristics as well as to a corporate entity. But once an aggregate is given a name, a closed-community model of society seems to take over, and unitary, group-like characteristics are taken for granted. In order to avoid the *a priori* presumption of an ethnic group, we speak of ethnic processes, which have internal as well as external aspects. An analysis of the dynamic interaction between internal and external processes is a major objective of this paper.

The Meaning of Ethnogenesis

The Social Science Research Council Conference on Ethnicity proposed that ethnicity involves past-oriented group identification emphasizing origins, includes some conception of cultural and social distinctiveness, and relates to components in a larger system of social relations (Bell 1974, p. 61). The report goes on to observe that "ethnicity provides an identification that gives meaning to life for a large proportion of the earth's people" (Bell 1974, p. 1; see also Said and Simmons 1976). The statement that ethnic identity gives meaning to life is a sweeping statement that strongly implies that ethnicity is the same phenomenon as culture.

Most discussions of ethnicity assume that "past-oriented group identification" is the most important determinant of present ethnic group identity. Thus, for Bennett, "the new ethnicity" refers to "the proclivity of a people to seize on traditional cultural symbols as a definition of their own identity" (Bennett 1975, p. 3). This emphasis tends to divert attention from the process by which traditional symbols emerge as the basis of a group-wide identity.

The historical connection between the rise of "ethnic" groups and European expansion and domination seems obvious, although as yet this fact has hardly entered as a major component of the theoretical discussions of ethnicity. Twenty years ago, for example, Wagley and Harris proposed that a majority of the populations which are now studied as ethnic groups "trace their origin to the expansionist activities of state societies" (Wagley and Harris 1958, p. 44). Conquering states do not often acknowledge the internal variation existing within a population to be subdued and reorganized in a colonial system. It is possible that what becomes the common background of an ethnic group may consist of generalized descriptions of native populations by the elites of conquering states (Skinner 1968, pp. 173-74).[2] What now are referred to as the Brazilian Indians, for example, originally included numerous separate tribal societies. And after the conquest of Mexico by the Spanish, "it became possible to establish a single national ideal for a great variety of Indian groups" (Wagley and Harris 1958, p. 244). The question is: What are the processes involved in establishing a single nation-like ideal from such variety?

The existence of a common emphasis on traditional symbols suggests that an ethnic group in its present form is not necessarily a new phenomenon but is a continuation of past structures and beliefs with minor modifications. Although Kolig agrees that pan-Aboriginality is a product of a white context, he argues that the preservation of the traditional ideology is located in a cognitive superstructure, and that

"Aboriginal identity appears as the logical final stage in a development of expanding traditional identity concept" (Kolig 1977, p. 49). As many writers note when ethnically categorized groups form as, or become, mainly political groups, the significance of cultural differences change (Barth 1969, Cohen 1969). Schildkrout holds that, like all social categories, ethnic categories presuppose some amount of consensus (Schildkrout 1974, p. 19). The ethnic boundaries, she continues, "are defined by both insiders and outsiders in terms of their common culture, not in terms of the distinct subcultures of any particular community". The quantitative dimensions of the consensus that presupposedly exist within an ethnic group presumably are not an important concern to Schildkrout. For her, ethnicity is relevant in a social situation if only one actor acknowledges its existence and acts according to the norms he associates with this categorization (ibid, p. 191).

We do believe that the quantitative dimensions of the consensus are particularly important, and they are especially significant to understanding the internal dynamics of ethnicity. The process of ethnic formation may indeed begin with a single individual, or a small set of individuals who begin acting in accordance with the new categories. But we are interested in the recruitment process that is implied in this, especially if the internal consensus is not great, a condition that can be expected to exist in the early stages of ethnogenesis where internal cultural variation exists and local loyalties remain strong. Thus we are concerned about the process whereby a "common culture" comes about and the manner by which it is defined. As to the degree to which past cultural tradition potentially provides the boundaries and norms of an ethnic group, we argue that the common culture of diverse subcultures is not "given" in a situation that is culturally diverse. The commonalities are first conceptualized and then "constructed". Since the Aborigines still retain a variety of distinct local cultural communities and are in the early stages of the process of ethnogenesis, it seems appropriate to shed light on these questions of the formation of consensus. It was important for research purposes to conceptualize just what mechanisms these processes might assume.

The processual and developmental aspects of ethnicity were addressed by Barth when he suggested that the "group" must select from among a *range* of traditional symbols available, and the process of selection itself may be surrounded by a considerable amount of internal conflict and debate. Since local community cultures are still strong in parts of Australia, we assumed that the process of selecting symbols would still be under way. Barth also links the process of symbol selection to innovators (Barth 1969, p. 34). In order to examine that linkage, the research focused on key individuals, as well as the organization they were connected with.

While Little (1970) has been foremost in exploring the role of associations in complex urban society and social change, he seemed in one case to separate the role and function of voluntary associations from ethnicity, viewing them as alternative to one another (Little 1976, p. 38). In the context of discussions of modern national development, many writers regard associations in which recruitment is based on ethnicity "as stopgaps, performing social and political functions that incipient national organizations, such as welfare departments and political parties, are expected to assume" (Schildkrout 1974, p. 188). In our view these discussions fail to make the further connection of similarity between the processes of building national identity and the processes of ethnogenesis. The role of voluntary associations in the consensus process can indeed be critical.

The parallel between nation building and ethnogenesis formed the basis of many of the questions addressed in this research (see Tilman 1969, pp. 247–505). We assumed that ethnic processes in the early stages would be similar to the process of nation-building with respect to the development of a wider loyalty and its competition with local loyalties. This theoretical posture suggested that the development and expansion of group-wide loyalties among the Aborigines would be centred in key associations, and would be advocated by the leadership of these associations. The relation between the leadership of these organizations and the general population is characterized, as Barth (1969) suggests, by recruitment, competition, and conflict. The Aboriginal situation was inspected in order to isolate key organizations and the key set of individuals attempting to guide and cultivate the spread of ethnicity. The nature of their relationship to the rest of the population and to the major institutions of Australian society was also a primary concern.

The Aborigine as a Category

Two facts about the modern Aboriginal situation are widely acknowledged. The first is the emergence of pan-Aboriginal organizations and processes (Berndt 1977; Kolig 1977; Rowley 1971c, 1973; McGuinness 1972, 1976). The second is continued existence of strong ties to local communities. And, according to Berndt, the gap between the two has not been adequately bridged, "in spite of formal statements to the contrary" (Berndt 1977, p. 8). It is possible that the statements about a situation, especially those made by policy-makers and social scientists, play a major role in the maintenance of that gap. This is an aspect of complex social systems that should not go unnoticed. There is a vast literature on traditional Aboriginal culture as well as on modern-day rural settlements, and much of this literature emphasizes the importance of local traditions. We will not review that literature here, since the situation is well covered in this volume as well as elsewhere (Berndt 1977, Turner 1974). However, there is a problem with respect to the ways in which the literature characterizes Aborigines and Aboriginal culture, and the empirical reality of their situation.

The literature that focuses on local communities emphasizes that the local context is more significant to most Aboriginal individuals than group-wide loyalties. Since group-wide activities are on the increase, these social conditions can be seen as opposing forces. Consequently, the contrast between local loyalties and group-wide identification is salient. A related issue is the degree to which the symbols that are beginning to operate as a basis for developing group-wide loyalty and identity can be traced to pre-contact tradition on the one hand, or may more accurately be traced to the common experience of modern-day Aborigines in white-controlled settings.

There is notable recognition that a great deal of diversity exists among Aborigines (Berndt 1977; Broom 1971, p. 21; Rowley 1971*a*; Tatz 1967, pp. 440—41), indeed, there is probably more recognization of this fact about Aborigines than for similar groups in other parts of the world. At the same time, along with the awareness of diversity there have been and are policies and practices which ignore it. Thus according to Tatz, "The ethnic culture, social values and environment of full-bloods in Central Australia do not correspond to those of Aborigines living in the northern Coastal regions. In the small sate of Victoria, with some 3,700 Aborigines, there are five distinct regional groups, each with its own differing contact with white society, each different in outlook" (Tatz 1967, pp. 440—41). But, Tatz concludes, government policies rest on the assumption that Aborigines are *one* people (ibid., p. 440). This *treatment* of the population as one people is, in our view, a fundamental element in bringing about the formative stage of Aboriginal ethnicity (see also Berndt 1977, p. 7).

The policies that treat Aborigines as a whole tend to focus on the problem aspects of Aborigines. Thus according to Guthrie, "Urban planners, with their white middle class bias, often regard Aboriginal migrants as a 'problem' in a manner in which Aborigines may not see themselves" (Guthrie 1975, p. 58).[3] Neither their internal variation nor the ways they view themselves alter this perception. "Those who ignore the human being and weep over the problems are forced to stereotype, for problems come in categories far more readily than people. The statement, 'you know what Aborigines are like' — is an oft-repeated phrase which purports to refer to people, but implicitly highlights a particular quality by which the speaker wishes to brand them" (Mitchell 1974, p. 57).

The Aboriginal population as a whole may constitute a common set of problems for the government, both federal and state, and various agencies of the Australian government have been set up to deal with these problems. Government policy regarding housing exemplifies the manner in which a problem is defined so as not to acknowledge internal socio-cultural differences (Wilson 1975, p. 460). The majority of the Aborigines living in urban centres live in inadequate housing (Lovejoy 1971). They are generally concentrated in economically depressed areas of the city and experience similar "psycho-social problems" (Davidson, Bryer and Gibson 1973, p. 243; Gale and Binnion 1975).

When a population comes to be characterized in terms of the set of social problems that the institutions of government must deal with, the study of the problem influences the definition of the aggregate, and discussion of both often takes a statistical form. Thus it is possible, as Broom (1971) does, to contrast and describe the occupations held by Aborigines with those held by non-Aborigines. It is true that this level of description of the generalizations is not in itself incorrect; it is, nevertheless, not always considered that such characteristics are as much an aspect of the larger political and employment structure of the larger society as they are of the structure and the characteristics of the target group that one has in mind (cf. Schapper 1964). The fact that the Aborigines constitute a special problem for the government is reflected in the existence of a single agency to deal with the full range of social concerns, ranging from employment to health, to housing, whereas these same problems are housed and handled in different agencies for white Australians.

While the Aborigines constitute a problem for the government, defined in terms of a set of economic, social, and health issues, the government constitutes a problem for Aborigines, defined in terms of oppression, discrimination, and exploitation. Thus an important dimension of the emergent pan-Aboriginal ideology is a description and definition of the status of Aborigines in Australian society, combined with an effort to mobilize individuals on the grounds of their common status and history of treatment, with the goal of altering the status of the group. Thus, Barth contends that "in most complex state systems ethnic identity implies a series of [macro-level] constraints on the kinds of roles an individual is *allowed to play,* and the partners he may choose for different kinds of transactions" (Barth 1969, p. 17; emphasis added). Barth implies here that the systematic nature of the constraints may form the basis that organized struggle *must* assume (see Kuper 1971). This fact, more than anything else, may explain why contemporary forms of ethnic movements are predominatly political (Barth 1969, p. 34). And in this analysis the political components of pan-Aboriginality is evident.

The Political Movements Among Aborigines

The Aboriginal population is still approximately 80 per cent rural, on a continent in which *rural* refers to vast and difficult areas. Thus, it was apparent from the outset that the number committed to group-wide identity would be small. This is an important condition for the position argued here that the process of ethnicity involves an ideology, created and spread by small groups and networks, linked to organizations, and that a small group of individuals engaged in ethnic activities can be and would be the vehicle for recruiting others to the ideology.

Politically inspired movements for Aboriginal rights are extremely old, much older than is often recognized. Examples of Aboriginal political movements can be found to have occurred sporadically in various parts and sectors of Australia (Horner 1972). The movement by Aborigines on behalf of their own rights is well illustrated by the activity of William Cooper, who was responsible for Sir Douglas Nicholls's involvement with Aboriginal legal and civil rights. Beginning in the early 1930s, Cooper's organizational work led to the formation of the Australian Aborigines' League, a voluntary association, "the first organization of its kind in Australia to be composed entirely of Aborigines" (Clark 1975, p. 91). Cooper left the reserve area of Cumeroogunga (located in Victoria near the border of New South Wales) and went to live in the urban setting of Melbourne, gathering other Aborigines around him to begin the onerous task of building the movement. "He could write a good letter, and much of his pension went on stamps for letters to the government, to the newspapers, and further afield to the Aboriginal settlements in Queensland and Western Australia, enlisting their support" (ibid., p. 87). Cooper recruited to the cause Douglas Nicholls, even then a public figure in the white world, saying, "You've got through to the whites Doug; they listen to you. Now you have to start wobbling your tongue on behalf of your own people. Lead them to better things" (ibid., p. 89).

The league's fight was for recognition of Aborigines as human beings, for full rights of citizenship, and for the same policies that were still being advocated and sought after in the recent militant Aboriginal movement: Aboriginal representation in both federal and state government; a Department of Native Affairs in the federal government to unify policy and law of all states with respect to the Aborigine in order that there might be a national policy for Aborigines; and a representative advisory council for each state. Cooper's group attempted to secure from the king of the British Commonwealth representation in the federal parliament, placing Australian Aborigines on the same footing as Maoris of New Zealand, who had had parliamentary representation since 1867.

However, communication on a national scale proved to be a prohibitive barrier to the expansion of the movement. Finding it a difficult matter to get signatures from Aborigines in remote missions and settlements in early 1934, Cooper sought assistance from the Commonwealth government for obtaining signatures in the Northern Territory. He was refused on grounds that those Aborigines were illiterate and unlikely to understand the meaning of or be able to sign such a petition. There were other movements, but this case underlines the fact that external factors, not cultural difference or the political backwardness of people of "little capacity for political organization and action" (Coombs 1978, p. 9), prevented the organized movements from reaching national proportion.

The movement stagnated into an essentially local effort, although its leadership intended it to be nationa in scope. And it could be argued that the socio-political context for a population-wide movement had not yet developed in Australia at that time. Key factors blocking such a development included the difficulty of communication, limitations on the movement of Aborigines, and the lack of a sufficiently large urban Aboriginal population. Subsequent changes in the status of Aborigines in Australian society included greater political freedom, their right to vote, and an increase in their migration to urban centres (Gale 1970, 1972). Although these gains led to the formation of organizations before the early 1970s, these groups were primarily controlled and dominated by whites. Similarly, in the United States the civil-rights movement had been controlled by whites, and one of the first signs of the birth of Black Power was the removal of whites from key organizations. The identical process took place in Australia in the early 1970s.

One informant related that they were always told by whites involved in these organizations that they would be "happy to step aside" as soon as blacks were ready to take over. The strategy in one situation was related as follows: "We waited until the election of officials, and every time a white candidate was put up for an office, we nominated a black. One of the whites was in on this plan with us, and when a black person was nominated to run against him he resigned and made a speech reminding everyone that the whites were waiting for blacks to move forward. We thought sure that the other whites would follow his example. Instead they protested against the idea. After we saw that they had no intention of stepping aside we became a little aggressive, almost violent. As a result most whites left the organizations." The strategy in another situation was to abandon the original organization and establish an all-Aboriginal group. Whatever the means, the important outcome was a series of organizations controlled by Aborigines (cf. Howard 1977, 1978).

There is little doubt that the modern movement for Aboriginal self-determination was greatly influenced by the Black Power movement in the United States. In fact there was some evidence that a member of the Black Panther Party paid a visit to Australia in the late 1960s and held a conference with some of the Aboriginal leaders. In the opinion of many, the first visible manifestation of this recent national level movement is to be traced to the massive demonstration of Aborigines at the seat of Australian national government in Canberra in February of 1972 (see *Identity* 1, no. 5, p. 13). Their brazen erection of an "Aboriginal Embassy" in the form of a tent on the very grounds of the Parliament House drew nation-wide attention. It was similar to the non-violent protest of the Southern Christian Leadership Conference in the United States, and led to similar responses on the part of the police force and to responses of outrage on the part of the general public.

Talking to people who were involved in the event reveals several significant aspects. First, it is apparent that the event was organized and carried out by a small group of militants. The first day a demonstration ended with an attack by the police and an attempt to destroy the tent encampment erected by the Aborigines. The event was widely covered by the national media, and the next day Aborigines from all over Australia, as well as sympathetic whites, joined the protest. This may have been the first nation-wide political protest event organized and controlled by Aborigines that included the participation of a broad spectrum of the Aboriginal population.[4] If this event marked the beginning of the Black Power movement in Australia, it also marked the intensification of governmental concern about Aboriginal affairs. Thus, a significant result of the Aboriginal Embassy affair was a meeting with the opposition leader, Gough Whitlam, whose party won the national election later that year, where a series of promises were made. Massive funding of Aboriginal organizations and projects began shortly after the Labor government came to power.

Both the interviews conducted during the period of field research and the documents of the period indicate that an important dimension of the ideology of Aboriginality was political in nature. Thus Rowley wrote in 1973 that the Aborigines had begun "to explode into a fury of defiance".

Aborigines are beginning to organize to advance their interests, often, necessarily, at the expense of short term interests of others. The Aboriginal, by his own organized protest, may eventually force the rest of us, and our government, to see him as he really is . . . a man with needs like everyone else, not someone who is to become a house-trained amenable asset to white Australia. [Rowley 1973, pp. 187, 191]

The platform and programme of the Black Panther Party of Australia proclaimed a desire for freedom, the power to determine the destiny of the black community, full employment, a guaranteed income, restitution "for the armed robbery of our land", decent housing, education that would expose "the true nature of this decadent Australian society", an immediate end to police brutality. "We want land, bread, housing, education, clothing, justice and peace. And as our major political objective, a United Nations–supervised plebiscite to be held throughout the black colony, in which only black colonial subjects will be allowed to participate, for the purpose of determining the will of the black people as to their national destiny" (McQueen 1974, pp. 34–35).

Statements of this nature were obviously both offensive and threatening to many white Australians as well as to some Aborigines. Individuals holding these views were widely condemned as not representing the views of the more tradition-oriented Aboriginal population. It should be noted, however, that any public statement by the ethnic elite, regardless of the nature of the ideology being advocated, could be made out to be not representative of all Aboriginal views. The abrasive and crude, politically oriented statements were frequently set in opposition to the culturally anchored Aborigines' more exclusive concern about the ritual system, and his symbolic and emotional ties to a territory which excluded concern for the political reality of economic, racial, and cultural oppression. Thus, we label the two major competing ethnic ideologies as the "cultural" and the "political" ideology.

The response of the Labor government to Aboriginal protest was probably based in part on a real concern for the conditions of the population, but the responses to the threatening nature of the protest cannot be discounted, especially in view of subsequent events. It is possible to isolate two factors that converged to produce an Aboriginal ethnic elite at the time social programmes aimed at dealing with the conditions among Aborigines were expanded. The first was Aboriginal assertiveness. Interviews conducted with individuals who had had a long-term involvement with Aboriginal rights revealed their concerted effort to develop organizations, recruit individuals, and establish a group-wide network of communications. The second factor was the government's response to political pressure. Thus, in the discussion that follows it is not argued that governmental policy created the first

Aboriginal ethnic elite. Rather, when the government responded, the emerging elite became a part of the governmental structure.

Before the development of massive governmental funding for a wider range of Aboriginal activities, it was possible to isolate a small number of viable organizations, only a few of which were controlled by Aborigines, and a handful of activists associated with them attempting to have an influence on social conditions affecting Aborigines. One long-time activist recalled how hard they had to work to raise money to keep organizations alive; but he related that those who were involved were actively involved and were strongly committed to the political goals of the organization. Government funding, he claimed, changed the character of individual involvement mainly by making political protest remunerative.

Another consequence of government funding was a tendency to develop greater uniformity among the more educated of the Aboriginal population. The most dramatic example of this is in the realm of employment itself. Before the massive funding of activities began, Aborigines with some degree of education were employed in a range of different kinds of occupations, although the kinds of occupations were always severely limited by discrimination. Now, most educated individuals are employed by organizations and agencies concerned with Aboriginal affairs.

Before 1972 the Aboriginal leadership participated in the movement for Aboriginal rights in addition to working for a living in other occupations. After 1972 positions in these organizations became salaried. Thus in 1976 not a single visible national-level Aboriginal leader was discovered who did not occupy a position in, or connected with, government or who was not connected with an organization funded by the government. The consequence has been a greater concentration and specialization of the most active leaders in a single occupational setting, financially dependent on the government. Conceptually this is seen in the context of this discussion as a condition in which the struggle of an oppressed population has become institutionalized. That is, they are integrated into the very structure of oppression that they are attempting to combat.[5] The selection of Aboriginal representatives to *advise* the government on policies pertaining to Aborigines was the ultimate step in this process and demonstrated that incorporation into the structure is, in the final analysis, their only option when the government itself controls their status as a political entity. In this instance the National Aboriginal Consultative Committee ventured beyond advising to political advocacy. The conflict between political ethnicity and cultural ethnicity played a prominent role in the strategic course of events surrounding the rise and decline of the NACC.

Aboriginal Representation

Shortly after the referendum in 1967 which accorded Aborigines the right to vote for the first time, a council for Aboriginal affairs, composed of white Australians, was formed that would advise the government on policies concerning Aborigines (Department of Aboriginal Affairs 1976, p. 10). The chairman of this council endorsed the idea that Aboriginal spokesmen should be chosen by Aborigines, and appointed four Aborigines as consultants to the council until the mechanism for selecting spokesmen could be arranged. The four Aboriginal consultants held their position in the Department of Aboriginal Affairs and were in fact public servants. This means that the process of establishing some form of Aboriginal representation preceded the Aboriginal Embassy affair and was advocated by whites as well as by Aborigines. Ultimately, however, it appeared that different motivation lay behind white as contrasted with black advocacy of black representation.

As early as 1962, proposals were offered for "the . . . training of Aborigines as leaders of their people" (Robb 1962, p. 38). It was ironic that a government that oppressed a people should be responsible for training its leaders. Robb combined the proposal with the suggestion that Aborigines should not be separated from their own people: "We have had many warnings from anthropologists that the Aborigine, full-blood or mixed blood, never entirely forgets his obligations to his group, and that when divorced from that group, no matter how successful the individual may be in white society, he suffers, sometimes disastrously, from loss of racial associations" (ibid.). Thus Robb combined his proposal with a definition of what it meant to be an Aboriginal, and implicit in this was a definition of the role that the trained leaders would play.

The late 1960s and early 1970s was a period of frequent assemblages of selected Aborigines on which the Australian government exercised indirect, if not direct, control (see Valadian and Barwick 1977 and *Batchelor Seminars* 1976). One significant aspect of the Aboriginal Embassy affair was that the selection of leaders was not controlled by whites. In fact, during the affair itself the minister responsible for Aborigines "convened a National Conference of Aboriginal Councillors from the States" (Department of Aboriginal Affairs 1976, p. 11). One of the stated purposes of the conference was to discuss the establishment of a centre for Aboriginal representation in Canberra.

However, one of the Aborigines involved in the Aboriginal Embassy described this act as an attempt to undercut the impact of the embassy protestors. The opening comments by the ministers to the conference included a remark which suggested that those involved in the Aboriginal Embassy only represented a small group of people: "I have spoken with various groups from time to time but I have never been completely sure whose views they were expressing. Certainly, at best, the views could have represented only small numbers of the total Aboriginal population. Now, I believe that we have a representative gathering of Aboriginal delegates" (ibid., p. 12). Spokesmen of the Aboriginal Embassy requested to attend the conference. The narrative continued: "The Gubas [whites] thought that they [the delegates to the conference] would not let us speak. Not only did they let us speak, but they supported us. It was beautiful" (ibid.).

One of the goals of the conference was to discuss a mechanism for Aboriginal representation. A result of the conference was the "appointment of a steering committee which later held discussions with the ministers on the formation of a national body of elected Aboriginal representatives" (ibid., p. 13). On 11 January 1973 the minister for Aboriginal affairs announced a plan to convene a consultative group of Aborigines from all parts of Australia to advise him on Aboriginal problems. The National Aboriginal Consultative Committee was proposed to advise the government on matters pertaining to Aboriginal citizens. Their representatives were to be democratically elected by the Aboriginal people themselves (Tatz 1977, pp. 392–93). By the very nature of the socio-cultural situation, even a democratically elected body cannot possibly be *truly* representative of *all* the Aboriginal people.[6] Thus, the grounds for the NACC's manipulation or destruction was built into the terms of its creation.

The NACC was to be composed of members elected by Aborigines from forty-one districts. (See Howard 1977 for a brief account of planning, enrolment, and election in south-western Australia.) The election was held on 24 November 1973, and its first meeting was held on 13–14 December 1973. Each elected member was paid a salary of seven thousand dollars a year, plus two thousand to three thousand dollars allowance. Although the NACC was seen as an example of Aboriginal self-determination, it was clearly controlled by the Australian government. Once elected and operating, however, the NACC was not satisfied to be merely an advisory lobby. At a meeting in February 1974 the NACC proposed that they be established as an independent congress to administer Aboriginal affairs, but they were informed by the government that they must remain an advisory group or funds for their operation would be withheld. This meant, in effect, that the group was to represent Aborigines but only within the limits defined by the government.

In addition to the constraints imposed on the NACC by the government, there were problems from the other direction, the culturally diverse Aboriginal population. One member of the NACC described the committee as the means of voicing the needs of the Aboriginal "communities". This goal, he went on, is hampered by the control of its resources by the Department of Aboriginal Affairs and by the criticism against it from the Aboriginal people. This criticism was in part due to the tremendous amount of diversity of the Aboriginal population (McGuinness 1976, pp. 10-13, 29). One of the forty-one electorates was described as having as many as seventy "distinct tribal communities" (ibid., p. 11). Another electorate was less culturally diverse but contained twelve "major Aboriginal organizations, each of which feels that their particular organization is more important than the other" (ibid.). Where the social characteristics, needs, and aspirations of a population are varied, adequate representation is difficult; moreover, the sources of diversity and difference are not merely those continued from the diversity of the cultural traditions of pre-contact and early post-contact periods, nor simply those of the socio-economic conditions of the present, but come from the diversity of interests organized into and represented by voluntary associational forms.

In an effort to contend with criticism from Aboriginal communities, an attempt was made by the NACC to increase communication and to convince Aborigines of its goals and intentions (McGuinness 1976, p. 29), an effort that was hampered by inadequate resources. The notion of an ethnic *group* implies that at least a social category, if not a social entity, exists that *already* shares a set of values and aspirations. Clearly, this was not then the case with the Aborigines. The intent of the communication between the NACC and the population was to create and build a common set of politically relevant values and aspirations, and communication was the major mechanism through which this could be accomplished. The problem was that the message of this elite reflected an underlying political ideology that was not compatible with the policies of the Australian government. Thus the government, using as its rationalization the problem of communication between the NACC and the Aboriginal communities, formed an independent committee to inquire into ways of improving the effectiveness of the NACC (Department of Aboriginal Affairs 1976).

The committee of inquiry on the role of the National Aboriginal Consultative Committee concluded that the NACC had "not functioned as a consultative committee and, to that extent, [had] not been effective in providing advice to government on policies and programs in

Aboriginal affairs (ibid., p. viii)." While the NACC was not fulfilling its role in the limited fashion the government wished, it *was* engaging in public actions and pronouncements and in organizing efforts that put constant pressure on the government for major changes in the political and economic situation of Aborigines in Australia. Their policy goals were often universalistic rather than particularistic. The terms of their pronouncements were far more political than cultural in nature. Their resolutions included proposals relating to the representation of Aborigines in parliament; the control of anthropological and social science research on Aborigines; the full education of Aborigines; effective modes of legal recourse against racial discrimination against Aborigines; improved housing conditions and arrangements, land rights (and property rights), and compensation for Aborigines; and control and elimination of police brutality towards Aborigines. When the NACC audaciously proposed that the Department of Aboriginal Affairs be made *its* secretariat, rather than NACC being merely "consultative" to it, the department began to view NACC as a rival rather than as an assistant body. The role pursued by NACC can be seen as appropriate or inappropriate depending on whether one takes the perspective of the government or the Aborigines.

The committee of inquiry makes much of the tribal versus non-tribal polarity and shifts the focus of attention to the cultural dimensions of Aboriginal ethnicity; it concludes that "proposals affecting tribal people have been less numerous than those affecting non-tribal people" (ibid., p. 45). This conclusion is only justified if it is assumed that the measures the NACC advocated have no relation to what tribal people also suffer. It implies that tribal people suffer *none* of the discrimination, exploitation, and oppression suffered by non-tribal, a conclusion often implicit in much of the anthropological literature. If it is assumed that Aborigines suffer from a common set of unusually subordinating socio-political and economic constraints in their context in Australian society, it makes little sense to separate tribal from non-tribal concerns with respect to those conditions. Given the persistence of the outcry in full public view, stimulated and sustained by the NACC, it clearly was far more comfortable for the government in power to shift the public eye to the localized, particularistic, and special needs of remote people, a very legitimate concern of effective policy-making.

The appeal to localism is an effective procedure for rousing a positive sentimental reaction from European Australians, who, despite a largely undisturbed and thus unconscious attitude of superiority towards Aboriginals, are inclined to romantic appreciation of Aboriginal past, walkabout, and Dreamtime traditions.[7] They can be easily aroused in favour of some policy effort to preserve the heritage, at least in the limited forms of arts and public performance. But such sentiments are *weak* grounds for support of campaigns in favour of land rights for Aborigines that also entail some effective control to be exercised by Aboriginal occupants of the land over arrangements to extract wealth from it. None but the most extreme of liberalist sentimentalizers would support such powers of decision for Aboriginals on the basis of sentiment for preservation of cultural ways and traditions from a Dreamtime past.

Thus, we return to a major issue in this paper, the relationship between the emergence of pan-Aboriginal processes and cultural diversity. The committee of inquiry pointedly focused on the NACC's difficulties with local "feedback" of information or "representativeness". The report itself described the reality of difficulties faced in attempting to "represent" traditional sectors of the Aboriginal population: "Delegation entails trust, which traditionally depended on kinship and proximity. Under the NACC electoral system, many people are expected to confer authority on an individual who comes from outside their own community and with whom at best their kinship and even cultural bonds may be tenuous or . . . non-existent" (Department of Aboriginal Affairs 1976, p. 60). The committee concluded that "the great majority of Aborigines knew practically nothing of the formal activities of the NACC" (ibid., p. 45). Discontinuity between a politically motivated ethnic elite and the rest of the ethnic population who are culturally diverse and have a traditional outlook is an integral aspect of the political circumstances of ethnicity. Most importantly, the attempt to bridge the gap falls to the elite and, as already noted, they were sensitive to that problem. This critical foray against the NACC, however, goes beyond realism and fairness, unless one accepts the presumption that NACC delegates are to be super representatives. A fair empirical comparison of Aboriginal knowledge of the NACC with European Australians' knowledge of the "formal activities" of their government representatives would very probably find them equally uninformed.

Representativeness to the full standard used by the committee in general would probably be impossible short of plebiscite on every issue. Certainly the NACC was cognizant of the problem of particularistic needs, demands, and views from local Aboriginal situations and settings; but their efforts in this initial stage of pan-Aboriginal formation was to bring pressure to ameliorate the general mechanisms of subordination. Formulations in their own terms, promulgated in public, were not viewed by the Australian government as "consultative". Had the NACC accepted the role of "respondent adviser" rather than independent initiator and formulator of advice, we submit that the issue of representativeness would never have arisen.

As the history of the effort to establish Aboriginal representation is inspected, it is apparent that its early development was managed and controlled by whites. The Aboriginal Embassy affair altered the course of events, adding a more independent Aboriginal component that diverged somewhat from governmental policies. Since it is apparent the radical element continued to dominate the NACC structure, strategic moves of the governments in power, of which the inquiry was a part, resulted in the dissolution of the NACC and its re-establishment along lines more compatible with governmental policies — that is, more controlled and more advisory.

Tatz compared the NACC to similar structures created to deal with colonized and subordinate populations (Tatz 1977, p. 396). He suggests that talk of self-determination and participatory decision-making is a pretence of talking with Aborigines while actually talking for them. "It is also a desire for Aboriginal approval of what they [the policy makers] decide is in their [own] best interest, for co-operative endorsement, not for hectic criticism — let alone a role reversal by which the Aborigines become the policy-makers and the department *their* civil service" (ibid., p. 395; emphasis added). The full sense of impasse and futility is struck by Marcia Langton, secretary of the Federal Council for the Advancement of Aborigines and Torres Strait Islanders, in her preface to the *Minority Rights Group* Report (which was composed in a more optimistic tone by H. C. Coombs). Her words outline the outcome of the processes just discussed.

> The fine words and the rhetoric of the new policies have reassured white Australians that, at last, their Government is doing the right thing by the people they dispossessed . . . The public relations exercise conducted by Australian Governments for the last ten years has been successful. But the position of Aboriginals in Australian society has not substantially improved. . . . the only positive aspect of this situation is that the political consciousness of the Aboriginal people has been raised . . . They have learnt to press their case more directly. [Langton 1978, p. 5]

Thus the formation of an ethnically based political constituency is the only real accomplishment of this decade. And the possibility of political action is her final note (cf. Said and Simmons 1976): "The extent to which we are forced to pursue our legitimate claims outside the Australian political system will depend on how long Australian politicians continue to confuse their success in expunging the guilt of white Australians with implementing their policies on Aboriginal affairs" (Langton 1978, p. 5).

Clearly the NACC was mobilizing the opinions and views of diverse and widely scattered sets of Aborigines to see the political subordination, exploitation, and repression. These conditions, of course, were known and recognized by Aborigines themselves and discussed among themselves. But transforming this consciousness into a public voice of national proportion has been a cause of the elite and most clearly was a *cause celebre* of the NACC.

Other Associations and the Ethnic Elite

Government support brought into being a host of Aboriginal organizations in addition to the NACC, in very much the same manner as the Office of Economic Opportunities supported community organizations in black communities in the United States in the late 1960s (local-level organizations are discussed in chapters by Howard and Pierson). At this point we are concerned with the many organizations and attendant processes that served to bring Aborigines from all parts of Australia together, setting in motion the mechanism of mobilization parallel to and redundant to the NACC's mobilization efforts. An important process of mobilization is the development of group-wide identity. To pinpoint the process we must identify individuals and groups responsible and the characteristics they are formulating to represent ethnic practice. Thus, an article in *The Aboriginal Child at School* (Aboriginal Consultative Group 1975b), noted how the Schools Commission came to the conclusion that there was no Aboriginal voice in educational policy-making. To assist it in its consideration of the problems, the commission formed an Aboriginal Consultative Group, choosing Aborigines from all parts of Australia. Among the organizations that operate on a national level are the Aboriginal Hostels Limited, the Aboriginal Legal Service, and the Aboriginal Housing Service. Regular meetings are held that bring together in a central place the leaders of local units of these organizations from all over Australia, facilitating the development of nation-wide networks. One individual who participated in one of these organizations suggested that the government was doing the Aborigines a big favour by bringing the Aboriginal leaders together. At no other time in the history of the movement for Aboriginal liberation have so many leaders been assembled in this manner, justifying description of them as the first Aboriginal Elite. In Barth's terms they are "innovators" (Barth 1969), the visible leaders of a categorically marked population set who are attempting to define the social and political goals that a population may set out to achieve and attempting to recruit and mobilize members of the population as a means of applying pressure to achieve those goals.

While the government may be doing the Aborigines a favour by bringing various sets of leaders together in the same place, it is also true that most of the time the government knows exactly in politically strategic terms where they are and what they are doing. As we noted earlier, not a single visible national-level leader was discovered who did not have some connection with the Australian government. Along with this economic dependency we observed growing signs of feelings among the rank-and-file that the visible leaders had become distant.

Throughout this paper an important distinction has been made between one segment of the ethnic population — those who define and attempt to spread the ideology of ethnicity — and other segments of the population, who may hold values and ideology that may be in conflict with the emergent ethnic ideology. But the ideology itself is the creation, in part, of a politically inspired ethnic elite, and from this core group it is spread to more and more members of the larger population. The extension of the ethnic ideology to more and more of the population is a process of recruitment, conversion, and mobilization.

This developmental and creative dimension of Aboriginal ethnicity was reflected in several seminars and workshops. An item that appeared in the journal *Identity* in 1972 expresses the process of creating ideology: "To help foster a strong and diverse Aboriginal identity, full-blood Aborigines and part Aborigines will get together at a seminar in Canberra to discuss their traditional culture. Aborigines in all parts of Australia are invited to nominate suitable people from their communities to take part" (*Identity* 1, no. 5: 13). Through discussion *they would define* the concerns and values common to all Aboriginal people, clarify which of the significant differences among Aboriginal cultures they wished to retain, and continue to establish what they wish in the way of Aboriginal culture in Australia.

Another such occasion was a six-week workshop entitled "The Culture, Identity and Future of Aborigines", sponsored by the Commonwealth Office of Aboriginal Affairs at the Australian National University in January–February 1971 (Valadian and Barwick 1977). The students were drawn from all the states and from urban and remote community settings, and included "a fair representation by age, and experience, and sex" (ibid., p. 322). Clearly the representatives of local variations of Aboriginal culture could meet, discuss, and exchange cultural information. "Rural as well as urban folk praised the workshop as a step towards unity because it had given them 'a chance to understand my people more'" (ibid., p. 324).[8] During an interview, one Aboriginal acquaintance spoke of an attempt to develop a new form of male initiation ritual that urban Aborigines could undergo. The idea was to work out the forms of this ritual with some of the older traditional Aboriginal religious leaders; the ritual, however, would not be strictly traditional but would be made compatible with urban patterns of life. Such a ritual, even if it were developed, would not automatically become acceptable to all Aborigines, either those located in traditional or in urban settings. It would have to compete with other ritual and cultural forms for personal commitment. In June 1975 the Aboriginal Consultative Group presented a report to the Schools Commission on Education for Aborigines in which the following statement appeared.

> We recognize the existence of an Aboriginal people consisting of many diverse communities and individuals, and that specific educational needs are different amongst different Aboriginal groups. But we see a common cohesion of cultural values and aspirations *that identify us as a distinct people, with aspirations often quite different from that of the non-Aboriginal community* (Aboriginal Consultative Group 1975a, p. 60; emphasis added).

On this occasion we witness the ethnogenic dynamic of formulating the common cultural heritage in terms of contrasts. The diacritica of ethnic identity are located in characteristics in which Aborigines *contrast* with whites. This process of defining ethnic identity in terms of traits that contrast with the dominant groups is as common as developing ethnic identity markers in contrast to other sub-populations (a process that receives much attention in a recent analysis of ethnicity by Despres and others [Despres 1976]).

While the ethnic elite were formulating the terms of a common set of norms that would be used to define pan-Aboriginal ethnicity, non-Aborigines were also involved in this process. In 1973 a seminar was held at the Australian National University to discuss Aboriginal affairs. Attending the seminar were thirty-two representatives from the departments of Aboriginal affairs, other Commonwealth departments, mission authorities, progress associations and other agencies. *Not until its final meeting did the seminar include representation of persons of Aboriginal descent.* One of the major recommendations was that "community self-determination should be the overriding principle of Government policy". And self-determination was defined as a situation where Aboriginal communities will decide the pace and nature of their future development within the legal, social, and economic restraints of Australian society (*Batchelor Seminars* 1976, p. 3). Community self-determination, an ideology of the European-dominated government, was to be instigated for Aborigines and presumably become their ideology. It is a move that accentuates diversity.

Data collected during the 1976 period of field research indicated the existence of strains among Aborigines caused by traditional cultural variations and different perceptions of Aboriginality. The strains at the interpersonal level were exemplified when a marriage broke up because, in part at least, the husband and wife developed different ideological positions on Aboriginality. The husband sought to recapture the more traditional practices of Aboriginal culture, while the wife saw this as a retreat from the modern world and the demands of the political arena.

Some of the internal problems did not relate to cultural differences so much as to structural characteristics. One social affair that took place in July 1976 brought a large number of Aborigines from surrounding areas together in Sydney. They arranged themselves around the hall in which they were assembled in a pattern corresponding to their region of origin, and within that to reserve and kinship relationship. One well-informed person pointed to each table and identified the people sitting there in terms of their reserve, commenting that several of these groups did not have much to do with other Aborigines in the past. Many of the local-level organizations receiving government funding to carry out some activity such as providing housing or health services for Aborigines were, in order of importance, organized around kinship groups, composed of people from the same reserve, or composed of people from the same region.

The propensity of groups to organize around aggregations based on local principles was reinforced by the support of government funds, and they were not always enamoured of the notion of joining a wider collective for co-operative activities. The "drip-feed" manipulation of funded programmes at a certain point of deprivation stimulated factional conflict along existing social boundaries. With the reduction of government funds for local Aboriginal action groups, the competition for the resources originally with non-Aboriginal action groups attempting to perform similar functions for both Aboriginal and non-Aboriginal populations had produced clear signs (in Sydney) at the time of our departure from the field that the reductions were then forcing competition among and between local Aboriginal action groups, particularly in urban settings. Not only existing social and cultural diversity, but the effects of strategic changes from external forces and resources posed further alignments of diversity out of which Aboriginal ethnicity had to be shaped.

Discussion and Conclusion

This discussion inspected the processes involved in the emergence of group-wide identity among the Australian Aborigines. We prefaced the empirical account of the Aboriginal case with a challenge to those who equate ethnicity with common cultural traditions. To the contrary, we proposed that the development of the definition of a new social category is a creative process. We noted, however, that the creation is not merely an effort of insiders. Outsiders too are critical and active participants. Moreover, the process is not merely a feat of an undifferentiated set of insiders. Conflict, factionalism, and leader-client gaps contribute dynamic dimensions and phases to the process. Ethnicity, then, is a continuous process of strategically negotiated identity and status.

Although culture is an important part of the process, the role it plays is neither simple nor direct. The Aboriginal case points up the interrelated problem of internal cultural diversity and the generation of a generalized common culture. We contend that the cultural dimension of pan-Aboriginality should not obscure the political aspects of the process. Nor should the political aspirations of an ethnic population obscure the important role of traditional practices in the quality of life of that population and the socio-economic and political status of Aborigines as a whole.

To some degree the liberation of Aborigines from economic and racial oppression is placed in opposition to the preservation of traditional Aboriginal culture. These polar positions, we claim, are the basic symbols competing to form the basis of group-wide identity. Indeed, it seems that the history of the relationship between Aboriginal political demands and the government's response has been an attempt to reduce the full scope of these demands – which include *freedom,* the ownership of all reserves and settlements, the title to mineral and mining rights as well as respect for the integrity of Aboriginal culture – to the more limited demand of the rights of Aboriginals to retain their racial and cultural heritage.

A parallel case exists in Mexico, according to Gonzalez-Casanova (1976), where the Indians' situation is often viewed as a problem of cultural differences. In that setting there is also a dominant population of a specific race and culture, separated from a dominated population of a different race and culture (ibid., p. 353). In addition to the cultural aspects of the Indian situation, one also finds prejudice, discrimination, and a colonial type of exploitation. The Aboriginal situation in Australia is similar to the Mexican Indian situation in that it is also treated as a cultural problem. An inspection of the Australian anthropological literature reveals scant consideration of racial discrimination as an important factor in cultural accounts of Aboriginal life. As indicated, Aborigines in various parts of Australia retain a degree of cultural distinctiveness, and the anthropological literature stresses this cultural component and its diversity. In this literature, however, emphasis is more often placed on the kinship and ritual system, less on the economic and political aspects of Aboriginal life.

Setting up a colonial system, according to Fanon (1976), does not mean the death of the native culture. He observes, however, that we may witness institutions that are functioning but ignore the fact that they are functioning under the supervision of the oppressors or within the context of constraints imposed by them (cf. Tonkinson 1977). The cultural belief system of any group constitutes important psychological and social dimensions, influencing how an individual sees himself as well as others.

The case account supported the substance of the claim that voluntary associations play a key role in the process of ethnogenesis. Reference to "ethnic group" and organized ethnic groups is only metaphoric and does not refer to the organization of a *total* population. Rather, there are loci and centres of organizations, voluntary associations, that attempt to act on behalf of populations, or sectors and segments of the population, by representing the variety and diversity of interests that can exist among several hundred thousand widely dispersed people. However, through certain mechanisms it is possible that the interests of an entire population are represented by a small group of individuals.

The Australian government in establishing the National Aboriginal Consultative Committee, acting externally to the group, supplied such a mechanism. But when the elite association engaged in acts that went beyond the constraints placed on their role definition by the government, the government turned to appeal to the diversity and variety in the Aboriginal population and the differences and conflicts that diversity perpetuated to justify removal of the ethnic upstarts. The very gap that is used as a device to remove an elite makes it possible for the government to manipulate the population. Thus the government, by changing the structure of the NACC, was merely searching for a different set of spokesmen, more compatible with their goals and aims. (For a similar account involving the leadership of a black community in an American city, see Arnstein 1972.)

The kinds of diversity that are manifested at the local level in the Australian case mean that any ideological basis of ethnicity must of necessity be of a general sort. The problem of abstraction in creating a common culture is critical. One way to address this question is to ask how a varied set of Aborigines from different parts of Australia would define themselves if they were not a subordinate social and political category in Australian society. The Australian case is only one of many where a dominant European population conceptually lumps a socially and culturally diverse population into a single category. The common treatment of a population, so defined, by the major institutions of power is the most important source of the *common experience* all members of that population share. This is the source of the political ideology that underlies pan-Aboriginal identity.

People within any social system use symbols to define and explain their own position with references to others and to rationalize acts that are committed with reference to others (Silverman 1970, p. 327). One of the first steps towards any kind of mass politically based movement for social change is for a group to define their position with respect to another group in terms of concepts such as oppression and exploitation.[9] Over and over in Australia, whites involved in Aboriginal affairs, including anthropologists, insisted that a sharp difference existed between the definition of the socio-political situation by Aboriginal radicals, who were urban based and relatively highly educated Aborigines, and the rural, more tradition-oriented tribal populations. We have no reason to doubt this. As the preceding discussion shows, this polarity is an integral part of the model used to analyze the Australian situation upon which this paper rests. Two key elements of this conceptual model is the role of the ethnic elite on the one hand and the function of internal diversity on the other. Successful ethnogenesis involves working through the distinctions and differences toward some kind of consensus around politically relevant definitions of the population.

It is the responsibility of the ethnic elite to define the conditions of the larger population and mobilize support for that condition. This requires intensive interaction with other members of the local populations over a period of time. It is facilitated by the existence of political enfranchisement that engages the *potentially ethnic population* in participation in political selection, election, and putting out. While it might be acknowledged that those living in more traditional areas of Australia may not now perceive of their condition in terms of racial discrimination, oppression, or exploitation, the politically oriented ethnic elite has been working to raise the political consciousness of those individuals to cause them to see the "true" nature of their condition. This necessarily requires radical changes from exclusive practice of traditional cultural patterns, although the view that this process necessarily entails the disappearance of all traditional practices is probably exaggerated, unless the practice of multiple culture codes is greatly stigmatized. Members of this ethnic elite must carry out their attempt in full view, and thus their definitions and their efforts are subject to constant criticism, counter-arguments, and obstructions from members of the dominant society. Thus, there is not only competition among different expressions of Aboriginality within the Aboriginal elite, but also competition between Aborigines and liberal whites about who is best equipped to speak for the Aboriginal population, particularly the traditional segments of the population (see Department of Aboriginal Affairs 1976, p. 39, for a similar statement).

This leads us to offer a general observation that in many cases ethnic ideology is primarily the property of an ethnic elite, a condition that makes it possible for the national government at times to ignore the existence of diversity at the local level but at other times to use it as a mechanism to manipulate that elite structure. The explanation for this paradox is simply that the degree to which any group-wide identity exists, it exists among the elite. An ideology at this elite level *may* indeed reflect the aspirations of the local population (Holden 1973) or may on the other hand reflect goals moulded by outsiders.[10] Another source of jeopardy for the ethnic elite comes out of a lack of economic resources to finance their own movement. In the process of attacking and challenging the government, they demand the financial resources so long denied them and now due them. But in accepting government positions and the financing of programmes (a notable condition of voluntary associations) the ethnic leadership exposes itself to strategic manipulation of allocations that places them in dependency relationships to the very government they are attacking.[11]

The examination of the history of Aboriginal movements reveals how tightly legal and economic constraints repressed and suppressed their many efforts. The enfranchisement of Aborigines in 1967 seems to form a watershed for the possibility of political organization and mobilization of pan-ethnic consciousness around a common ideology.

Moreover, the changing nature and disappearance of formal (legal) and then informal control of the movement of Aborigines into cities and urban settings has played an important role in facilitating recruitment and in consolidation of a population that in turn can sustain a leadership of a movement. The critical mass of Aborigines required to support and sustain an elite activity on behalf of nation-wide ethnicity seems now to be present in the major cities of Australia. Their associational activity provides a core of resources and potential for ready mobilization of an ethnic constituency. The urban voluntary associations are potentially also part of the competitive processes that place constraints and limits on elite leadership, helping to anchor them in the ethnic population. But the associations themselves can be co-opted and manipulated (Jones 1982).

The comparison between ethnogenesis and nation-building is especially important in this respect, for the search for a national identity is hampered by variations in the local settings, traditional cultural practices being only one source of that variation (Emerson 1969, Shaplen 1969, Skinner 1968). Barth's suggestion that an ethnic category has a range of traditional symbols available from which to choose its ethnic definers, where choice is often a matter of internal conflict and debate (Barth 1969), is also an important problem confronting the process of nation-building.

One of the major problems facing any social system is the management and control of diversity. From the perspective of the national society it means managing the centrifugal tendencies of minority populations such as Aborigines; from the point of view of the Aboriginal elite, attempting to achieve an ethnic unity, it means managing the centrifugal tendencies of local groups to go it alone. From the point of view of the national government, it is understandable that they cannot stand idly by and allow an ethnic elite to develop and spread an ideology that might smack of a splinter "nation". It is in this connection that the agents of government and public personnel enter into the debate concerning formulation of characteristics. Thus, if an ethnic elite can persuade members of an ethnic population to accept an ideology, so can the national government. This addresses a more general problem of how a population can produce changes in their status while the consciousness is controlled by the institutions of the larger society (Jay 1973, p. 59). Social scientists, including anthropologists, psychologists, and educators, debate which characteristics will be attributed to the population even to the point of implying that such experts as anthropologists can sort out the genuine from the spurious attributes by which an ethnic population is to define itself.

Thus, Berndt, an anthropologist, writes that anthropological studies have played a significant role in "helping to establish a tangible system of values and concepts which together could add up to a contemporary 'Aboriginal' identification" (Berndt 1977, p. 11). He goes on to observe that anthropologists through the medium of the Australian Institute of Aboriginal Studies, an organization supported by the Australian government devoted to the study of Aboriginal culture, society, and history, may serve appreciably in forging a *real* Aboriginal identity and in "transforming that vision into a reality", while dissipating "the present mirage by helping to replace it with a more substantial and meaningful image" (ibid., p. 12). Thus not only have anthropologists been involved historically in defining Aboriginal culture; they are also involved in formulating Aboriginal policies. Thus there is great significance in the NACC's proposals to control both the Institute of Aboriginal Studies and anthropological research among Aborigines.[12] The scholarly descriptions have a definitive legitimacy that could add force to the Aboriginal elite's own efforts to develop a pan-Aboriginal identity.

The pendular moves of public argument between political and cultural ideology of pan-ethnicity reflect strategic efforts of government to contain and control the economic and political demands and victories of a rapidly consolidating political minority. Thus, as we noted in the discussion in the paper, in the course of Aborigine's making political demands and the government's responses, there is a persistent shift toward reducing the full scope of demands to the more limited demand of rights of Aborigines to retain their racial and cultural heritage. The relationship between ethnicity and the organization of diversity from the perspective of national institutions is a double-edged sword.

Notes

1. This chapter is based on research supported in part by City University of New York, Faculty Research Award Program, by the National Institute of Mental Health (MH 7052303); and by The Center for International Comparative Studies, University of Illinois, Urbana, Illinois.
2. Skinner noted the following about the African situation: "Africans found new if often contradictory identities during the colonial period. The most pervasive of these new identities was that of 'native' or 'indigene' or 'indigenous', a label which often classed all colonized people together as distinct and inferior to their white colonizers" (pp. 173–74).
3. There is a further irony beyond the point made by Guthrie that white middle-class biases regard Aborigines' problems in a way Aborigines do not see themselves. It must be noted that behaviour on the part of Aborigines that comes to constitute a "problem" is often the *same* behaviour that on the part of white Australians is regarded as an element of the lusty life style of white Australians.
4. One long-term activist related his experiences with being one of two or three Aborigines involved in earlier political protests. Not only did Aboriginal friends and family refuse to joint the protest, he claimed; they stood on the sidelines taking pictures and heckling. To see the kind of turn-out of Aborigines that the Aboriginal Embassy affair stimulated was obviously gratifying to this individual.
5. An interview with a director of a Black Resource Centre in Melbourne contained the following:

   > Do you think Aboriginal Public Servants such as Charles Perkins have usefully assisted the Black Movement?
   >   I think there was a time — was a time — when Charles Perkins had a great deal of power in the liberation struggle. Nearly every black you ran into was saying: "Charlie Perkins is really showing these bugs what it's about." He appeared to be supporting the slogan of black control of black affairs. He should have left the government and gone out and mobilized on the reserve and everywhere else — perhaps even marched on the building in Canberra, destroying the files and smashed the bureaucracy. He could have done it — he had that much power, that much credibility among blacks.
   >   Now he's completely lost the support of many of us. People realize that he'll have to suppress his convictions because of his $17,000 a year. He had his chance and he stuffed it. [Aboriginal and Islander *Forum* 1, no. 2 (May 1975)]

An incident surrounding Perkins highlights several aspects of the relationship between public servants and Aboriginal spokesmen. Perkins, an assistant secretary in the Department of Aboriginal Affairs, was "charged with improper conduct under the Public Service Act . . . The charge resulted from his outburst . . . that the Liberal and Country Party were the 'biggest racist' political parties the world has ever seen" (Brisbane *Courier-Mail,* 29 February 1974). The charges were finally dropped, but the issue generated a great deal of debate in the press, including ridicule and condemnation. And while Aborigines generally came to the support of Perkins, one news account reported the following: "Suddenly a sharp backlash is setting in among Aborigines against the attempt to elevate Charles Perkins to folk hero-martyr status." The report went on to say that one of the leaders of the movement, who had long been a spokesman for Aborigines in Sydney, said, "I support him as a public servant, but not as a black person. His behaviour has been quite hysterical and has done the cause no good." Another individual, a "full-blooded Aboriginal actress, called on Charles Perkins to take a more balanced view of the Aboriginal problem". The account ended with the comment that messages of support for the criticism was received from twenty-five Aborigines (*Courier-Mail* 1974).

6. The issue of representation and who really speaks for the Aborigines was always present. Once established, the NACC never seemed to have been recognized as a legitimate mouthpiece for Aboriginal concerns. Thus a newspaper article appearing on 23 January 1973: "The Aboriginal Affairs minister (Mr. Bryant) intends to establish direct lines of communications between Canberra and Aborigines throughout Australia." In another story a similar statement was attributed to the minister for Aboriginal Affairs, Senator Cavanagh, who felt that the opinions of the NACC members were unrelated to the views of the Aboriginal people: "The whole structure of the committee will be put back to grass roots level where we will hear the voice of the Aboriginal people."

7. Several aspects of this problem, the process of manipulating public opinion by appealing to the romantic, is illustrated in a newspaper story in the Brisbane *Courier-Mail* of 23 June 1976, which contained the following:

    The State and Federal were accused yesterday of attempting to eradicate the Aboriginal race. The Anglican priest at Nomation . . . said that the public should be made aware of what the government's economic policies were doing to the Aborigines. "We have given them too much too quickly," he said. "We have given them too much without any sense of how to handle it." In a similar vein Mr. Wentworth (Lib., N.S.W.) said in a story on 20-3-74 in the *Courier-Mail* that the Aboriginal population would be "decimated" if unemployment benefits were introduced in the northern territory . . . He claimed that Aborigines would not work once they realized they would be paid for unemployment. The statement was in reaction to a plan to phase in award wages and unemployment benefits to Aborigines.

8. We found many indicates during the research project that the gap between the urban-based, politically oriented elite and the tribal people was not nearly as great or serious as many "well informed" Australians claimed. Although we have no real proof of this suspicion, we were struck by the following from an article in the *Newsletter on Aboriginal Affairs,* no. 4 (p. 8), by Barrie Pittock:

    The Minister for the Northern Territory (Dr. Rex Patterson), publicly claimed that increasing consumption of alcohol by Aborigines, along with militant "stirrers" from the south, were inciting Northern Territory Aborigines to violence". Excessive consumption of alcohol is part of the vicious circle of poverty, both economic and of the spirit. It can only be taken as a measure of the personal insecurity, loss of self-respect, lack of life satisfaction, and alienation experienced by many Aborigines . . .

As for the militant "stirrers" from the south — have you ever tried to stir someone who doesn't want to be stirred?

9. Among the complaints of those we talked to was not the lack of awareness. An article in the *Courier-Mail* of 2 February 1973 noted: "A central Australian Aboriginal rights leader has urged his people to unite in an effort to get what they want. . . . 'we have to stand up to the white people and tell of our problems. Don't be frightened of them.' " In a letter to the editor of the Melbourne *Herald* of 22 February 1974, entitled "An Open Letter to the People of Victoria" a member of NACC bemoaned:

> Regarding the fact that our people are speaking out; this is not fully or widely correct, even in this state. Only a few of us have the socialization and courage and independence although limited, to speak out for the recognition of our Aboriginal sovereign rights. [Some of] those who are aware, for reasons best known to themselves, do not speak out when they should.

As many a budding revolutionary has learned to his cost, 'stirrers' can only succeed where injustice and grievance are rampant, and one might add, when the oppressed feel some hope of change. Injustice and poverty, coupled with new awareness through education and modern communication, are the great stirrers. Given these, the Aboriginal people of northern Australia will stir themselves.

10. The process of moulding is to discredit, to ridicule, to demean existing spokesmen in public, and especially to make them seem dangerous and unreasonable. Thus a newspaper account of 13 July 1974 contained the warning: "Communists were stirring up the radical element in the Aboriginal population, Mr. John Budge said yesterday." But charges such as this are more effective if they come from other members of the population. On 14 June 1975 the *Courier-Mail* reported: "Many young Aboriginal militants are behaving violently because they are under the influence of hard drugs, the Aboriginal senator Neville Bonner claimed yesterday. Arms and drugs were being supplied to them by Trotskyites and other subversive groups, he said." A headline in the *Courier-Mail* on 21 January 1974 proclaimed: "Extremist Aborigines 'get rifle and grenade training'. The story began, "A group of Aboriginal leaders warned yesterday that some militant aborigines armed with machine guns, shotguns and grenades — has been carrying out regular, secret training manoeuvres in the Brisbane Valley." In a subsequent story on 24 January 1974 the activist leader denied the story.

11. Another important aspect of the debate in the public arena is the creation of suspicion among the population. Thus, statements of the following kind were often published: "Mr. Wentworth (Lib. N.S.W.) said yesterday he was worried that 'half-breed carpet-baggers', associated with the Government, would get control of Aboriginal land allocation in the Northern Territory" (11 July 1975).

12. But the cultural aspect of the problem is even more complicated. One indication of the interaction between the cultural and the political surrounded the proposal that the Institute of Aboriginal Studies should be controlled by Aborigines and that more Aborigines should be employed at the institute. When the employment issue was raised, a discussion developed around the issue of employing Aborigines in an institution where sacred and secret materials from different Aboriginal groups were housed. The issue was not decided on that basis, but when we raised the question in interviews with one Aboriginal spokesman, the response was to explain the cultural basis

that gave rise to the problem, not to charge what we would have considered the obvious answer: that it was a political manoeuvre. We were struck by the possibility that, even for the politically minded, an appeal to cultural practices could be blinding.

We inquiried if it was the practice for Aborigines to attempt to look at the sacred artefacts of other tribes. The reply was that that was not the case. In fact as we learned later, individuals take special precautions when they are in situations, such as museums, where sacred objects might be present and exposed. But whites were careless about these displays. Thus, if whites could be trusted to keep sacred objects concealed from those who should not see them, why could not Aboriginals be trusted to take precautions against violating their own cultural principles?

References

Aboriginal and Islander *Identity*. 1976. 2(7): 10–13, 29.

Aboriginal Consultative Group. 1975*a*. Education for Aborigines: Report to the Schools Commission by the Aboriginal Consultative Group – June 1975. *The Aboriginal Child at School* 3, no. 4: 60–64.

———. 1975*b*. Education for Aborigines: Report to the Schools Commission. *The Aboriginal Child at School* 3, no. 5: 3–26.

Arnstein, S. R. 1972. Maximum Feasible Manipulation. *Public Administration Review* 32: 377–402.

Barth, Fredrik. 1969. *Ethnic Groups and Boundaries: The Social Organization of Cultural Differences*. Bergen-Oslo: Universitets Forlaget.

Batchelor Seminars 1973–74. 1976. New Policies in Aboriginal Affairs. Canberra: Centre for Continuing Education, Australian National University.

Bell, Wendell. 1974. *Comparative Research on Ethnicity: A Conference Report.* SSRC *Items* 26: 61–64.

Bennett, John W. 1975. *The New Ethnicity: Perspectives from Ethnology.* 1973 Proceedings of the American Ethnological Society. Saint Paul: West.

Berndt, R. M., ed. 1977. Aboriginal Identity: Reality or Mirage. In *Aborigines and Change: Australia in the 70s,* ed. R. M. Berndt. New Jersey: Humanities Press.

Broom, Leonard. 1971. Workforce and Occupational Statuses of Aborigines. *Australian and New Zealand, Journal of Sociology* 7: 21–34.

Clark, Mavis Thorpe. 1975. *Pastor Doug: The Story of Sir Douglas Nicholls, Aboriginal Leader.* Adelaide: Rigby.

Cohen, A. 1969. *Custom and Politics in Urban Africa.* London: Routledge & Kegan Paul.

Dagmar, Hans. 1978. "Marginal Australians: A Prelude to Political Involvement." In *"Whitefella Business",* ed. Michael C. Howard. Philadelphia: Institute for the Study of Human Issues.

Davidson, G. R., F. X. Bryer and V. Gibson. 1973. Anticipation of Urban Migration Amongst Young Australian Aborigines. *Australian Journal of Psychology* 25, no. 3: 243–49.

Department of Aboriginal Affairs. 1976. *The Role of the National Aboriginal Consultative Committee: Report of the Committee of Inquiry.* Canberra: Australian Government Publishing Service.

Despres, Leo, ed. 1975. *Ethnicity and Resource Competition in Plural Societies.* The Hague and Paris: Mouton.

Dizard, J. E. 1970. Black Identity, Social and Black Power. *Psychiatry* 33: 195–207.

Duke, C., and E. Sommerland. 1976. Design for Diversity: *Further Education for Tribal Aborigines in the North.* Canberra: Australian National University.

Emerson, Rupert. 1969. Paradoxes of Asian Nationalism. In *Man, State, and Society in Contemporary Southeast Asia,* ed. R. O. Tilman. New York: Prager.

Fanon, Frantz. 1976. Racism and Culture. In *Racial Conflict, Discrimination, and Power: Historical and Contemporary Studies,* ed. William Barclay, Krishna Kumar, New York: AMS Press.

Francis, E. K. 1976. *Interethnic Relations: An Essay in Sociological Theory.* New York: Elsevier.

Gale, Fay. 1970. The Impact of Urbanization on Aboriginal Marriage Patterns. In *Australian Aboriginal Anthropology,* ed. Ronald M. Berndt. Nedlands: University of Western Australia Press.

———. 1972. *Urban Aborigines.* Canberra: Australian National University Press.

Gale, Fay, and Joan Binnion. 1975. *Poverty among Aboriginal Families in Adelaide.* Commission of Inquiry into Poverty. Canberra: Australian Government Publishing Service.

Glazer, Nathan, and Daniel P. Moynihan. 1976. *Ethnicity: Theory and Experience* Cambridge: Mass.: Harvard University Press.

Gonzalez-Casanova, Pablo. 1976. Internal Colonialism in Mexico. In *Racial Conflict, Discrimination, and Power: Historical and Contemporary Studies,* ed. William Barclay, Krishna Kumar, and Ruth Simms. New York: AMS Press.

Gray, W. G. 1974. Decentralization Trends in Arnhem Land. In *Aborigines and Change: Australia in the 70s,* ed. Ronald M. Berndt. New Jersey: Humanities Press.

Guthrie, G. 1975. Aboriginal Migration: A Survey Amongst Cherbourg Residents. *The Aboriginal Child at School* 3, no. 4: 49–59.

Handleman, Don. 1977. The Organization of Ethnicity. *Ethnic Groups* 1: 187–200.

Holden, M., Jr. 1973. *Politics of the "Black Nation".* New York: Chandler.

Horner, Jack. 1972. Steadfast Pioneers. *Identity* 1, no. 5: 10–11.

Howard, Michael. 1977. Aboriginal Political Change in an Urban Setting: The N.A.C.C. election in Perth. In *Aborigines and Change,* ed. Ronald M. Berndt. New Jersey: Humanities Press.

———. ed. 1978. *"Whitefella Business": Aborigines in Australian Politics.* Philadelphia: Institute for the Study of Human Issues.

Iris, Mark, and Shama Avraham. 1977. *Immigration Without Integration: Third World Jews in Israel.* Cambridge, Mass.: Schenkmen.

Jay, Martin. 1973. *The Dialectical Imagination: A History of the Frankfurt School and the Institute of Social Research, 1923–1950.* Boston: Little Brown.

Jones, Delmos. 1982. Communities and Organizations in the Community. In *Anthropology in the United States,* ed. Leith Mullings. New York: Columbia University Press.

Kolig, Erich. 1977. From Tribesman to Citizen: Change and Continuity in Social Identities Among South Kimberly Aborigines. In *Aborigines and Change: Australia in the 70s,* ed. Ronald M. Berndt. Social Anthropology Series No. 11, Australian Institute of Aboriginal Studies, Canberra. New Jersey: Humanities Press.

Kuper, Leo. 1971. Theories of Revolution and Race Relations. *Comparative Studies in Society and History* 13: 87–107.

Langton, Marcia. 1978. Self-Determination as Oppression. Preface to H. C. Coombs, *Australian's Policy Towards Aborigines, 1967–1977.* Australian Rights Group, report No. 35, London.
Little, Kenneth. 1970. *West African Urbanization: A Study of Voluntary Associations in Social Change.* Cambridge: Cambridge University Press.
——— . 1976. Comment on James N. Kerri, Studying Voluntary Associations as Adaptive Mechanisms: A Review of Anthropological Perspectives. *Current Anthropology* 17: 23–48.
Lovejoy, F. H. 1971. Costing the Aboriginal Housing Problem. *Australian Quarterly* 32: 79–90.
McGuinness, S. B. 1972. Black Power in Australia. In *Racism: The Australian Experience,* ed. F. S. Stevens, vol. 2. Sydney: Australia and New Zealand Book Company.
——— . 1976. National Aboriginal Congress. *Identity* 2, no. 7:10–13, 29.
McQueen, Humphrey. 1974. *Aborigines, Race and Racism.* Victoria: Dominion Press.
Mitchell, I. S. 1974. Paradoxes in Aboriginal Welfare. *Australian Journal of Social Issues* 9: 56–60.
Robb, L. C. 1962. Leadership Training for Aborigines. *Australian Journal of Social Issues* 1: 38–40.
Rowley, C. D. 1971a. *Outcasts in White Australia.* Canberra: Australian National University Press.
——— . 1971b. *The Reconstruction of Aboriginal Society.* Canberra: Australian National University Press.
——— . 1971c. *The Remote Aborigines.* Canberra: Australian National University Press.
——— . 1973. From Humbug to Politics: Aboriginal Affairs and the Academy Project. *Oceania* 43: 182–95.
Said, Abdul A., and Luis R. Simmons. 1976. *Ethnicity in an International Context.* New Jersey: Transaction Books.
Schapper, H. P. 1964. Administration and Welfare as Threats to Aboriginal Assimilation. *Australian Journal of Social Issues* 3, no. 4: 3–8.
Schildkrout, Enid. 1974. Ethnicity and Generation Differences among Urban Immigrants in Ghana. In *Urban Ethnicity,* ed. Michael Banton. London: Tavistock.
Shaplen, Robert. 1969. *Time Out of Hand: Revolution and Reaction in Southeast Asia.* London: Andre Deutsch.
Silverman, Sydel F. 1970. "Exploitation" in Rural Central Italy: Structure and Ideology in Stratification Study. *Comparative Studies in Society and History* 12: 327–39.
——— . 1976. Ethnicity as Adaptation: Strategies and Systems. *Reviews in Anthropology* 3: 626–35.
Skinner, Elliott. 1968. Group Dynamics in the Politics of Changing Societies: The Problem of "Tribal" Politics in Africa. In *Essays on the Problem of Tribe,* ed. June Helm. Seattle: American Ethnological Society.
Tatz, Colin. 1967. Equal Rights for Aborigines: Australian Slow Progress. *Round Table* 57: 439–47.
——— . 1977. Aborigines: Political Options and Strategies. In *Aborigines and Change: Australia in the 70s,* ed. Ronald M. Berndt. New Jersey: Humanities Press.
Tilman, Robert O. (ed.) 1969. *Man, State and Society in Contemporary Southeast Asia.* New York: Praeger.

Tonkinson, Robert. 1974. *The Jigalong Mob: Aboriginal Victors of the Desert Crusade.* Menlo Park, Col.: Cummings.

————. 1977. Aboriginal Self Regulation and the New Regime: Jigalong, W. A. In *Aborigines and Change: Australia in the 70s,* ed. Ronald M. Berndt. New Jersey: Humanities Press.

Turner, David H. 1974. *Tradition and Transformation: A Study of Aborigines in the Groote Eylandt Area, Northern Australia.* Canberra: Australian Institute.

Valadian, Margaret, and Diane Barwick. 1977. Aboriginal Identity: Instruction and Interaction at an Experimental Training Workshop. In *Aborigines and Change: Australia in the 70s,* ed. Ronald M. Berndt. New Jersey: Humanities Press, 320–326.

Wagley, Charles, and Marvin Harris. 1958. *Minorities in the New World.* New York and London: Columbia University Press.

Wilson, John. 1975. *Review of Housing for Aborigines.* Canberra: Australian Government Publishing Service.